WOMEN RIGHTS AND GENDER JUSTICE

WOMEN RIGHTS AND GENDER JUSTICE

Editors

PROF. (DR.) N.B. CHANDRAKALA
DR. G. INDIRA PRIYADARSINI
DR. K. SUNITHA

REGAL

REGAL PUBLICATIONS
New Delhi

WOMEN RIGHTS AND GENDER JUSTICE

ISBN 978-81-8484-426-9

Typeset by
RAHUL COMPOSERS
New Highway Apartments, Lakshmi Niwas
760, Pocket-D, Lok Nayak Puram, New Delhi - 110 041

Printed in India at
MAYUR ENTERPRISES
WZ Plot No. 3, Gujjar Market, Tihar Village, New Delhi - 110 018

Published by
REGAL PUBLICATIONS
F-159, Rajouri Garden, New Delhi - 110 027
Phone : 45546396, 25435369
E-mail : regalbookspub@yahoo.com, regaldeepbooks@yahoo.com

Contents

Other, unwritten, hierarchical practices place further constraints on Indian women. At the international level, the United Nations Charter, the Universal Declaration of Human Rights and Convention on Elimination of All Forms of Discrimination Against Women (CEDAW) sought to guarantee better legal status to women. Despite the Charter of United Nations, the UDHR, the International covenants on Human Rights and other instruments of the UN and of the specialised agencies and despite the progress made in matter of equality of rights, there continues to exist considerable discrimination against women. Independence of India heralded the introduction of laws relating to women. The Constitution provided equality to men and women and also gave special protection to women to realise their interests effectively. Special laws were enacted to prevent indecent representation of women in the media and sexual harassment in workplaces. The law also gives women equal rights in the matter of adoption, maternity benefits, equal pay, good working conditions, etc. Though the above mentioned measures have been taken by the government the position of Indian women in social, economic and political arena has not been meted out on par with the international standards. The women protection laws are also proved to be in vein as the crime rate against women in India is increasing day-by-day.

Gender injustice, taking the shape of crimes against women without punishment of the criminal, is escalating the world over. In India, it has ancient roots and modern malignant manifestations where legislative, executive and judicial wings who are the operators of protective legislations are acting perfunctorily. This distortion in the role justice calls for militant action and correction through conscientisation of the people, empowerment of women and statutory status and punitive functions granted to Social Action Groups and women police. The social and legal culture *vis-a-vis* the female gender has not elevated her to an equal level, breaking with the past, insisting on egalite and making her role autonomous. Women's "Vimochana", in its semantic fullness and as a personality development project is still distances away from her. Whatever the Constitution may intone, whatever the Universal instruments may inscribe, we have miles to go and promises to keep if gender justice is not to be mere dope but sure hope.

N.B. CHANDRAKALA
G. INDIRA PRIYADARSINI
K. SUNITHA

Preface

Woman is the greatest gift of God to humanity. She possesses the power to create what is good and destroy what is bad. Tulsidas, Kalidas and Surdas, the great Indian poets, were also inspired by their better halves in their literary ventures. Empowerment of women and their parity with men in all walks of life and spheres of activity, be it political, economic, cultural or social, is a *sine quo non* of gender justice. Justice does not distinguish between men and women

The founders of the constitution realized that majority of the women in India are generally ill-treated in the areas of employment. They realized that religion, caste and class played a main role in establishing the status of the women. They therefore felt it is essential to incorporate some provisions to improve the status of women in India and check on the discrimination between men and women. The Constitution of India gives women right to equality. Moreover, powers were given to State Governments to make special provisions for women. Thus, the framers of the Constitution of India put the best of their efforts in breaking away the walls of old customs and traditions which governed the women on their empowerment.

The origin of the Indian idea of appropriate female behaviour can be traced to Manu in 200 BC: "*by a young girl, by a young woman, or even by an aged one, nothing must be done independent, even in her own house*". Throughout history, women have generally been restricted to the role of a home-maker; that of a mother and wife no religion has spared her. Despite major changes that have occurred in the status of women in some parts of the world in recent decades, norms that restrict women to the home are still powerful in India, defining activities that are deemed appropriate for women. India is a multifaceted society where no generalization could apply to the nation's various regional, religious, social and economic groups.

List of Contributors

A. Aswini, Research Scholar (P.T.), Department of Law, S.P.M.V.V., Tirupati, Lecturer-in-Law, Dr. Ambedkar Law College, Tirupati (A.P.).

Adapa Sarada, St. Ann's. Hr. Secondary School, Panagudi, Thirunalveli Dt. (T.N.).

Aruna Sri Lakshmi, B.Com. M.L., Principal, DNR College of Law, Bhimavaram, W.G. District (A.P.).

B. Yuvakumar Reddy, Principal, S.S. Maniyar Law College, Jalgaon (A.P.).

Ch. Venkateswarlu, Lecturer in Law, N.B.M. Law College, Visakhapatnam (A.P.).

D.B. Krishna Kumari, Centre for Women's Studies, S.P.M.V.V. (Women's University), Tirupati (A.P.).

G. Indira Priyadarsini, Academic consultant, Department of Law, Sri Padmavati Mahila Visvavidyalayam (Women's University), Tirupati (A.P.).

Haripriya Susmitha B., M.B.B.S., Medical Practitioner, Tirupati (A.P.).

I. Rama Sundari, Lecturer-In-Law, MRVRGR Law College, Vizianagaram (A.P.).

K. Deepthi, B.Tech., (Final), Siddartha Engineering College, Vijayawada (A.P.).

K. Samatha, Research Scholar, Department of Law, S.P.M.V.V., Tirupati (A.P.).

K. Sita Manikyam, Assistant Professor, Dr. B.R. Ambedkar College of Law, Andhra University, Visakhapatnam (A.P.).

K. Sudha, Faculty, Damodaram Sanjivayya National Law University, Palace Layout, Pedawaltair, Visakhapatnam (A.P.).

M. Deenadayal, Research Scholar, Department of History, S.V.U. College of Arts, Sri Venkateswara University, Tirupati (A.P.).

N. Victoria, Research Scholar, Department of Law, S.P.M.V.V. , Tirupati (A.P.).

N.B. Chandrakala, Head, Department of Law, Sri Padmavati Mahila Visvavidyalayam (Women's University), Tirupati (A.P.).

N.B. Chandrakala, Professor & Head, Department of Law, Sri Padmavathi Mahila Viswavidyalayam (Women's University), Tirupati, Chittoor Dist. (A.P.).

P.B. Pankaja, Reader, Law Centre 1, Faculty of Law, University of Delhi, Delhi.

Padma Ragam K., M.S.W. Student, Rodamistry College, Gachi Bowli, Hyderabad (A.P.).

R. Srinivasan, Assistant Professor, P.G. Department of Constitutional Law & Human Rights, Tamil Nadu , Dr. Ambedkar Law University, Chennai (T.N.).

Rani Manda, Assistant Director, TCR & TI, Tribal Welfare Department, DSS Bhavan, Masab Tank, Hyderabad (A.P.).

S. Drakshayani, Research Scholar, SPMWW, Tirupati (A.P.).

S. Faizunnisa, Faulty of Law, Sri R.K.M. Law College, Chittoor (A.P.).

S. Padmaja, Research Scholar, Faculty of Law, Adarsha Law College, Kakatiya University, Warangal (A.P.).

Sridhar Ganji, Assistant Professor in Law, Sri R. K.M. Law College, Chittoor (A.P.).

Sunitha Kanipakam, Academic Consultant, Department of Law, SPM University (Women's University), Tirupati, Chittoor Dist. (A.P.). (Formerly worked as Assistance Professor of Law, Gujarat National Law University, Gandhinagar, Gujarat).

T. Divya Sravani, B.Tech., (Final) Siddartha Engineering College, Vijayawada (A.P.).

T. Keerthi, Faculty of Law, Sri R.K.M. College, Chittoor (A.P.).

T. Tagore Dinesh, B.Tech., Vignan University, Visakhapatnam (A.P.).

T.Y. Nirmala Devi, Faculty, Damodaram Sanjivayya National Law University, Palace Layout, Pedawaltair, Visakhapatnam (A.P.).

V. Sasi Kala, Lecturer, Sri. R.K.M. Law College, Chittoor (A.P.).

V. Sowbhagya Rani, Department of HR & SD, Sri Venkateswara University, Tirupati (A.P.).

V. Sunitha, Research Scholar, Department of Law, S.P.M.V.V., Tirupati (A.P.).

V. Vijay Lakshmi, Associate Professor, Dr. B.R. Ambedkar College of Law, Andhra University, Visakhapatnam (A.P.).

Y. Arunavalli, Professor, Department of Law, S.P.M.V.V., Tirupati (A.P.).

Y. Padmaja Rani, Asst. Professor, Department of Law, Kakatiya University, Hanamkonda (A.P.).

1

Normative Hierarchy under International Law

With Special Reference to Women's Environmental Rights

N.B. CHANDRAKALA

INTRODUCTION

Women represent more than half the world's population. They stand in the front line in terms of poverty, yet provide invaluable contributions to sustaining communities around the world and managing the earth's biodiversity and natural resources. Despite their role and know-how, women's contribution is regularly undervalued and ignored. Furthermore, women are uniquely vulnerable to environmental degradation. For example, it is well established that environmental hazards are among the major causes of global death and disease, and that the burden falls disproportionately on women and young children, especially in less developed countries.[1]

The role of women and their 'know-how' is often undervalued and ignored. All too often they are treated as second-class citizens with fewer rights and lower status than men. It is high time that national and international policies reflected gender differences and gave far greater weight to the empowerment of women Gender dimensions. So we must breathe life into the gender dimensions enshrined in the United Nations Millennium Development Goals. We must build on the outcomes of the 1992 United Nations Conference on Environment and Development, the 1994 International Conference on Population and Development (ICPD), the 1995 World Conference on Women and the 2002 World Summit on Sustainable Development, and cement them at this tenth anniversary of ICPD. For if we ignore the role of women, all our hopes and aspirations for a better and more stable world will be harder to achieve.

It is important to underline that women should not be seen as just instruments for environmental conservation and management. The burden of environmental destruction can not be put on the shoulders of women alone. The role of men in environmental conservation and management was stressed throughout the Online Discussion on Women and Environment (UNEP/DAW, 2005).[2] The responsibility for women's participation and empowerment in environment, as well as for gender sensitive environmental policies and practice is a common responsibility of men and women. As the United Nations concluded in 1995: Policies that only target women cannot achieve the best results, nor can those which assume that public actions are gender-neutral in their effects, hence, promoting gender equality implies a profound change in socio-economic organization of societies: not only in the way women work, live and care for the other members of the households, but also in the way men do, and in the way their respective roles in the family and community are articulated with the need to earn a living".[3]

INTERNATIONAL HUMAN RIGHTS INSTRUMENTS

The main global instrument dealing with women's rights is the Convention on the Elimination of All Forms of Discrimination Against Women (CEDAW, 1979), which prohibits sex discrimination and provides for affirmative action (Arts. 2 and 4). The principle of non-discrimination is stated in a very broad way, applying not only to state-enacted laws and regulations, but also to the behaviour of private individuals. Women's rights under the CEDAW include the right to a legal capacity identical to that of men, including equal rights to conclude contracts and administer property (Art. 15); gender equality in relation to marriage and family (Art. 16);

and non-discrimination in employment and training (Arts. 11 and 12). Article 14 specifically protects the rights of rural women, including the right to "equal treatment in land and agrarian reform".[4]

A major development in relation to the CEDAW has been the adoption of an Optional Protocol (1999) allowing individuals and groups claiming violations to submit complaints to the Committee on the Elimination of All Forms of Discrimination Against Women. After hearing such complaints, the Committee communicates to the parties its views and recommendations, and states are to "give due consideration" to these and provide a written response. (Protocol, Arts. 1, 2 and 7). Moreover, the Committee may on its own initiative start confidential inquiries on "grave or systematic violations", although states may opt out of this procedure (Arts. 8-10).

Soft law instruments have also been adopted by United Nations human rights institutions. For instance, Resolution 15 (1998) of the Sub-Commission on the Promotion and Protection of Human Rights states that discrimination against women with respect to acquiring and securing land constitutes a violation of human rights law. The Resolution urges governments to amend or repeal discriminatory laws and policies and to encourage the transformation of discriminatory customs and traditions.

Women's rights are also protected by regional human rights treaties, such as the European Convention for the Protection of Human Rights and Fundamental Freedoms (1950, as amended), the American Convention on Human Rights (1969), the African Charter on Human and Peoples' Rights (1981) and the Arab Charter on Human Rights (adopted in 1994 but not yet in force).

INTERNATIONAL ENVIRONMENTAL INSTRUMENTS

The first mention of women in the environmental treaties was in 1968 during the *African Convention on the Conservation of Nature and Natural Resources* held at Algiers. In the1980s the relationship between women and the environment had received considerable attention and since then the impact of the international environmental crisis on women has been an important subject of study. The parallel workshop of NGO's along with the first World Conference on Women in Nairobi (1985) was symbolic of the interlinked concerns of women, development, and environment. Both recognized and stressed women's concerns and their incorporation as an integral part of the policy planning. Women's Action Agenda 21 as part of the 1992 UN Conference on Environment and Development (UNCEDA), reflected a cross sectoral approach including women's issues. The focus was on the strong links between women and environment. But it was the International Drinking Water Supply and Sanitation Decade and the UN Conference on Environment and Development (UNCED) that has been hailed as promoting the role of women in natural resource management in a major way. Later, the Beijing conference in 1995 listed a greater need to involve women in issues of sustainable development and environment. In 1998, the World Conservation Union (IUCN) framed a "*Gender Policy Statement*" that recognized the need to consciously enlist women's concerns for sustainable use, management, and conservation of natural resources. Gender equality and equity were felt to be fundamental to human rights and social justice issues and a foundation paving the way for sustainable development. Understanding the linkages between gender relationships and the environment became a major theme for advocacy and shifting paradigm. It concluded that only with a gender perspective in place can a complete picture of human relationships and ecosystems be built up.[5]

Some Rio and post-Rio international environmental instruments contain provisions specifically addressing gender. The preamble of the Convention on Biological Diversity recognizes women's "vital role" in the conservation and sustainable use of biodiversity, and affirms the need for their participation in policies concerning these issues. Among Rio soft law instruments, principle 20 of the Rio Declaration states that "women have a vital role in environmental management and development", and "their full participation is therefore essential to achieve sustainable development". The Non-Legally Binding Authoritative Statement of Principles on Forests calls for women's participation in the planning, development and implementation of national forest policies and in the management, conservation and sustainable development of forests (principles 2(d) and 5(b)). Moreover, Chapter 24 of Agenda 21 is specifically devoted to gender.

An example of a gender-sensitive post-Rio instrument is the 1994 Convention to Combat Desertification, which provides for the facilitation of women's participation in efforts to combat desertification at all levels, and specifically for their effective participation in national action programmes (Arts. 5 and 10). Women's participation in national action programmes is also required by Article 8 of the Regional Implementation Annex for Africa, an associated instrument to the Convention.

During the second UN World Conference on Women (Nairobi, 1995) the International Environment Liaison Centre organized a series of workshops on 'Women, Environment and Development'. The expert meeting concluded that: "*The growth of women's power and sustainability of development are ecologically tied.*"(ELC, 1985) The Forward Looking Strategies of the UN Conference mentioned that 'the environment' was an area of concern for women. It was the first time in history that at global level the linkages between gender issues and environment were highlighted: two streams were converging (merging)—the one on gender and development, with the one on environment and sustainable development.

Not only did the outcome document of the United Nations Conference on Environment and Development (UNCED) in Rio de Janeiro, 1992, have 145 references to the specific roles and positions of women in environment and development, but it also recognized women as one of the nine major groups to achieve sustainable development, and included a separate chapter (24) in Agenda 21 entitled: 'Global Action for Women towards Sustainable and Equitable Development.' Maurice Strong, the Secretary General of the 1992 Earth Summit, played a major role in putting gender on the UNCED agenda and beyond: "*There is a pressing need to continue to centralize women's issues and to ensure the incorporation of their collective perspectives, experiences and contributions to sustainable development. The implementation of the programme areas of Agenda 21 which extensively incorporates the important role of women in SD will help to meet this need.*"[6]

In New York the 1995 UN Conference on Women that brought thousands of women (government delegations, non-governmental organisations and civil society) together in Beijing. Section K of the Beijing Platform for Action focuses on Women and the Environment, and has three strategic objectives:

K1. Involve women actively in environmental decision-making at all levels.
K2. Integrate gender concerns and perspectives in policies and programmes for sustainable development.
K3. Strengthen or establish mechanisms at the national, regional and international levels to assess the impact of development and environmental policies on women.

These days we are reviewing how far we are in meeting these objectives and identify areas that need renewed action and leadership.[7]

Recent international conferences have adopted soft law declarations and plans of action revealing increased attention in the international community to gender issues. Particularly important are the 1994 Cairo Plan of Action on Population and Development, the 1995 Beijing Platform for Action adopted by the Fourth World Conference on Women and the 1996 World Food Summit Plan of Action. Some provisions of these documents relate directly to environment and agriculture. For instance, the Beijing Platform for Action envisages legislative and administrative reforms to ensure gender equality in access to natural resources, including inheritance rights (para. 61(b)). The World Food Summit Plan of Action also envisages measures to enhance women's access to natural resources (para. 16(b)), and affirms the goal of ensuring gender equality and women's empowerment (objective 1.3).

INTERNATIONAL LABOUR CONVENTIONS AND DECLARATIONS

The rights of women agricultural workers are addressed in several conventions adopted by the International Labour Organization (ILO), particularly the Equal Remuneration Convention 100 of 1951, the Maternity Protection (Revised) Convention 103 of 1952, the Discrimination (Employment and Occupation) Convention 111 of 1958 and the Plantations Convention 110 of 1958 with its 1982 Protocol.

A major recent development in this field has been the adoption of the 1998 ILO Declaration on the Fundamental Principles and Rights at Work, which reaffirms some principles and rights to which all ILO member states must adhere by the very fact of their ILO membership, regardless of their ratification of the relevant conventions. The principles include the elimination of discrimination in employment and occupation, which encompasses sex discrimination.[8]

CONCLUSION

In the last decade, gender has received considerable attention. At the international level, the Beijing Platform for Action has provided comprehensive policy directives, the Optional Protocol to the CEDAW has strengthened international human rights mechanisms and international environmental instruments have addressed gender issues. Domestic measures have also been adopted in various forms. At the policy level, plans of action have been adopted by most countries to follow up the Beijing Platform for Action. In the legislative arena, efforts have been made to eliminate discrimination and to improve women's legal position, e.g., by reforming family and succession law, by revising agrarian law, by protecting women's labour rights and by prohibiting discrimination and providing affirmative action in certain contexts. Judicially, discriminatory norms have been declared unconstitutional, and women's rights have been enforced.

Notes and References

1. United Nations Environment Programme Environment for Development, Français, 'UNEP, Gender and the Environment'.
2. United Nations Division for the Advancement of Women (DAW).
3. UN, 1995.
4. *Convention on the Elimination of All Forms of Discrimination Against Women.*
5. *Kiran Soni Gupta, Gender and International Environmental Negotiations—How Far and How Much More?*, www.oas.org/dsd/Tool-kit/Documentos/.../Gupta%20Reading.pdf
6. UNIFEM, 1993.
7. Irene Dankelman M.Sc., Radboud University, Nijmegen, IRDANA advices, irene.dankelman@hetnet.nl
8. FAO Corporate Document Repository, Law and sustainable developemnt since Rio, Produced by: Office of Director-General.

2

Gender Analysis of the Indian Penal Code

Y. ARUNAVALLI

INTRODUCTION

The Indian Penal Code 1860 (IPC) has been amended only sparingly since its enactment. The substantive penal provisions contained therein are applicable to the whole of India except the State of Jammu and Kashmir. The IPC originally had twenty-three chapters. Three more chapters, namely, offences relating to criminal conspiracy, election and cruelty to married women, have been added later. Thematically, the IPC may broadly be divided into four sections. Chapters one to five contain general matters relating to the extent, definitions, principles of liability, etc. Chapters six to fifteen deal with public matters between individuals and the state. Chapters sixteen to twenty-two are primarily concerned with offences committed by individuals against individuals or legal persons other than the state. The last chapter twenty-three is residuary in nature, laying down the principle of punishment for attempt to commit an offence if no specific provision has been made therefore. In this scheme of chapters more serious offences precede the lesser offences, e.g. offences relating to state policy precede offences affecting individuals; offences relating to body precede those affecting property and so on. Placement and the punishment provided for an offence by the IPC indicates the legislative perceptions about its nature and seriousness.

Serious offences are classified as cognizable and non-bailable by the Criminal Procedure Code, 1973 (CrPC). Classification of offences as cognizable means that the police can initiate investigation into the offence on its own and arrest the accused without a warrant. In the case of a non- cognizable offence the victim is required to obtain an order from the magistrate for even an investigation to begin. The procedure requires the complainant to be present in the court on all the days of the hearing for the trial to continue. If such an offence is also declared as bailable, the accused is entitled to be released on bail as a matter of right. The victim may be more afraid to file the complaint for fear of harassment by the accused. The non-cognizable and/or bailable offences require the victim to have more perseverance, better resources and greater determination to prosecute.

This scheme of things applies equally to all persons irrespective of them being men or women. When presented in this manner, the IPC seems essentially an inherently gender neutral. This approach, however, does not take into account the differential impact of the scheme on men and women due to the differential status, socialization, role expectations and resources available to men and women in reality. A preliminary reading of the interpersonal offences between men and women and the punishments provided therefor in the IPC indicates the public-private dichotomy and patriarchal values to be at their base. A close examination of the extent to which the IPC has followed the private-public dichotomy and incorporated patriarchal values ensuring male domination, power and authority is, therefore, necessary. The primary focus of analysis in this paper is the provisions of the IPC though incidental references have been made to the CRPC, the Evidence Act, 1872 and other relevant special laws. The provisions relating to sexuality, procreation and marriage are the main focus of analysis as these areas are most affected by the private-public dichotomy and the resultant discriminatory application of law to men and women.

ANALYSIS OF THE INDIAN PENAL CODE PROVISIONS

Before analyzing the specific provisions of the IPC, it is important to remember the distinction in the usage of 'he' by the

IPC in contrast with 'man' and 'woman'. The general explanations in the IPC mention that the pronoun 'he' and its derivatives are used for any person whether male or female.[1] The word 'man' denotes a male human being of any age and woman' denotes a female human being of any age.[2] Usage of 'he' or 'man' in a section, therefore, determines whether it is applicable to both the males and females or it applies to either males or females.

SEXUALITY

The provisions relating to obscenity,[3] sexual assault,[4] flesh trade,[5] kidnapping and abduction[6] and custodial intercourse[7] have been included in this section for closer analysis. Legal notions of sexuality of married women have been discussed under the section dealing with offences relating to marriage.

The following discussion brings forth the patriarchal values and Victorian morality underlying these provisions.[8] It shows clearly that the criminal law does not interfere with their lives as long as people maintain heterosexual consensual relationships within marital boundaries in the private spheres of their lives. However, the law does not allow the emergence of sexuality in the public sphere or any kind of sexuality even within the private sphere contrary to the heterosexual norm obscenity.

In the Indian context, pornography and obscenity have become synonymous. The IPC declares any representation as obscene which is "lascivious or appeals to the prurient interest or if its effect ... is, if taken as a whole, such as to tend to deprave and corrupt persons who are likely ... to read, see or hear the matter contained or embodied in it".[9] This provision incorporates the Hecklings test[10] based on the then prevalent narrow moral considerations and is not reflective of the current thinking on the subject.

At least four different positions have emerged among feminists concerning obscenity, namely, liberal, moral right, anti porn and feminists against censorship.[11] The liberal position defines pornography "as sexually explicit material designed for sexual arousal", and argues "that there is no scientific evidence that pornography causes harm to society and there are no sound reasons for banning it or taking any other action against it'.[12] The position of the moral right is that pornography is a preoccupation with sex that is not related to the purpose of sex. They view pornography as a threat to traditional family values which reserve sex for procreation and within marital relations.[13] The antiphon feminists too take a similar position and view pornography as "the material which depicts violence against women and is itself violence against women".[14] The approach taken by feminists against censorship is that it is not the images that cause men to rape but the fact that the pornographic genre is becoming the dominant form of representing women. The experience of Denmark demonstrates that when pornography is exposed to the light of day it loses its power, while censorship or suppression of such images brings pornography into existence, gives it power and invites policing.[15]

Censorship curtails the space for other forms of representation and alternative erotica. Feminists against censorship argue in favour of a multiplicity of images and the creation of space for alternative images. Suppressing existing images will end up simultaneously silencing alternative representations and interpretations that could help in promoting feminist, anti-racist or egalitarian values. This approach exposes the danger of resorting to legal strategies to fight pornography. Such recourse, in their opinion invariably collapses feminists' concerns about degradation and objectification into the discussion on how sex depraves and/or how representations of violence cause actual violence.

The Indian law does not reflect any of these new developments and continues to be limited to narrow moral considerations. The conception of depravity being limited to sexual depravity, images denigrating to women's equal status, reinforcing sexism, gender discrimination and misogyny are ignored by the legal regime. Sexually explicit images are interpreted as tending to deprave and corrupt persons and therefore to be prohibited but the sexist, gender discriminatory or misogynous messages of other images are not considered as tending to deprave or corrupt persons. The sexism in non-sexually explicit representations remains untouched by any penal liability. Even the comparatively recent Indecent Representation of Women (Prohibition) Act, 1986 has focused on the "depiction ... of the figure of a woman ... as to have the effect of being indecent'.[16] 'Indecency' too, is guided closely by conceptions of morality. Its focus on what is explicitly indecent diverts the attention from derogatory messages as well as from other derogatory though not explicitly indecent images of women. Such derogatory messages and images are much more harmful to women and responsible for increasing violence against women, but they remain outside the purview of legislation. The following standard of indecency has been suggested[17] for inclusion in the Indecent Representation of Women Act—

> The depiction in any manner of the figure of a woman, her form or body or any part thereof in such a way, as the effect of being indecent, or derogatory to, or denigrating women or is likely to deprave, corrupt or injure the public morality or morals. 'Derogatory Representation of Women' means the depiction in any publication in any manner, visual or otherwise, of the figure of a woman, her form or body or any part thereof in such a way as to have the effect of being indecent or derogatory to her dignity as a person.

Recent censorship and the litigation thereafter relating to the film Bandit Queen[18] do reflect the conflicting perceptions about what constitutes obscenity. It is time for the law in India to recognize at the least that the words 'deprave and corrupt' are clearly capable of bearing a wider meaning. It has been held in other countries that depravity and corruption is not confined to sexual depravity and corruption.[19] *Miller* v. *Califomia*[20] has expanded the test laid down in Heckling. What is obscene can be determined by asking—

- whether the average person, applying contemporary standards, would find that the work, taken as a whole, appeals to prurient interest,
- whether the work depicts or describes, in a patently offensive way, sexual conduct specifically defined by the applicable state law, and
- whether the work, taken as a whole, lacks serious literary, artistic, political or scientific value.

RAPE AND SEXUAL ASSAULT

Various provisions in the IPC relating to sexuality reinforce not only Victorian morality but also the non-agency of women. In case of rape the general principle is that if a man has sexual intercourse with a woman below the age of sixteen years with or without her consent, he is guilty of rape.[21] But if the woman is his wife and above fifteen years of age, the act is not rape.[22] A nominal punishment is provided if the wife is between twelve to fifteen years of age[23] or is living separately from him under a decree of separation or under any custom or usage.[24] The undeniable conclusion is that a wife is presumed to have given irrevocable consent to sexual relationship with her husband even though there is no presumption of consent for any other purpose, including the marriage itself. The option of puberty given by Hindu and Muslim laws relating to marriage allows women to revoke their marriages performed before attainment of majority but there are no sanctions against a husband establishing sexual relationship within such a marriage. The husband is punishable at par with other rapists only if the wife is too young physically for sexual intercourse. Her mental maturity or her clear withdrawal from matrimony by living separately is of little protection to the woman against aggressive sexual access of her husband.

A woman may successfully prosecute a man for rape who had sexual intercourse with her consent when the man knew that he was not her husband and that she had consented believing him to be someone else to whom she was or believed herself to be lawfully married.[25] A similar mistake about the identity of the accused made by an unmarried, widowed or divorced woman provides her with no protection even if the man knows that she consented to the sexual intercourse believing him to be someone else. The message is clear. The tie between marriage and sexuality is unmistakable. The law protects virgins and chaste married women. A woman who is not married if she decides to be sexually active, she does so at her own peril. A man can swindle her for her promiscuity without any risk to himself. Any sexual activity beyond the private sphere of marriage is not worthy of legal protection. In fact, as the past sexual conduct of the prosecutrix is admissible in evidence[26] her promiscuity may be and is raised in cross examination to injure her character as to shake her credibility. The assumption of the law apparently is that if she has an immoral or sexually promiscuous history, her cry of rape has to be a lie.

The assumptions under Sections 155(4) and 146 of the Evidence Act have been characterized as (i) women lie about rape; (ii) women deserve to be raped; (iii) women provoke rape. These assumptions reinforce the view that a woman is responsible for male sexual behaviour, that is, she is not only responsible for her sexual behaviour but also for a man's misbehaviour. The linking up of chastity to the requirement of consent has resulted in denial of women's sexual autonomy and dignity.[27]

The definition of rape itself also does not reflect a woman's experience. The existing law requires proof of penetration of the vagina by the penis. The penetration requirement is linked to conservative notions of chastity and the fear of pregnancy by someone other than the legitimate father. In other words, the priority given to penetration by the penis over all other forms of penetration or sexual assault is historically based on the need to defend the rights of the legitimate father rather than the woman's integrity. The requirement excludes all sorts of other ways in which women experience sexual abuse or violence that are no less humiliating, for example, insertion of the penis into the woman's mouth or anus or insertion of fingers or other objects into her vagina.

The availability of legal protection to sexual activity is not determined by whether it is happening in private or in public but whether it meets the traditional standards of morality. Homosexual relations are declared 'unnatural' and 'offences' irrespective of whether these are occurring in the private or public sphere. Such a declaration directly imposes a heterosexual marital code of sexuality.

It may be noted that the provisions relating to rape assume that women alone may be raped and that it is only a man who can rape a woman and not *vice versa*. A woman can seduce a man, but not rape him. However, new Sections 376-B to 376-D[28] make a person in authority liable for inducing or seducing a woman only and not a man, for sexual intercourse. It is apparent that these provisions do not recognize any sexual initiative and agency in women. These provisions suggest that either women in authority do not/cannot exploit men in their custody or subordinate to them or even if the women may do so, men are capable of handling it themselves without the protection of law while similarly placed women are weak and in need of protection.

Sections 354 and 509 of the IPC lay down punishments for assault, use of criminal force, words or gestures intended to outrage the modesty of a woman. These sections clearly recognize gender-based assumptions of male and female sexuality. Any public gesture of sexuality towards women is outrageous to their modesty but similar actions by women towards men are outside the purview of law. The law seems to presume that either men have no modesty or their modesty is impossible to outrage or even when it is outraged they can take care of themselves without needing protection from law.

Further, the fact that only nominal punishment has been provided for outraging the modesty of a woman[29] gives the message that the law does not take a serious view of such actions. The rationale for this approach can only be the sexist assumption that male sexual urges are naturally irrepressible.

PROSTITUTION, TRAFFICKING AND ILLICIT INTERCOURSE

The criminal law as contained in the IPC and the Immoral Traffic Prevention Act, 1986 perceive prostitution as a necessary evil which should be contained but not be completely prohibited. The laws do criminalize the outward manifestations like soliciting, brothel-keeping, trafficking in women for prostitution, but do not ban prostitution *per se*. Formulated in this manner, women in prostitution are exposed to harassment by the police and exploitation by pimps and customers.

The law still has not responded to women's demands for recognizing that women in prostitution have made the best economic choice possible in the circumstances and that prostitution should be decriminalised to protect their legal rights.[30] It continues to view prostitution as a necessary social evil nurtured by immorality and illicit relationships.

Sections 372 and 373 of the IPC declare as offences the selling or buying of minor/s for the purpose of prostitution. These sections apply to males and females below the age of eighteen years but provide extra protection to women. Explanations to these sections lay down the presumption that possession of a female by a prostitute or a brothel-keeper is for the purpose of prostitution. These sections also apply if the minor is sold or purchased with the intent that such minor, at any age, shall be employed or used for illicit intercourse or for any unlawful and immoral purpose. For the purposes of these sections illicit intercourse is limited to heterosexual intercourse between two persons not united by marriage.

It may be noted that while Sections 372 and 373 recognize that a minor, either male or female, may be sold or purchased for the purposes of illicit intercourse or for any unlawful and immoral purpose, Sections 366, 366-A and 366-B of the IPC, dealing with kidnapping, abduction, inducing, procuring, importing for the purpose of illicit intercourse, apply only when such actions are directed against women. Though Sections 366-A and 366-B apply to a girl below the age of eighteen and twenty-one years respectively, Section 366 applies to females of all ages. The rationale for excluding men from these provisions may be traced to the notions of morality, virginity and chastity applicable to women. Men found in situations of illicit intercourse do not suffer either a social stigma or a psychological scar, as it is acceptable behaviour given the assumptions about the nature of male sexuality. But women lured into such situations will perhaps end up being prostitutes due to the social and psychological repercussions of illicit intercourse with them. That also explains the inclusion of prostitution, and illicit intercourse in the same sections.

All offences relating to sexuality, except rape of a wife between 12-15 years of age, are cognizable even though the punishment prescribed for some of these offences is as low as imprisonment up to three months,[31] one year[32] and two years.[33] Among these the more serious offences punishable by up to ten years of imprisonments[34] and life imprisonments[35] are declared as non-bailable while others are bailable. These provisions are a clear indication that the state takes a very serious view of the exploitation of women for illicit intercourse by coming down heavily on the persons accused or found guilty of these offences. However, nominal punishments actually imposed by courts in rape cases and the gender biases operating in their determination led to the demand for prescription of mandatory minimum punishments and changes in the principles of evidence[36] resulting in amendment of the law.[37] A new provision has been incorporated which makes disclosure of the identity of a rape victim punishable.[38]

PROCREATION

Sections 312 to 318 of the IPC relate to miscarriage, injuries to unborn children, exposure of infants and concealment of births. Abortion (except for the purpose of saving the life of the woman[39]), causing death of the woman in an attempt to abort,[40] preventing a live birth or causing death of child after[41] birth, causing death of quick unborn child[42] and exposure and abandonment of a child under twelve years of age[43] are all offences under the IPC as the scheme of these sections indicates that those offences are considered as serious by the IPC. The periods of imprisonment prescribed are quite substantial ranging from seven years to ten years and life except under Sections 312 and 318. All offences except that under Section 312, are cognizable and non-bailable—another indicator of the framers' perception of their serious nature. These sections are formulated in gender neutral terms adopting the sameness approach and deal with men and women in the same manner. In fact, they seem to be protective of women as they lay down a greater punishment if the offence is committed without the woman's consent. A deeper analysis of the operations and the assumptions underlying the law bring out the gender biases inherent in these provisions.

The gender-neutral terms of these provisions concerning the sex of the fetus aborted or the infant banned or killed ensures their equal application whether the fetus or child victim in question is male or female. Male feticide and infanticide, however, are exceptional in India. The problem is of female feticide and infanticide. These provisions by their gender neutrality hide the real problem. In fact, the instances of female infanticide and feticide were found to be far too many to be dealt with under a gender-neutral law and special penal statutes, namely, the Female Infanticide Act, 1864 and the Prenatal Diagnostic Techniques (Regulation and Prevention of Misuse) Act, 1994 were required to be enacted to deal with both these evil practices.

Nature has ordained a primary role to women in procreation of children. It is women who bear and give birth to children. Logically they should, therefore, be able to decide whether to have a child or not and be equally responsible for aborting a fetus or injuring an infant. The social and physical child-bearing experiences of Indian women, however, require a different approach.

The majority of the Indian population is Hindu, mostly patriarchal and within Hindu thought sons are required to carry the family name. The belief and practices of the majority community influence the attitudes of other communities as well. Most Hindus believe that they will go to heaven if their son performs the last rituals after their death. It is considered almost a scared duty of a married Hindu woman to give birth to a son. As daughters they are less wanted, less taken care of, less fed, less educated and so on. Women are denied the opportunities for development of basic social and psychological abilities needed for decision-making. At the end of the road as women they have a lower social status than men. They get fewer chances to deal with the world on their own and depend heavily on men even for their survival. In most instances women do not have the social status, economic standing and psychological strength to go against the decision of the men.

The gender-neutral terms of the IPC provisions making women equally liable for abortion or injury to foetus and infants ignore that women in India are socialized in the religious and cultural environment of 'son preference'. Women suffer numerous pregnancies and abortions injurious to their own health under the tremendous social and psychological pressure generated by this belief. The law further ignores women's experiences by keeping certain other aspects of childbearing outside its ambit. For example, impregnating a woman regardless of her wishes or against the advice of a doctor remain outside the realm of the IPC. It is also not an offence to abandon a pregnant woman or to deny her required medical care and attention during pregnancy or at childbirth or soon thereafter.

A comparison of the assumptions underlying the provisions relating to sexuality with those relating to procreation reveals the double standard of law not only between men and women but also among different subject matters concerning women. In matters relating to her sexuality within or outside marriage it is assumed that she is incapable of forming a will. When it comes to pregnancy whether through a forced or consensual sexual intercourse, it is assumed that she has the capacity to take decisions with or without the agreement of the man responsible for such pregnancy. Not only is this differential approach to 10 women's agency based in the private-public dichotomy and patriarchy, it also does not give any space for a differential experience in either situation.

The underpinnings of the policy of the law against abortion have another gender dimension also despite its apparent moral basis in the natural right to life. Women's right to life includes the right over their body and should give them an absolute right to decide whether to bear a child or not. The right to life for the unborn means the right to be born. The Medical Termination of Pregnancy Act, 1971 allows abortion only in specified circumstances, e.g. where the health of the pregnant mother is endangered, failure of contraceptives. The grounds permitting abortion of a fetus do not have even a semblance of balancing the right of the unborn to be born and the right of the woman over her body. The Act curtails the right of the unborn to be born, without recognizing women's right over their bodies. The Act was and continues to be a population control measure and does not recognise a woman's right over her body.

MARRIAGE

Prior to 1983, Chapter XX of the IPC dealt with offences relating to marriage. It included offences relating to cohabitation and sexual access by persons through deceitful inducement of belief of marriage, bigamous marriage, adultery and enticing or taking away a married woman. In 1983, a new Chapter XX-A 'Of Cruelty by Husband or Relatives of Husband' consisting of only one Section 498-A was added in the IPC. In 1986, Section 304-B dealing with dowry death was inserted in the IPC.

Offences Relating to Marriage

Three of the six sections included in this chapter are concerned with sexual relationships and marriage and may be committed only by men.[44] The exclusion of women from penal liability for these offences is directly linked to stereotyping and role socialisation of male and female sexuality.

The sections relating to offences of bigamous marriage[45] and fraudulently going through marriage ceremony without a lawful marriage[46] use the word 'he'. In contrast, the sections dealing with inducement of a belief of marriage in order to cohabit or to have sexual intercourse use the word 'man'.[47] As usage of the word 'he' in contradistinction to 'man' changes the scope of a provision in the IPC, the former set of offences may be committed by either a man or a woman but it is only the man who is liable for the latter offence. There are two plausible explanations for exclusion of women from this offence. Either the law does not believe that women can induce a belief of marriage in a man in order to cohabit or to have sexual intercourse or even if they can do so men will not suffer any adverse consequences because of that. Men can look after themselves in such situations.

The provisions relating to adultery make liable only the man in the adulterous relation and not the married woman.[48] It is further provided that the aggrieved person entitled to file a complaint of the matter is the husband.[49] The underlying patriarchal notions are too apparent to be ignored. First, these provisions look at married women as victims, incapable of either expressing their sexuality or to protect themselves against the lecherous behaviour of other scheming men. Second, the husband is conceived as having the sole proprietary rights over his wife's sexuality, which are violated by the intruder. Third, the law does not take cognizance of the situation when the man committing adultery with another married woman, may himself be married. By denying a criminal remedy to the wife of an adulterous husband, the law monopolizes access of the husband to his wife's sexuality. The wife has no legal protection to secure similar reciprocal monopoly over her husband's sexuality. Interestingly enough, one of the justifications offered for this discriminatory approach is that whereas a wife by an adulterous affair can burden her husband with an offspring not his own,[50] no such possibility exists with the husband's sexual relationships outside marriage. This rationale is offered despite the fact that all parents are obligated to maintain not only their legitimate but also illegitimate children.[51]

A comparison of Section 375 fourthly and Section 493 bring out another discrepancy. Both sections punish the man who cohabits with a woman to whom he knows he is not married and that she has given the consent for cohabitation believing herself to be married to him. Section 493 applies when the man deceitfully created the belief of marriage but the woman was not mistaken about the identity of the man.[52] But if she was under a misconception as to his identity, even though he did not create that misconception, the man is liable for rape.[53] With the introduction of mandatory minimum punishment of seven years imprisonment for rape, the man convicted under Section 493 may receive very much less punishment even though the substantive nature of the activity under both sections remains the same. In fact, the man liable under Section 493 is more devious as he not only exploits the wrongful belief but also deceitfully creates that belief in the woman according to the requirement of the section. Further, it is provided that cognizance of this offence cannot be taken by any court unless the complaint is made by the aggrieved party,[54] i.e. the woman deceived, while court's jurisdiction can be invoked in rape cases by information of the offence by anyone.

Section 498-A makes a husband and his relatives liable to imprisonment up to three years if they subject the woman to cruelty. Cruelty includes two kinds of actions : (a) any wilful conduct of a nature which is likely to drive a woman to commit suicide or cause grave mental or physical injury or danger to life, limb or health; and (b) harassment for meeting unlawful demand for property or valuable security or on account of failure to meet such demand.

At the outset it may be noted that this chapter has been inserted between the chapter dealing with offences relating to marriage and another dealing with defamation. Thematically this placement indicates that the offence contained therein is considered closer to offences relating to marriage 'rather than offences affecting the human body and that it is not a serious offence.'

This perception is further fortified by the fact that limitations on initiation of prosecution under this chapter are similar to those provided for offences relating to marriage. Section 198-A of the

CRPC requires that courts can take cognizance of this offence only on a police report or complaint by the woman, her closest relatives or with the leave of the court by any other person related to her by blood, marriage or adoption. By this provision the state continues to show its hesitation to intervene in the realm of family and marriage even if it is likely to cost the woman's life. The state machinery comes into operation *suo moto* after she loses her life and not on a reasonable possibility of such an eventuality if she or her kith and kin do not complain.

Section 498-A itself has further limitations on its scope and does not take cognizance of a woman's day-to-day experience of violence in the household. The section takes cognizance of cruelty only by husbands and his relatives, precluding imposition of any liability if an unmarried, widowed or separated woman is subjected to cruelty by members of her natal family. Reports of brothers subjecting their sisters to cruelty to sign off their share in property are not unknown. Further, it takes cognizance of only such conduct which is likely to drive a woman to commit suicide or to cause 'grave' injury or danger to life. Women are subjected to such cruelty but almost all women suffer from cruelty of lesser degree in the household. A woman subjected to occasional beatings not causing 'grave' injury is not entitled to any protection from the state. The family ideology, stereotyping of woman's role and behaviour are further hindrances to getting any action initiated for a non-cognizable offence like hurt caused by a husband, even if a woman chooses to file a complaint before a magistrate.

DOWRY DEATH

Section 304-B of the IPC read with Section 113-B of the Evidence Act deals with a married woman's death within seven years of marriage due to bums, injuries or in circumstances other than normal. These provisions lay down that if soon before her death she was subjected to harassment for dowry by her husband or his relatives, such death shall be presumed to be dowry death and such person shall be deemed to have caused her death. Mandatory minimum imprisonment of seven years but which may extend to life has been prescribed for the offence.

The assumptions under the section and its formulation are also far from being unproblematic. It assumes that a woman is harassed in marriage only for dowry or that harassment for dowry alone is worthy of legal protection. A woman in India may be harassed because she is of dark colour or because some disaster befell the household with her entry into the household or that she is infertile or that she has failed to give birth to a son and so on. If she is found dead in the circumstances mentioned in Section 304-B, conviction of her husband or his relatives for murder or abatement to commit suicide is almost impossible in the absence of enough proof. As the harassment and death occurs in the husband's house, proof of such harassment or how actually the death occurred, is not available to the prosecution. The same problem was faced in case of harassment for dowry and that is why the presumption of harassment was laid down in the case of dowry death. However, death of a woman in unnatural circumstances preceded by harassment for any reason other than dowry, has not been taken cognizance of by the legislature. It may be noted that Section 304-B applies if a woman harassed for dowry dies 'within seven years of her marriage'. If she survived the torture and bore the harassment for seven long years but dies in abnormal circumstances after that, her death is dealt with at par with other deaths in similar circumstances. The assumption of the law is that once the magic seven years of marriage are over, either the torture/ harassment ceases or it was non-existent in the household for the woman to have survived that long or it was not grave for the woman to have endured it. *Prima facie*, no presumptions may be raised if a woman dies of bums etc., or in circumstances other than normal even if there was proof that she was being harassed for one or the other reason before her death.

The section further poses new interpretational challenges. When can a person be said to have died "otherwise than in normal circumstances"? Suicide may be included and sudden heart failure excluded but what about a woman who dies in the absence of proper medical care? Further, what is the meaning of 'soon before her death'? When will an instance of harassment be soon enough to qualify for proving this requirement of dowry? If a woman was being harassed for dowry for three years but was not so harassed for the last one, two or six months before her mysterious death, will earlier harassment constitute 'soon before her death'? A comparison of the penal, procedural and evidentiary provisions relating to Sections 498-A and 304-B shows that the state has followed the policy of symbolic intervention in the private sphere of family at the request of the woman aggrieved by severely injurious conduct of her husband or his relatives. A married woman is required to lose her life for the state to swing into action. Even though the state responded to the demand of the women's movement of the early and mid-eighties and amended the laws relating to rape, marital rape and dowry harassment, the provisions fell short of women's expectations.

It is also necessary to take note of the fact that all offences relating to marriage under Chapter XX, marital rape and rape of the separated wife are noncognizable and bailable,[55] even though the punishment prescribed for some of the offences is up to seven and ten years of imprisonment.[56] The non-cognizable nature of these offences not only makes initiation of investigation possible only after an order to that effect by a magistrate but also conveys a message to the investigating agency that the offence is not considered serious enough. It also provides the magistrate an opportunity to exercise discretion in ordering initiation of investigation. In view of the generally prevalent and accepted patriarchal norms, it is not unlikely that the order is guided by such considerations rather than by an objective assessment of whether *prima facie* a case is made out. The offence of cruelty against married women is cognizable if the persons specified therein file the complaint. It is only after a married woman loses her life for dowry that the offence within marriage is considered serious enough to be fully cognizable.

Classification of a majority of these offences as bailable.[57] Suggests that these are considered to be not serious and may also dissuade a victim from filing a complaint for fear of reprisals from the accused who can avail as a matter of right in these offences.

The combination of long sentences with classification of offences as non-cognizable and bailable in case of offences relating to marriage are in interesting contrast to the punishments and classifications concerning offences relating to sexuality. Obscenity under Section 294 is punishable with as low a punishment as imprisonment up to 3 months but the offence is cognizable. In fact, almost all offences relating to sexuality are cognizable though the punishment ranges from imprisonment up to one year to 10 years or life imprisonment. The link with the private-public dichotomy in these hands-off and hands-on pattern in relation to marriage and sexuality is apparent.

MISCELLANEOUS

Some other provisions too reflect the values and norms of the time when the IPC was enacted. The definition in Section 27 of the IPC clarifies that when property is in possession of a person's 'wife', (clerk or servant), on account of that person, it is in the person's (husband's) possession within the meaning of this Code. As some other sections in contradistinction have used the words 'wife or husband', e.g. Section 52-A, it is pertinent to ask whether the same rule will apply to the property of a wife in possession of the husband on her account and will she be considered to be in possession for the purposes of this Code?

Section 477 lays down, among other things, punishment for willful destruction of a document that is an authority to adopt a 'son'. The reference to adoption of a son was justified in the period when the section was enacted as at that time the old Hindu law permitted adoption of sons only. But in today's era when either a son or daughter may be adopted, the continued reference to son only in the section is outdated. It may justifiably be asked today whether wilful destruction of a document authorizing adoption of a daughter will be an offence under this section? Positive answers to these questions may be given by a liberal construction of 'wife' as referring to 'spouse' and 'son' to 'child' but in criminal law the rule applied is of strict interpretation and all benefits accrue to the accused. Further interpretational difficulties may be faced in view of the distinction expressly mentioned in the usage of man and woman. As a section using the word man or woman does not connote a reference to a human being, it will be difficult to interpret 'son' as 'child' or 'wife' or 'husband' as 'spouse'.

Section 361 lays down the cut-off ages of sixteen and eighteen years for boys and girls respectively for the purposes of kidnapping from lawful guardianship. The section adopts a projectionist approach reinforcing the idea that women are weak and require protection for a longer period. By the same token, it curtails the liberty of the females between the age group of sixteen to eighteen while leaving the male of that age group free of legal regulations. It may be recollected that a woman above 16 years is considered capable of giving valid consent to sexual intercourse but she cannot give consent to be taken away from lawful guardianship. The interplay of the public-private dichotomy and patriarchal alues has operated to give advantage to males in both situations. If a young unmarried woman indulges in extra-marital sexual activities, the law looks at her with suspicion and allows evidence of her moral character to the advantage of the man charged with rape. But if she remains a virgin and under the lawful control of her guardian (usually her father), the law protects the rights of the guardian by punishing the intruder. The consent of the girl of 16-18 years of age does not absolve an accused charged with the offence of kidnapping while it can in case of rape.

REASONABLE MAN/WOMAN

Another important aspect that needs to be examined is the concept of reasonableness that permeates the administration of criminal justice. Reasonableness of the behaviour of the accused and victims at and around the time of offence plays an important role in determining the guilt of the accused and the quantum of punishment. Depending on the judge's perception of what is reasonable or unreasonable, an accused may be convicted/acquitted, his/her punishment reduced increased. Western feminist lawyers and writers have been challenging the male standards underlying the concept of 'reasonable man'. In the English case of *R.* v. *Ahluwalia*[58], Kiranjeet Ahluwalia sprinkled petrol on her husband after he had gone to bed and set him on fire. She was convicted for murder by the lower court. On appeal the charge was reduced to manslaughter by reference to diminished responsibility in view of her long-term battering. She had been married for ten years and was frequently and severely abused physically by her husband during that period. Cases of battered women who kill tend to follow a pattern. The woman waits till the batterer is drunk or in bed before striking. The theory of slow bum and battered woman syndrome have been advanced before the US courts as justifying and excusing defences when such women kill the aggressors.[59]

Katherine O'Donovan[60] brings out the male experiences and male standards underlying the very formulation of the defences of grave and sudden provocation and private defence. The defence of grave and sudden provocation may reduce the charge of murder to culpable homicide if the victim was killed whilst deprived of the power of self-control due to sudden and grave provocation. It took 274 years from the first announcement of the defence of grave and sudden provocation to recognise that wives who killed their husbands or their husbands' lovers too may suffer a jealous rage similar to men and avail themselves of the defence.[61] In case of battered wives the very nature of prolonged violence, the apparent initial tolerance by the victim, and her failure to respond violently immediately is contrary to 'the heat of the moment' requirement of the current definition of provocation. Delay in reacting to the violence and waiting till her tormentor went to bed denote 'revenge'.

The law of private defense requires existence of an imminent danger and use of reasonable force to repel that force. The idea of force proportional to the attack is based on the notion of persons roughly equal in strength and aggression. Use of a weapon by a woman in response to a fist or a boot does not satisfy the proportionality test. For a woman smaller in size and lighter in weight than her aggressor, use of physical force to repel the attack is not practicable. Use of poison in such instances indicates a strong element of planning to the male view of the situation. For a woman violently battered over a long period of time, temporary withdrawal of the batterer from active aggression does not signify cessation of danger. She may have a well-founded fear of future attack based on previous experience but that is not imminent danger as formulated by law. Given women's lesser violence, it is likely that the law of self-defense evolved in the context of male patterns of behaviour. And it continues to judge a woman's reaction to what she perceives as an imminently dangerous situation by male standard of reasonableness.

There are numerous instances in the Indian case law to show that when it comes to offences involving women victims and women offenders, rhetoric and passion guide the decision instead of objectivity and reason. The standards applied to judge a woman's behaviour are male centric. At other times stereotypical role expectations and patriarchal values decide the issue.

For example, in a bride burning case, the Rajasthan High Court ordered public hanging of the accused for this barbaric offence and directed amendment of the jail manual for the purpose if need be. The Supreme Court reversed this decision saying that it had been made more out of anger than on reasons. Judicial discretion should not be swayed by emotions and indignation.[62] The Delhi High Court imposed the sentence of death on the paramour and life imprisonment with a fine of rupees one lakh on the wife for having killed her husband. On appeal the Supreme Court found the trial court had been guided by the unrepentant attitude of the accused whilst the High Court was more on the moralistic aspect of the matter. Even if these two aspects were allowed full play, the apex court ruled, the case did not come within the criterion of rarest of rare required for the imposition of the death sentence. The death sentence of the paramour was therefore reduced to life. The woman never appealed and ended up with life imprisonment and the huge fine.[63]

In Sathin's case,[64] from Rajasthan, the sessions judge acquitted the accused because, among other things, immediate report of her rape by the victim, Bhanwari Devi, straight to the police without first informing her in-laws was 'unnatural'. In *State of Haryana* v. *Prem Chand*[65], the judges gave less than the mandatory minimum punishment because of the victim's conduct in reporting the rape five days later. The sessions judge in Bhanwari's case expected her to take some time before reporting, and the Supreme Court judges gave benefit to the accused when the victim delayed the reporting of the matter in Prem Chand.

In *Raju* v. *State of Karnataka*[66] the sessions judge considered imprisonment till the rising of the court and fine of rupees five hundred adequate punishment for rape. The High Court increased the imprisonment to seven years. The Supreme Court reduced it to three years. It said that the victim had agreed to sleep in the same room with the accused and the young accused were overpowered by lust during the course of the night. The victim was to be responsible not just for her own but for their sexuality as well.

Another woman, Gyarsibai jumped into a well with her children due to continuous bickering with her sister-in-law. Her children died and she was convicted for murder.[67] Her action did not constitute a reasonable excuse for mitigating the charge to culpable homicide. She could have moved out from the unhappy situation is the usual refrain. Moving out of an unhappy marriage is an option from a mate perspective. There is complete absence of any psychological and physical support structure for women in such an eventuality. Women experience many more unending and insurmountable problems rather than the end of their problems by moving out.

Criminal law in India needs to control the double standards and male-centered standard prevailing under the concept of 'reasonable man' and 'reasonableness'.

CONCLUSION

The above analyses show the latent and patent gender biases operating in the conceptualization, formulation and operation of criminal law. In its present form it excludes perspectives, interests, and experiences of women to a large extent by maintaining the private-public dichotomy and incorporation of patriarchal values. It also reinforces the typical stereotypical image of women as weak and in need of protection. With its current patriarchal nature and gender biases, it is not surprising that the law enforcement officers have negative attitudes towards offences against women, resulting thereby in their refusal to register complaints, or in frivolous and delayed investigations or acquittal or imposition of nominal punishments in case of conviction. As a result, women who take recourse to legal remedies find the system to be more cumbersome than supportive. This in turn results in hesitation to take recourse to criminal law in times of distress.

Gender injustice resulting from the patriarchal nature of the law has led to active discourses for reconceptualization and reformulating of the law. The National Commission for Women has proposed enactment of a comprehensive code on criminal laws relating to women and had nation-wide consultations on its advisability. The proposal has been mooted "in order to obtain justice to women in the true sense of the term.... This venture ... is an exploratory exercise, as many of the crimes being perpetrated against women today, has (sic) not found an adequate place in any of the existing laws".[68] The Commission is seeking to: examine the inadequacies and adequacies of criminal laws relating to women and efficiency of their administration; draw out either a separate comprehensive code or a separate chapter in the IPC relating to crimes against women; emphasize payment of compensation to women victims of atrocities; draw sentencing guidelines; emphasize setting up of special courts to handle atrocities against women.[69]

Many debates took place in the Conference organized by the National Commission for Women in Delhi on whether the proposal was for codification or rather consolidation or compilation of relevant existing laws relating to women. Though the National Commission for Women did clarify that its ultimate objective is codification, the proposal in its present form neither contains an exhaustive list of all criminal laws relating to women nor the concrete amendments to such provisions or suggestions of new sections nor has it found much support from participants either in Delhi or in Hyderabad.

The Law Commission of India is in the process of finalizing its report on the IPC. It has already submitted its report on the CRPC to Parliament. The Commission has made various suggestions for special protection for women victims and offenders. The main thrust of the suggestions is to involve women, as many and as often as possible, in the various stages of proceedings. The suggestions proceed on the assumption that integration of women during investigation and trial will automatically result in feminization of proceedings. (What it ignores is that men and women are the product of similar socialization processes.) Their value patterns are the result of their upbringing and not only their sex. Women may be as paternalistic as men once they are in position of power. The criminal procedure needs to be changed to bring in democratization and empowerment of its subjects rather than its enforcers.

Paternalism and exclusion of women have been the main focus of feminist critique of the legal system. The Law Commission does very little to change that through its suggestions. The Law Commission has suggested exclusion of women prisoners sentenced to life imprisonment from Section 433-A of the CrPC. The suggestion betrays the paternalistic and stereotypical notions of women at the base. Section 433-A has been held not to apply to juveniles convicted under the Borstal Schools Act applicable in Andhra Pradesh. Consequently, the Commission had recommended that a similar approach should be adopted in regard to women prisoners, particularly because long and continuous imprisonment of women prisoners might prejudicially affect the welfare and well-being of other members of their families.

The suggestion in its essence equates women with children. It also reinforces their role as homemakers. The objection is not to the suggestion but to the logic of the suggestion. The emphasis on having only women, as far as possible, as investigators and judges will lead to another kind of exclusion from the legal system-exclusion from the mainstream of the law. What we need is not soft and segregated justice for women but integration of women's experiences and concerns in the entire legal system. It is not possible at this juncture to predict the fate of the proposals made and about to be made by the Law Commission. It is certain though that the criminal law needs an exhaustive review. It has long been recognised that law is an instrument of social change as well as of the maintenance of *status quo*. Criminal law too serves both the purposes. It is used to curb certain social practices considered as evil, inhuman, oppressive, etc., by a given state at a particular time. Criminal law and policy, like any other law, is influenced by and incorporates the values and norms of the dominant groups in the state. Feminist writings have brought to light how the public-private dichotomy of various political theories have kept women out of realm of law and legal regulations to their detriment.[70] More and more feminist writings continue to expose the patriarchal biases incorporated in various laws and legal principles securing better rights to men and reinforcing stereotypical inferior images of women.[71]

The history of legislation in India does show that laws have been amended numerous times pursuant to social movements and pressure from elite groups. Such amendments, however, have been piecemeal and not aimed at structural changes. The criminal law needs to be gender sensitized in its conception, formulation and administration to actually ensure equal protection to women. Criminal law or for that matter any other law, is not a solution to all the problems facing women but its importance in laying down new norms cannot be ruled out.

Equality has been accepted as the basic principle of civil society. All laws need conceptual scrutiny but criminal law needs it the most. Criminal law in India for far too long has ensured law and order by maintaining *status quo* among various groups in the state. As in other societies, men as a group in India have enjoyed a better social and political status compared to women. Piecemeal amendments and innovative interpretations introduce a perception of equality to women without bringing any structural changes in the law. A protective approach is entrapped in paternalism and the sameness approach ignores the difference in the social reality for men and women. The challenge is to ensure equality while respecting the differences between men and women to ensure substantive equality to women.

Notes and References

1. Section 8, IPC.
2. *Id.* Section 10.
3. *Id.* Sections 292 to 294.
4. *Id.* Sections 354, 375, 376, 376-A, 376-B, 376-C, 376-D, 377, 509.21
5. *Id.* Sections 372, 373.
6. *Id.* Sections 366, 366-A, 366-B.
7. *Id*, Sections 376-B, 376-C and 376-D.
8. The Victorian middle class ideal of womanhood made women 'the angel in the house', the 'relative creature' who maintained the home as a haven. The transition of society from feudalism to capitalism involved a recodification of women's roles as mothers and wives. Evangelicalism provided a crucial influence on the definition of home and family and women were projected as custodians of mortality and spirituality. Evangelicals expected women to sustain and even to improve the moral qualities of the opposite sex. See, generally, Catherine Hall, White, Male and Middle Class: Explorations in Feminism and History, Polity Press,

U.K., 1992, pp. 75-93; Roberta Hamilton, The Liberation of Women: A Study of Patriarchy and Capitalism, Allen and Unwin, London, 1978, pp. 23-49.

9. *Id.* Section 292.
10. R. *v.* Hicklin (1868) LR 3 QB 360, namely, whether the tendency of the matter charged as obscene is to deprave and corrupt those whose minds are open to such immoral influences and into whose hands a publication of this sort may fall.
11. Comments by the Centre for Feminist Legal Research on the First Report of the UN Special Rapporteur on Violence Against Women, including its causes and consequences, Centre for Feminist Legal Research, New Delhi, 1995, pp. 6-7.
12. *Id.* at p. 6
13. *Id.* at pp. 6-7.
14. The anti-porn approach has been criticised by other feminists on the following grounds: (a) the anti-porn position reduces misogyny and sexism to sexuality and its representations; (b) it diverts attention from the sexism and misogyny at work within the traditional institutions like family, religion, judiciary; (c) the focus on explicitness assumes that it is the explicitness that causes men to rape; (d) it poses the danger of providing a ground for mitigation of sentence of rapists; (e) it also risks forming alliances with the moral right which are pro-family and anti-feminist.
15. *Id.* at p. 7.22
16. Section 29(c) of the Indecent Representation of Women (Prohibition) Act 1986.
17. See the amendments proposed by students of National Law School of India University, included in Shifting Boundaries: A report and commentary on the workshop on women, law and media, Centre for Feminist Legal Research in association with the Asia Pacific Forum on Women, Law and Development, Annexure N, Centre for Feminist Legal Research, New Delhi, 1994.
18. Bobby Art International *v.* Om Pal Singh Hoon, (1996) 4 SCC 1.
19. E.g. in Calder (John) Publications Ltd. *v.* Powell 1965 (1) All ER 159, it was held that Cain's Bookmight property be found obscene, on the ground that it"...highlighted as it were, the favourable effects of drug-taking and, so far from condemning it, advocated it, and that there was a real danger that those into whose hands the book came might be tempted at any rate to experiment with drugs and get the favourable sensations highlighted by the book".
20. 413 US 15 (1973).
21. Section 375 sixthly, IPC.
22. *Id.* Exception to section 375.
23. *Id.* Section 376(1) lays down imprisonment of either description up to two years or fine or both.
24. *Id.* Section 376-A lays down imprisonment of either description up to two years and fine.
25. *Id.* Section 375 fourthly.

26. Sections 155(4) and 146 of Evidence Act 1872.
27. Shomona Khanna and Ratna Kapur, Memorandum on Reform of Laws Relating to Sexual Offences, Centre for Feminist Legal Research, New Delhi, 1996, p. 11.
28. Inserted by Criminal Law (Amendment) Act, 1983.
29. Section 509, IPC lays down simple imprisonment up to one year or fine or both.
30. See Submissions Pertaining to the Discrimination Against Women in response to the GOI Third Periodic Report under the International Covenant on Civil and Political Rights, Centre for Feminist Legal Research, New Delhi, p. 7 and Comments by Centre for Feminist Legal Research, supran.11 at pp. 4-5.
31. Section 294 IPC.
32. *Id.* Section 509.
33. *Id.* Section 292, 354.
34. *Id.* Sections 366, 366-A, 366-B, 372, 373, 375.
35. *Id.* Sections 375, 376.
36. See Upendra Baxi *et.al.*, "Open Letter to the Chief Justice", (1979) 4 SCC (Jour).
    "Memoranda for Amending the Rape Law" (Mimeo)·1980; 8th Law Commission Report on Rape and Allied Offences: Some Questions of Substantive Law Procedure and Evidence, Controller of Publications, New Delhi, 1980.
37. E.g., Section 376, IPC; Section 114-A, Evidence Act.
38. Section 238-A, IPC.
39. *Id.* Sections 312, 313. The Medical Termination of Pregnancy Act 1971 has legalised abortion in case of failure of contraceptives and in case the pregnancy will be against the mental or physical well-being of the mother.
40. Section 314, IPC.
41. *Id.* Section 315.
42. *Id.* Section 316.
43. *Id.* Section 317.
44. *Id.* Sections 493, 497 and 498.
45. *Id.* Sections 494, 495.
46. *Id.* Section 496.
47. *Id.* Section 493.24
48. *Id.* Section 497.
49. Section 198(2) of the CrPC.
50. Section 112 of the Evidence Act provides a presumption of legitimacy of a child born during subsistence of a valid marriage or within 280 days after its dissolution.
51. Section 125 of the CrPC.
52. Section 493 of the IPC reads: Every man who by deceit causes any woman who is not lawfully married to him to believe that she is lawfully married to him and to cohabit or have sexual intercourse with him in that belief, shall be punished with imprisonment of for a term which may extend to ten years, and shall also be liable to fine".

53. Section 375 fourthly of the IPC reads with her consent, when the man knows that he is not her husband, that her consent is given because she believes that he is another man to whom she is or believes herself to be lawfully married.
54. Section 198 of the IPC.
55. Except for offence under Section 493 of the IPC.
56. E.g., *id.* offences under Sections 493 to 496.
57. Except for offences under Sections 304-B, 493 and 498-A of the IPC.
58. 1992(4) All ER 889.
59. L. Walker, The Battered Women, Harper, New York, 1979; The Battered Women Syndrome, Springer Pub. Co., New York, 1984. The idea of slow burn has been considered by the California Court in People *v.* Berry18 Cal. 3rd 509 concerning male defendants.
60. Katherine O'Donovan, "Defenses for Battered Women who Kill", 18(2) Law and Society, Summer1991, p. 219.
61. *Id.* at p. 226.
62. Lichma Devi *v.* State of Rajasthan1986 Raj LR 83; Lichma Devi *v.* State of Rajasthan(1988) 4 SCC 456: 1988 SCC(Cri) 978.25
63. Ashok Kumar *v.* State1995 Supp(4) SCC 513.
64. For an extract of the Sessions Court judgement See 11(1) The Lawyers' Collective, January 1996, pp.7-12 and 26-28.
65. (1990) 1 SCC 249: 1990 SCC (Cri) 93.
66. (1995) 1 SCC 453: 1994 SCC (Cri) 538.
67. Gyarsibai *v.* StateAIR 1953 MB 61.
68. Report on National Debate on Codification of Criminal Laws Pertaining to Women, National Commission for Women, New Delhi, July 27, 1996, p. 1.
69. Proposal for Codification of Criminal Law Pertaining to Women, National Commission for Women, New Delhi, 1996, p. 2.
70. See generally, Mary Lyndom Shanley, and Carole Pateman (eds.) Feminist Interpretation and Political Theory, Polity Press, U.K., 1991, for the analysis of various political thinkers' assumptions about women's inferiority at the base of the natural law human beings by nature are ordained to attain their full potential. Becoming male is attaining full potential of birth. Female body does not have than potential and, therefore, he assumed natural inferiority of the female. She is who failed to become male. He excluded females from the rights of citizenship and thereby, involving themselves in the governance of state because of their inferior intellectual capacity. When he said that the state is natural and its function is to bring out the best in men, he was talking literally of propertied men to the exclusion of slaves and women. See also; Carol Patman, The Sexual Contract, Polity Press, U.K., 1988, for the feminist critique of the social contract theory. The standard commentaries on the classical social contract theory do not usually mention that women were excluded from the original pact. But it was men who made the original contract. The device of the state of nature was used to explain why, given the characteristics of the inhabitants of the natural condition, entry into the original contract was a rational act. Only masculine beings were

endowed with the attributes and capacities necessary to enter into contracts, the most important of which was ownership of property in the person. Only men were 'individuals'. State was created by thinking rational human beings for protection of life and its functions were limited to its preservation. Beyond that every person was free to do whatever one linked without any interference from the state. Keeping law out of the private sphere of family ensured liberty of men. However, this private-public division considered so essential for man's fell in the private sphere where man was the monarch without any control of law. Women found themselves at the mercy of men. See Maria Mies, *et al.* Women: the last Colony, Zed Books Ltd., London and New Jersey, 1988, for a feminist analysis of the Marxist theory of society. Marxist theory of society is based, in essence, on the assumption that overcoming oppression and exploitation depends on the development of the productive forces. Exploitation of propertyless wage-workers resulting in surplus value and capital accumulation in the hands of the owner of the means of production are of central concern to the theory. Women's work of producing and raising children are essential for the capitalist in order to have the labour force but not of direct importance as they are concerned with increasing profit. Marxist theory too gives only secondary importance to the women's work and its appropriation. Women's salvation lies in the forward march of the productive forces.

71. L. Sarkar and B. Sivaramayya (eds.) Women and Law: Contemporary Issues, Vikas, New Delhi, 1994; Brendra Cossman and Ratna Kapur, Subversive Sites Feminist Engagements with law in India, Sage, New Delhi, 1996.

3

Gender Justice in India

Women's Property Rights under Hindu and Christian Laws

SUNITHA KANIPAKAM

INTRODUCTION

Gender has been an issue in India during the colonial rule. With the effect of western culture and the status of their counterparts in European nations an overwhelming preoccupation with the woman's issue from the beginning of 19th century was emerged in India. This has been gave momentum to social reform movement in India. The Hindu Women's Right to Property Act, 1937 was one of the most important enactments that brought about changes to give better rights to women in India. This Act was the outcome of discontent expressed by a sizeable section of society against the unsatisfactory affairs of the women's rights to property. Even this Act did not give an absolute right to women. Under this Act of 1937 widow was entitled to a limited interest over the property of her husband—what was to be termed as Hindu widow's estate. The Act was amended in 1938 to exclude the widow from any interest in agricultural land. But after Independence the Government of India has enacted the Hindu

Succession Act, 1956 which introduced many reforms and it abolished completely the essential principle that runs through the estate inherited by a female heir, that she takes only a limited estate. The Supreme Court put a lot of controversy at rest by holding that[1] the woman becomes the absolute owner and the object of Section 14 is two-fold: (1) to remove the disability of a female to acquire and hold property as an absolute owner, and (2) to convert the right of woman in any estate held by her as a limited owner into an absolute owner. The provision was retrospective in the sense that it enlarged the limit of the estate into an absolute one even if the property was inherited or held by the woman as a limited owner before the Act came into force. Any property acquired under the 1937[2] Act held in capacity of a limited owner was now converted to her absolute estate.

The Hindu Succession Act, 1956 abrogates all the rules of the law of succession hitherto applicable to Hindus whether by virtue of any text or rule of Hindu law or any custom or usage having the force of laws in respect of all matters dealt with in the Act. Therefore, no woman can be denied property rights on the basis of any custom, usage or text and the said Act reformed the personal law and gave woman greater property rights. The daughters were also granted property rights in their father's estate. In 1974, the Indian government published a report, Towards Equality, that put status of women forcefully on the national agenda by arguing that the position of Indian women had declined, not improved, since 1911[3]. As a result development and progress became gender issues. According to this report there is no change in the status of women governed under other persona laws. According to the Indian Succession Act, 1925, everyone is entitled to equal inheritance, except Hindus, Sikhs, Jains, Buddhists and Muslims. Under this act, the daughter of a person dying intestate would be entitled only to one-fourth of the son's share, or Rs. 5,000 (Sthree Dhan), whichever is lesser.

THE EMERGENCE OF GENDER ISSUES

An effective social reform movement does need the help of law and a sympathetic judiciary to achieve its objectives. Women empowerment, equal rights to both men and women, equal share of property, etc., are some of the issues which we discuss everyday, in life, newspaper and on television. But the reality which bites is that these issues are still unresolved. Not much has actually been done to create equality between the male and female gender. The male still dominates society. If it's a matter of property, then legally male dominate the society. There are numerous laws that say that there should be no discrimination between the sexes, but in reality none are effective enough to actually bring about a revolution; a change in society.

HINDU SUCCESSION [ANDHRA PRADESH] AMENDMENT ACT, 1985

Several legal reforms have taken place since independence in India, including on equal share of daughters to property. Yet equal status remains illusive. It is not easy to eradicate deep seated cultural values or to alter traditions that perpetuate discrimination and even after with the enactment of Hindu Succession Act, 1956. To this existing situation a remarkable change was made by the Hindu Succession [Andhra Pradesh] Amendment Act, 1985, which initiated a remarkable development. This law states that, in any circumstances, the rights of the daughter are equal to that of the son[4]. This new law found the Mitakshara system in violation of the fundamental right of equality bestowed upon women in Indian Constitution. Following Andhra Pradesh, the States of Tamil Nadu, Maharashtra and Kerala subsequently also amended their laws by including women as members of the coparcenaries. The Rajya Sabha on August 16, 2005, passed the Hindu Succession (Amendment) Bill, 2004, (Hindu Succession (Amendment) Act, 2005) which is now a law, giving daughters and sons equal rights to property. According to this law, any woman, irrespective of the marital status, has full right to inherit ancestral property just like a son of the family. This law has completely abolished the Hindu Succession Act, 1956 by giving equal rights to daughters in the 'Hindu Mitakshara Coparceners property, as sons have. If however, any of the parents have built some property and have made a will of their own, this law would be ineffective.

Judicial Activism

The recognition of gender as an issue forms the basis for India's women's movement. To quote *Justice Sujatha* v. *Manohar* of Supreme Court of India, it is not easy to eradicate deep seated cultural values or to alter traditions that perpetuate discrimination. It is fashionable to denigrate the role of law reform in bringing about social change. Obviously law, by itself, may not be enough. Law is only an instrument. It must be effectively used. And this effective use depends as much on a supportive judiciary as on the social will to change. An active social reform movement, if accompanied by legal reform, properly enforced, can transform society.

The application of the State Act[5] was challenged in the Supreme Court in the famous Mary Roy's Case[6]. The Court ruled that the Cochin and Travancore Christian Succession Acts had ceased to be operative on the Reorganization of States and that automatically made the Indian Succession Act applicable to all Kerala Christians bestowing on them equal inheritance rights.

Hindu Succession Act 1956, sections 6 and 14 recognizes equality of sexes and elevates the women from subservient position in the field of economy to a higher pedestal, this was held by the Apex court in the case of *Bai Vijaya* v. *Thakuribai Chela Bhai*[7]. The best approach that is followed by courts gives standing to the actual intent of the legislature that was followed while incorporating section 6 in the Act. As per the liberal interpretation, the effects of a real partition should follow once the share of the deceased has been ascertained and if there are female members who would have been entitled to receive a share if a real partition had taken place, they must be given such share, irrespective of whether the primary purpose of presuming this partition was only to determine the share of the deceased coparcener[8]. A Hindu woman or girl will have equal property rights along with other male relatives for any partition made in intestate succession after September 2005, the Supreme Court has ruled.A bench of justices R.M. Lodha and Jagdish Singh Khehar in a judgment said that under the Hindu Succession (Amendment) Act, 2005, the daughters are entitled to equal inheritance rights along with other male siblings, which was not available to them prior to the amendment. The apex court said the female inheritors would not only have the succession rights but also the same liabilities fastened on the property along with the male members[9].

Equal Right a Myth

Earlier, the law use to put the male heirs on a higher footing by providing that they shall inherit an additional independent share in co-parcenary property over and above what they inherit equally with female heirs; the very concept of co-parcenary was that of "an exclusive male membership club". Now this concept has been abolished . But surprisingly, even today, even after the new law, co-parcenary remains a primary entitlement of males; no doubt law provides for equal division of share between all heirs, male and female on the death of a male co-parcener, but in practice the scene is totally different. Legally, Intestate self acquired property devolves equally between male and female heirs; but, even toady female heirs are asked to relinquish their share by making relinquishment deeds on their signature and are commonly submitted in courts. If the intestate property includes a dwelling house, the female heirs have no right to partition until the male heirs choose to divide their respective shares. If a Hindu female dies intestate, her property devolves first to husband's heirs, then to husband's father's heirs and finally only to mother's heirs; thus the intestate Hindu female property is kept within the husband's lien[10].

CONCLUSION

Even where law has given a right, conventions and practices do not recognize them. Women themselves relinquish their rights. Women, as daughters, wives, daughters-in-law, mothers or sisters tend to lose out and often suffer deprivation. This further gets accentuated when they lose the security of the family, as single woman, divorced/separated or widowed. Social awareness of the rights under law, attitudes to adhere to it and a mindset to change law and practice to ensure social justice is therefore urgent.

Notes and References

1. Under Section 14 of the Hindu Succession Act, 1956.
2. http://www.prajendran.com
3. (Committee on the Status of Women 1974).
4. G.C.V. Subba Rao, (Revised by SubbaRao, T.V., Vijendra Kumar) Family Law in India, S. Gogia & Company, 2006, pp. 466-69.
5. The Travancore Christian Succession Act, 1916.
6. Mary Roy *v.* State of Kerala, AIR 1986 SC 1011; 1986(2) SCC 209.
7. AIR 1979 SC 993.
8. Rangubai Lalji Patil *v.* Laxman Patil (1966) 68 Bom LR 74. Also see Govindram Mithamal Sindhi *v.* Chetumel Villardas AIR 1970 Bom 251; Ananda *v.* Haribandhu AIR 1967 Ori 194; Vidyaben *v.* J.N. Bhatt, AIR 1974 Guj 23; Chandralata *v.* Sarat Kumar AIR 1973 MP 169; Kanahaya Lal *v.* Jamna Devi, AIR 1973 Del 160; Karuppa Gounder *v.* Palaniammai, AIR 1963 Mad 245; Controller of Estate UP *v.* Anari Devi Halwasaiya, AIR 1972 All 179 13 AIR 1978 SC 1239s.
9. *The Hindu*, 2011 October 13.
10. Rakesh J. Saxena, Women's right to property in India: A myth or reality, (Hindu Personal Laws of India), 2011.

4

Mainstreaming Gender Perspectives in Environmental Sustainability

Role of International Organisations

G. INDIRA PRIYADARSINI

> *"A gender sustainable development perspective should be infused with a commitment to change the cultural values and sexual division of labour, to attain, in the near future, a state where men and women share power and labour in the management and control of fragile ecosystems."*
>
> —Mariam Abramovay and Gail Lerner
> (Abramovay and Lerner, 1996, p. 11)

INTRODUCTION

Gender equality and equity are not only a question of fundamental human rights and social justice, and that is also through in the environmental area. As several studies have underlined (e.g. World Bank, 2002): gender equality is essential for countries' economies and the success of development initiatives. As Lorena Aguilar (2002)—senior gender advisor of IUCN—argued, sustainable development is not possible without equity.

Worldwide, women have manifested themselves as agents of change for environment and sustainable development. This has resulted in a gender-specific approach in environment and sustainable development policies and practices. Women's active participation and empowerment are important prerequisites for such an approach. The paper combines empirical developments with some theoretical reflections on the social movement of women for environment. In the final section it will explore some outstanding challenges for the near future.

Gender mainstreaming is a process that calls for change in our attitudes and practices, particularly how we carry out our work, be it in development of programmes or in management of human resources. Being a process of change therefore makes it a long-term venture.[1] Gender mainstreaming has been on the United Nations institutional agenda for almost two decades. A series of mandates starting in the 1980s—catalysed largely by the UN "Decade of Women" conferences—directs UN agencies to implement gender mainstreaming across their operations. At the United Nations Fourth World Conference on Women, held in Beijing in September 1995, this commitment was unequivocally renewed: participating governments undertook commitments to enact comprehensive "platforms for action" intended to ensure, in the words of the conference declaration, "that a gender perspective is reflected in all policies and programmes" and that "governments and other actors promote an active and visible policy of mainstreaming a gender perspective in all policies and programmes so that, before decisions are taken, an analysis is made of the effects on women and men, respectively." Additionally, gender-mainstreaming efforts have been developed by a wide array of UN agencies, by international organizations, by NGOs, and by national governments.

The main objective of incorporating gender in environment is to enable women and men perform their roles in the best cost effective methods that will conserve the environment, accelerate sustainable development consequently lead to the improvement in people's quality of life. Women have been estimated to make up 60 to 80 percent of membership in mainstream environmental organizations and even higher percentages in grassroots movements.[2]

WOMEN'S ORGANIZATIONS

Since the early 1980s international, regional, national and local women's organizations were important actors in empowering women and bringing a gender perspective towards sustainable development. It is often through women leaders and organisations, those women's voices are speaking out against environmental destruction and for a peaceful and healthy planet. International organisations such as WEDO (the Women's Environment and Development Organisation) have followed the international agenda closely, and tried to influence it through their advocacy work. Since 1992 particular thematic networks have been formed and developed in centres of expertise, such as the Gender and Water Alliance, ENERGIA (gender and sustainable energy), the Gender and Climate Change Network, Diverse Women for Diversity (gender and biodiversity). These groups are instrumental in promoting the integration of gender into specific sectors and enhancing women's voices in those areas.

Also regional networks on women and environment have played key roles in enhancing environmental security and at the same time contribute to women's empowerment; e.g. the Women in Europe for a Common Future (WECF). Organizations like WECF, have been advocating for safe chemical and health policies, and also look into issues such as energy and climate change, safe water, and sustainable agriculture—with particular emphasis on the European context, regulations and institutions.

Professional women's organizations have been established, such as the Women Leaders for the Environment of women environment ministers, and the recently established WOCAN: a global network of professional Women in Agriculture and Natural Resource Management, an alliance to support a process of change for equality in programs and organizations.

The endurance of innumerable local groups that have organized to address local environmental challenges and concerns is amazing. Publications such as UNEP's *Women and the Environment*, try to catch the rich experience and endurance of many of these groups.

In rural Romania, over 7 million people draw drinking water mostly from wells. These are often polluted with nitrates, bacteria and pesticides that flow in from latrines, waste dumps and agriculture. The health effects are long-term (thyroid and brain dysfunctioning) and immediate (blue-baby syndrome, diarrhoea, hepatitis) and can be lethal to small children. In the late 1990s a woman, expert in water quality and doctor, together with local women's groups formed the NGO Medium & Sanitas (Environment and Health). They not only test the water, organize multi-stakeholder consultations, but also start projects for improvement of the water quality in villages and in schools. Promotion of ecosanitation and of organic agriculture, including training and education, are important parts of the projects.

In October 2004 more than 150 professionals and activists came together in Nairobi for the first WAVE conference: Women As the Voice for the Environment, hosted by UNEP (United Nations Environment Programme). It was the second time since 1985 that UNEP organized a meeting on the nexus between environment and gender. Participants in WAVE identified areas that needed priority attention: gender aspects of global environmental change (focus: climate change), gender in the conflict and environment interface, environmental health and gender, gender in the urban environment, and strengthening local-global linkages, with particular emphasis on the role and position of indigenous women.

Participants identified the following requirements for gender mainstreaming in environment:

- political will (also to share power),
- institutional adaptations,
- information: availability (incl. cases, analysis, data) and access to information,
- enhanced women's leadership and capacity building (incl. mentorship programmes),
- gender-sensitive international environmental agreements, and
- and building an environmental dimension in B+10 and in the CEDAW-convention.

The WAVE assembly resulted in a Manifesto, Recommendations and a Portfolio of project ideas to enhance women's position in environment and sustainable development.

> "*We women, from all regions of the world, call for urgent action from all stakeholders, especially the UN system, to achieve sustainable development, which requires harmony between economic policies, human rights, gender equality and environmental conservation and management.*"

The UNEP 23rd Governing Council took place in Nairobi. Women had to lobby hard, but we are very happy to announce also here that the GC adopted a Decision on Gender Equality, which requires governments to work mainstream gender into their environmental policies, and requests UNEP to develop an Action Programme on Gender and Environment and include gender issues in their overall work. Specific activities are requested in the field of conflict-environment-gender, mentoring young women leaders and in developing an environmental angle to the CEDAW convention.[3]

LOCAL LEVEL MOVEMENTS

Environmental change has itself been a source of gender role changes. Men and women tend to occupy, use and manage aspects of the biophysical environment in a gender differentiated manner. At the local level women have often played leadership roles more or taken the lead in promoting an environmental ethic, reducing resource use, and reusing and recycling resources to minimize waste and excessive consumption, e.g., Wangari Mathai's green belt movement and Chipko movement in India. Wangari Mathai led the green belt movement in Kenya by organizing women to plant trees and preserve resources. The process of mobilizing people to action addresses a wide range of issues that directly affect the lives of individuals, particularly women, including education, access to water, equity, and reproductive health. People then begin to stand up for their rights and those of their communities. It is their empowerment that leads them to decide to prioritize the environment and good governance.

The Chipko Movement started in the 1970s and 1980s as a resistance to the destruction of forests. The first Chipko action took place in April 1973 and over the next five years it spread through the entire Himalayan range in Uttar Pradesh. The name of the movement comes from a word meaning "embrace": the villagers hug the trees, saving them by interposing their bodies between them and the contractor's axes. The Chipko protests in Uttar Pradesh achieved a major victory in 1980 with a 15-year ban on green felling in the Himalayan forests of that state by order of India's then Prime Minister, Indira Gandhi. Since then the movement has spread to the entire country. The movement is an important milestone in the environmental preservation.[4]

INTERNATIONAL ORGANISATIONS

Several International Organisations have played promotional roles in bringing a gender perspective into environment and sustainable development thinking. In the 1980s United Nations Environmental Programme (UNEP) was a leader in connecting the issues of women and environment. Women play important roles in environmental management, but are not recognized as such. In 1986, the UN Division for the advancement of women, designated UNEP as lead agency for women and the environment in UN system. In 1991 UNEP women advisor's were instrumental in organizing the 'Global Assembly on women and the environment' in Miami. Since 1992 role of UNEP in gender and sustainable development has become less and focused on its own internal functioning. Some strong women leaders in the organization took up the issue and pushed the agenda and supported management.

United Nations Fund for Women (UNIFEM) has been instrumental in putting gender high agenda during the UNCED, preparatory process. Its approach was two-fold: first to mainstream a gender perspective in UN preparations for the UNCED, and to strengthen the environment-gender linkages into its own work programme. In Agenda 21 UNIFEM was assigned a specific task in integrating gender and sustainable development.

INSTRAW, the United Nations International Research and Training Institute for the Advancement of Women, was among the pioneers in the area of women, with UNICEF, INSTRAW assumed joint responsibility for the inter agency task force on women. More recently, INSTRAW carries out its programme through information and communication technologies namely GAINS—Gender Awareness Information and Networking System. Through GAINS, the Institute has continued with its programme on environmental management and sustainable development.

The International Union for the Conservation of Nature and Natural resources (IUCN) guaranteed better representation of women. IUCN is successful in mainstreaming gender in environmental issues.

In addition, other organizations, such as the Food and Agriculture Organisation (FAO), International Fund for Agricultural Development (IFAD), United Nations Educational, Scientific and Cultural Organisations (UNESCO), United Nations Population Fund (UNPF), United Nations Development Fund (UNDP), etc., have developed specific programmes in the area of gender and sustainable development.[5]

CONCLUSION

The successful mainstreaming of gender contributes to the efficiency and quality of environmental work and to gender equality in society. Gender mainstreaming requires institutional capacity in all of the areas detailed in this report. Institutions must have the knowledge base, staff expertise, political commitment, resources, capacity, institutional structure, monitoring system, and external partners to incorporate gender into all aspects of environmental work. A few countries question the relevance of the gender-specific approach in the environmental sector, while others excel in specific areas and can be considered as role models. Overall, the areas in greatest need of attention, or the 'first tier' requiring action related to gender mainstreaming in environment ministries, include organizational commitment, resources, gender expertise and capacity, and women's equal participation. The second tier for action includes tools for gender mainstreaming, gender indicators and systems for monitoring, evaluation, and reporting. The third tier for action, where the majority of governments in this group have excelled at some level, involves gender policies, and organizational structures including gender focal points, and external contacts.

Notes and References

1. The Educator, UNEP, Vol. 2, Issue 2, Mainstreaming Gender in UNEP Exclusive Interview with UNEP's Senior Gender Advisor, Ms. Janet Macharia on Mainstreaming Gender in UNEP's Programmes.
2. Seager, Joni, 1993. Earth follies: Coming to feminist terms with the global environmental crisis. New York: Routledge.
3. Irene Dankelman M.Sc., Radboud University, Nijmegen, IRDANA advices, irene.dankelman@hetnet.nl
4. *Kiran Soni Gupta, Gender and International Environmental Negotiations – How Far and How Much More?*, www.oas.org/dsd/Tool-kit/Documentos/.../Gupta%20Reading.pdf
5. Irene Dankelman, United Nations International Research and Training Institute for the Advancement of Women, Gender, Environment and Sustainable Development: Theoretical Trends, Emerging Issues and Challenges, Review paper prepared for INSTRAW.

5

Women Empowerment in India

The Role of Information and Communication Technology

T. DIVYA SRAVANI, K. DEEPTHI AND N.B. CHANDRAKALA

INTRODUCTION

Women play a pivotal role in the development of any country. Women's status is the best indicator of progress of any nation. Status and development of women influence the development of country, as they not only constitute half of its population, but also influence growth of the remaining half of its population.

It is necessary to build up women capacities to involve them in productive activities, institutional building, family and social transformation, decision-making process, political representation, trade and commerce, entrepreneurial development and social leadership. There is a need to enhance opportunities to women to enable them to own, manage and control industries and service enterprises including IT-based units. There is also need to provide more opportunities in related sectors to them in higher managerial, technical positions in government and non-government agencies, research, educational institutions in private and public sectors, without confining their role to only call centers, data-entry level and lower levels in the organizations. ICT has to address to all these problems of women as a whole and has to be used to facilitate to build a women empowered society.[1]

The Information and Communication Technology (ICT) revolution has not only opened up new opportunities for economic growth and social development but has also posed problems and challenges. It can shape and enhance wide range of developmental applications in agriculture, industry and social sectors and is influencing all sections of the society. ICT provides unique opportunities for human development. At the same time, ICT has been widening the gaps between and within countries, regions and gender while increasing disparities divide between the rural-urban, rich-poor, elite neglected and also within the different categories of women in various spheres of activity.[2]

Despite the numerous challenges to equity in the ICT arena, many social actors have exploited ICTs as tools for social transformation and gender equality. Women artisans are directly accessing global markets through e-commerce initiatives and are using the Internet to support their activities with market and production information. E-governance programmes have been initiated using ICTs for delivering government services; in some cases with an explicit strategy to ensure these services reach women and others who face barriers to access. Health educators have used the radio to communicate information related to women's sexual and reproductive health. Email, online newsletters and List Serves have enabled women to communicate on a global scale, resulting in increased collaboration to push the agenda of gender equality. New technologies do offer remarkable advantages in terms of ease of communication, unprecedented possibilities for interaction, and efficiency in information storage and retrieval; however they are not universally available. New initiatives have been most effective where they go beyond issues of access and infrastructure to consider the larger social context and power relations.[3]

KNOWLEDGE NETWORKING SYSTEM—WOMEN

Women stand to benefit tremendously from the inroads laid by ICT in the domain of knowledge networking. The pertinent question is not whether they stand to benefit but how do they benefit and what are the mechanisms to ensure that the benefits accrued to the women community do not remain restricted to mere trickle-down effects? At the very conceptual level, ICT have the potential to digitally link each and every woman in the world in a star topology network, which opens up endless possibilities for information exchange. This mechanism could be used by women in creative ways, both to communicate with other people who are online, and also to disseminate information to people in the outside world who are not online through the use of convergence and hybrid technologies such as community emails, community radio broadcast, tele-centres, newsletters, videos, etc. This mechanism forms the skeletal process through which women communities could overcome the constraints of seclusion, mobilise resources and support, reach out new markets, and open up avenues for life-long learning. We could broadly classify the spaces in which women stand to gain under the spheres of Empowerment and Governance. This condition forms the basis of evolution of women as equal contributors and end-users of knowledge in a knowledge society.[4] NGO's and the Government bodies have to come forward to setup and build a hierarchical network comprising of social groups which are successful in a venture from the village level to the state level. The success stories should be circulated to emulate them. Training groups have to be built up from these groups to percolate the knowledge to the different levels.

IMPACT ON WOMEN'S WORK

Information and communication technologies are both enabling as well as a contributing factors to globalization. Information and communication technologies made global financial markets possible. Examining the issue of the impact of information technology on women's work in the context of globalization underlines the differences in the issues of information technology and women's work between developed and developing countries. In developed countries, most of the literature on the impact of information technology on gender and work deals with the association of men with technology and power whereas in developing countries, women are looking at the issue not only in terms of gender relations with the men in their society, but also at Western dominance over innovation and as the source of technology. Some argue that the new technologies are not appropriate for women because they are imported. However, this position seems to be head-in-the-sand.

Information technology is no more foreign than air travel or electricity. The technologies are there and will not be displaced. It is more appropriate and effective for women to devise ways of dealing with them to improve the situation of women than to reject them for being foreign. As with globalization generally, the impact of information technology on women's work through globalization has been most evident in Asia first, than in Latin America and the Caribbean. Africa is effectively absent from this process.[5]

GENDER IN THE INFORMATION ECONOMY

Women have relatively little ownership and control of the ICT sector. While data is lacking, it is clear that women are underrepresented on the boards and senior management of IT companies, policy and regulatory organizations, technical standard-setting organizations, industry and professional organizations and within government bodies working in this area. Women's participation as employees in the sector presents a more complex picture. The new economy rides on the power of ICTs. Job outsourcing is an important business strategy today and has given rise to a new global division of labour. Internationally outsourced jobs, such as medical transcription work or software services, have made a considerable difference to women's work opportunities in developing countries. According to UNIFEM, women hold 9 per cent of mid- to upper-level IT-related jobs in engineering and make up 28.5 per cent of computer programmers and 26.9 per cent of systems analysts. Only among data entry workers the women form the majority at 85 per cent.[6] Information technology has brought employment gains for women, but trends highlight many challenges. The ILO Report on Work in the New Economy 2001 makes the following observations about the IT sector: Patterns of gender segregation are being reproduced in the information economy where men hold the majority of high-skilled, high value-added jobs, whereas women are concentrated in the low skilled, lower value-added jobs. Therefore, a Policy should encourage girls and women to use ICTs early in education, and pursue higher studies in ICTs as well as technical careers as scientists, researchers, administrators and educators. In addition to policies that ensure gender equality at the firm level, within the ICT sector, a strong role for state regulation of job security, insurance, maternity leave, and healthy and safe working conditions is vital for gender equality in the information economy.[7]

ICT TOOLS—WOMEN EMPOWERMENT

Livelihoods: New ICTs provide opportunities to reorganize economic activities in ways that can bypass the traditional dependence of women producers on male-dominated and exploitative market structures, including "middle-men". In many places, initiatives are being tried that link women artisans directly to global markets through the Internet, as well as support their activities with market and production information. The 'Inter-city Marketing Network of Women Entrepreneurs' project in Chennai, India has set up a communication network among women's community-based organizations (CBOs) to market their produce. The CBOs are provided with cellular phones, and women have been trained to maximize the use of telephones for selling not only in their immediate neighbourhoods but also reaching new markets within the city. The impact is that poor women from CBOs constrained by pressures of time and mobility are able to assess and aggregate market demand by trading through their peer CBOs, and evolve cost-effective mechanisms to increase business turnover by making the most of business networking.[8]

Capacity Building of Women: Several organizations are building the capacities of girls and women to make ICTs accessible and useful to them. At one level, girls and women are being provided general training in ICTs for ICT-related jobs; at another, women in business, women entrepreneurs and women in the professions, are systematically being supported for skill enhancement, career growth and greater work efficiency. In the Deccan Development Society, in South India, socially disadvantaged women have used radio and video to document and disseminate traditional farming practices, to reach policy-makers, and to archive their community-based development work. Such development activities in fact have deeper meanings; they reflect the recording by women of their own history and reclamation of their knowledge.[9]

Health: The technologies are being successfully used in many places for information dissemination about health. The Self-Employed Women's Association (SEWA), a trade union of women workers from the informal sector in India uses video to convey basic health information to its women members. Women themselves have produced video footage on how to address diarrhea through oral rehydration therapy, and they distribute this through their networks. New ICTs can also play a critical role in health delivery. The use of networked information exchange systems, and offline information tools like CD ROMs, databases and mobile ICT devices can enhance public health delivery. They can enable health education and information dissemination, bring communities and health facilities closer to each other through regular and systematic information exchange, and offer simple solutions for collecting and analyzing information about disease and health-seeking behaviour to help health interventions become more locally relevant. ICTs are being used in response to the crisis posed by HIV/AIDS. ICTs promote better access to AIDS advice, counseling, and test results without fear of being stigmatized.[10]

E-Education: ICTs like satellite, radio and TV offer many possibilities for non-formal and continued education, which can have important gender implications. They can deliver education content to the doorstep, which, for women with constraints on mobility and access to public places, can be a significant starting point. Technologies are being used the world over for open and distance learning. Azim Premji Foundation in India is among the few NGOs that work with the government to strengthen the public education system. The organization produces CD ROMs of creative content based on the primary school curriculum, which is gender-sensitive, uses local dialects and is designed to appeal to rural students. In India, computers are being introduced in schools, as a tool to support the learning process and ICT interventions is a precondition to ensure equal access and effective use by girl students of computers in the classroom environment. In the formal education at the graduation level the educational system should introduce Job Oriented Certificate courses as an add-on course and should be made mandatory for a student to get trained at least in one of them. Apart from direct employment, ICT has benefited women in a number of ways. It is a viable tool of information and communication which goes a long way in empowerment of women. Immense amount of information is obtained through the internet. Effective and efficient use of information technology like internet can help in assimilating information about variety, range and quality of products, publicity and marketing of products and services. Apart from being used as a tool of information and communication and employment, application of ICT has created avenues for women empowerment. Noteworthy examples are that of Gyandoot, Embalam, SEWA, Datamation and Smile.[11]

Rights-based information for women: ICTs have been used by gender equality advocates the world over for putting out rights-based information. From multilateral agencies like UNIFEM to feminist activists at local levels, actors at different levels are involved in creating, collating and disseminating material on rights – legal rights, sexual and reproductive rights, women's human rights. This is done through websites, e-magazines and email. In many developed countries, websites provide assistance to women seeking help on domestic violence.[12]

CONCLUSION

The majority of women in the developing world do not have access to ICTs due to variety of barriers as such the infrastructural, social, cultural and linguistic. While it may be necessary for the progressive elite to mediate information dissemination, real democratization of information depends on making ICTs relevant to the majority and accessible to every woman. Today, print media and radio are used extensively by feminist groups for information dissemination. ICTs can strengthen these media strategies. Community access points such as telecenters can be a simple tool for conveying information to women that supports their social and political empowerment. Telecentres need to be used as strategic spaces where information on the law (e.g. violence, religious law), on worker rights (e.g. minimum wages), and citizenship rights can be obtained. Governments and NGOs have to take a lead in this process of universal access to rights-based information, especially in rural areas. ICTs can provide spaces for diverse, bottom-up and low-cost communication. They can amplify women's voices, help publicize women's experiences and perspectives and integrate their specific concerns with the mainstream policy-making and development process. Engendering ICTs is not merely about greater use of ICTs by women. It is about transforming both gender politics and the ICT system. It is evident that the ICT system is organized on elitist, patriarchal, techno-centric, non-democratic lines and based on capitalist values. Transformatory gender politics will need to question these values and search for ethical alternatives. This calls for synergy between a new bottom-up culture of ICT production and use and the re-engineering of the global ICT system that will guarantee sustainable changes towards gender equality. Addressing the ICT arena is part of a larger struggle to build an information society based on protecting people's right to communicate, own and use knowledge for their own ends, and resisting curtailments on freedom to use, share and modify information tools and content.

Notes and References

1. Lal, B. Suresh, B. Rama and Hussain S.K. Ahmed, Information Technology for Rural Development: An Overview, *The Economic Challenger*. No. 6, Issue 23 April-June, 2004, pp. 34-37.
2. CARE, Women's Empowerment : www.care.org/../women Empowerment.pdf,U.S.
3. Acharya, K., Flaws in Bhoomi, India's Model e-Governance Project, Pune, India: Infochange India, 2003. http://www.infochangeindia.org/features120.jsp.
4. Chandrasekhar, C.P., Promoting ICT for Human Development in Asia: Realizing the Millennium Development Goals, India Country Paper, for Regional Bureau for Asia and the Pacific, UNDP, 2003.
5. *Ibid.*
6. UNIFEM and UNU/INTECH, Gender and Telecommunications: An Agenda for Policy, 2000. http://www.unifem.undp.org/conferen.htm.
7. International Labour Organization (ILO), World Employment Report 2000: Life at Work in the New Economy, Geneva: International Labour Office, 2001. http://www.ilo.org/public/english/support/publ/wer/index2.htm (accessed 28 April 2004).
8. Gurumurthy A., Bridging the Digital Gender Divide: Issues and Insights on ICT for Women's Economic Empowerment, New Delhi: UNIFEM, 2004. http://www.itforchange.net/resources/Pat.htm
9. Vikas Nath, Empowerment and Governance: Women's Perspective, 2001. http://www.cddc.vt.edu/digitalgov/gov-menu.html
10. *Ibid.*
11. Sify, Internet Usage in India, *Sify News*, 31 July, 2003.
12. Lal B. Suresh, Ms. B. Rama, Hussain S.K. Ahmed, Information Technology for Rural Development: An Overview, *The Economic Challenger*, No. 6, Issue 23, April-June, 2004, pp. 34-37.

6

The Girl's Rights

Implementation Under International Law

V. Sowbhagya Rani

> *"I always want girls to know their full potential by understanding the depth of girl's strengths, and how she can change the world."*
>
> —Whitney

INTRODUCTION

In India, right from her birth, a girl child is treated by the society, including her parents as a burden because of various traditional beliefs and misconceptions of the society. The reaction of the family members is different towards the girl's rights right from the birth. Often, the girl is born and brought up in an atmosphere where the family would have rather preferred a boy in her place. This attitude of acceptance to large extent affects her existence. Those who survive are also discriminated against and neglected in numerous ways.

CEDAW Convention insists that the state parties have the obligation to ensure the equal rights of men and women to enjoy all economic, social, cultural, civil and political rights. The Beijing

Platform for Action, adopted at the Fourth World Conference on Women, included "the Girl Child" in its 12 critical areas of concern. It recognises that in many countries, the girl child faces discrimination in all stages of life from birth through childhood and into adulthood. It urges the government to take action to provide access for girls to training and information, to enable them to articulate their views and to promote the equality and participation of girls. Despite the government's ratification of numerous international treaties that prevent discrimination against the girl child, the Indian Census show a sharp decline in the child sex ratio in many regions in India.

POSITION OF THE GIRL CHILD IN INDIA

The bias is rooted in a complex set of religious, economical, social and cultural factors. The degree of bias may vary but it definitely exists at various levels at different stages in girl's life affecting the fundamental rights of the girl child to survival, development, protection and participation. The mortality rate of young girls of different age groups is much higher than young boys because of the preference for male children, resulting in the neglect of girl children. The hat redness towards a girl child has grown up so much and brought into the system of eliminating the girl child — the vulnerable and unwanted gender, in the womb, before she sees the world. The sex ratio is already precarious owing to the discrimination against daughters. Abortion of unborn daughters is bound to accelerate the downward slide of female along the demographic ladder.[1]

Thus, in our society where systematic neglect and discrimination against daughters and 'son preference' attitude are so deep-rooted, the very birth of the girl children and their survival are at stake leading to declining sex ratio. The pathetic situation is that women are forced to endanger their own species either in the womb by practicing female feticide or at birth by practicing female infanticide or after birth by way of neglect. This also indicates the denial of women's reproductive rights as human rights, which recognises that personal freedom and social entitlements are essential to the advancement of human welfare. It is a very denial of women's right to control their own fertility, their own lives, their reproductive freedom to have children when they want, to be confident that they will survive and to avoid unwanted child being.[2]

Though the practice of killing female child soon after birth has existed in certain pockets of our country and more in particular communities, female feticide—the practice of silent killing of female foetuses in womb is wide across regional boundaries and castes. Indicating a continuing preference for boys in society, the child ratio in India has dropped to 914 females against 1,000 males since independence, from 927 females against 1,000 males in 2001 to 914. Kerala with 1084 has the highest sex ratio followed by Puducherry with 1038. Daman and Diu has the lowest sex ratio of 618. According to the Census Report 2011 the child sex ratio in Andhra Pradesh has dropped 961 females against 1,000 males in 2001 to 943 in 2011. (Census Report 2011)[3]

The persistent of social attitude and prejudices against girls continues to raise considerable concern for human rights defenders of Girl Children. Girls are often neglected in their access to nutrition, health care and education. They are deprived of their childhood by being domestic workers or farm workers or child labourers in different work places. They are often the target and victims of gender discrimination, violence, sexual exploitation and abuse.[4] Amongst all her very right to be born and right to life is taken away by practices of sex selective abortion and infanticide, which is a human rights violation and violation against the provisions enshrined in the Constitution and Child Right Convention. The World Conference on Human Rights affirmed that the rights of the girl child are inalienable, integral and indivisible part of human rights and the eradication of all forms of discrimination on the ground of sex is to be considered a priority objective of the international community. The final document on the International Conference on Population and Development held at Cairo has encouraged the government to raise the minimum age of marriage and recognized that the age of marriage was a factor contributing to the violations of human rights.[5]

IMPLIMENTATION OF INTERNATIONAL LAWS FOR THE PROTECTION OF GIRL'S RIGHTS

An important aspect of a woman's life is her girlhood. It is, therefore, but right to enact laws addressing that stage of her life. This need is emphasized by the fact that there had many complaints by minors about abuses committed by their parents, guardians or the very people who they are supposed to trust and who supposedly are the ones who will uphold their rights.

Over history there have been a number of international treaties and documents that outline the rights of girl child. Prior to World War II the League of Nations had adopted Geneva Declarations of the Rights of the Child in 1924. United Nations (UN) took its first step towards declaring the importance of the child rights by establishing the United Nations International Children's Emergency Fund in 1946 (UNICEF). Health has become an increasingly central part of its work over the decades. At present, UNICEF has five priorities embedded within its programmes: girls' education; immunisation; HIV/AIDS; early childhood development; and child protection.[6]

United Nations Convention on the Rights of the Child (CRC), 1989[7]

United Nations adopted its first international legally binding document concerning of child rights. It came into force on the 2nd September 1990. The convention has been ratified by 192 countries becoming the most ratified of all international Human Rights Treaties. India signed and ratified the convention in 1992 except US and Somalia. The articles of the Convention may be grouped into four categories of rights and a set of guiding principles. Additional provisions of the Convention (Articles 43 to 54) discuss implementation measures for the Convention, explaining how governments and international organizations like UNICEF will work to ensure children are protected in their rights.

Guiding principles: The guiding principles of the Convention include non-discrimination; adherence to the best interests of the child; the right to life, survival and development; and the right to participate. They represent the underlying requirements for any and all rights to be realized.

Survival and development rights: These are rights to the resources, skills and contributions necessary for the survival and full development of the child. They include rights to adequate food, shelter, clean water, formal education, primary health care, leisure and recreation, cultural activities and information about their rights. These rights require not only the existence of the means to fulfill the rights but also access to them. Specific articles address the needs of child refugees, children with disabilities and children of minority or indigenous groups.

Protection rights : These rights include protection from all forms of child abuse, neglect, exploitation and cruelty, including the right to special protection in times of war and protection from abuse in the criminal justice system.

Participation rights : Children are entitled to the freedom to express opinions and to have a say in matters affecting their social, economic, religious, cultural and political life. Participation rights include the right to express opinions and be heard, the right to information and freedom of association. Engaging these rights as they mature helps children bring about the realization of all their rights and prepares them for an active role in society. The equality and interconnection of rights are stressed in the Convention. In addition to governments' obligations, children and parents are responsible for respecting the rights of others—particularly each other. Children's understanding of rights will vary depending on age and parents in particular should tailor the issues they discuss, the way in which they answer questions and discipline methods to the age and maturity of the individual child.[8] To help stem the growing abuse and exploitation of children worldwide, the United Nations General Assembly in 2000 adopted two Optional Protocols to the Convention to increase the protection of children from involvement in armed conflicts and from sexual exploitation. The Optional Protocol on the involvement of children in armed conflict establishes 18 as the minimum age for compulsory recruitment and requires States to do everything they can to prevent individuals under the age of 18 from taking a direct part in hostilities. The Optional Protocol on the sale of children, child prostitution and child pornography draws special attention to the criminalization of these serious violations of children's rights and emphasizes the importance of fostering increased public awareness and international cooperation in efforts to combat them.

Beijing Convention[9]

The Beijing flat form for Action, adopted at the Fourth World Conference on Women, included "the Girl Child" in its 12 critical areas of concern. It recognises that in many countries, the girl child faces discrimination in all stages of life from birth through childhood and into adulthood. It urges the government to take action to provide access for girls to training and information, to enable them to articulate their views and to promote the equality and participation of girls. The strategic objectives formulated under Girl Child are as follows:

1. Eliminate all forms of discrimination against the girl child.

2. Eliminate negative cultural attitudes and practices against girls.
3. Promote and protect the rights of the girl child and increase awareness of her needs and potential.
4. Eliminate discrimination against girls in education, skills and development and training.
5. Eliminate discrimination against girls in health and nutrition.
6. Eliminate the economic exploitation of child labour and protect young girls at work.
7. Eradicate violence against the girl child.
8. Promote the girl child's awareness and participation in social, economic and political life.
9. Strengthen the role of the family in improving the status of the girl child.

The General Assembly Resolution on Girl Child, adopted on 9th December 1998, regarding the rights of the Girl Child:

> It urges all States to enact and enforce legislation protecting girls from all forms of violence including female infanticide and pre-natal sex selection, female genital mutilation, rape, domestic violence, incest, sexual abuse, sexual exploitation, child prostitution and child pornography and to develop age appropriate safe and confidential programmes and medical, social and psychological support services, to assist girls who are subjected to violence.

A comprehensive overview of the issues concerning the rights of the girls and women—reviewed by CRC and Beijing Convention:

- The status of girls and women in general raises serious and unresolved questions of inequality and indifference manifested by discrimination, neglect, exploitation and violence.
- The rights of the girl are fundamental rights inherent to the human dignity and they should be seen as individuals.
- In order to breakdown the cycle of harmful traditions and prejudices against women, there should be a comprehensive strategy to promote and protect the rights of girls and building a share and lasting efforts to promote the self-esteem of women and acquisition of skills for all round participation.

- If the platform for action was to be an agenda for change and advancement of women, it could only be meaningful if it placed the human rights of girls at its core.
- The persistent tradition, prejudices and traditional role distributed within the family are the key factors affecting the enjoyment of girls' fundamental rights. The son preference often manifested itself in the form of neglect, less food and less health care. Such as situation of inferiority often favoured violence and sex abuse within the family as well as problems associated with early pregnancy and marriage. It has even resulted in the elimination of girl children in the form of feticide and infanticide.
- The situation of girls is of particular concern in rural and remote areas under the strong influence of community and religious leaders.
- The educational programmes should be launched to eradicate all forms of discrimination against the girl children and the participation of customary religious and community leaders must be ensured to overcome the negative influences of traditions and customs.
- Effective to educational and vocational system will allow for the harmonious and informed development of children and skills to make free choices in their life and to act in a context of gender partnership both at work and family.
- Eliminate stereotype in educational material and incorporate the CRC in the school and training curriculum to enhance the promotion and protection of rights of girls and to eradicate gender discrimination.
- Eradicate degrading and exploitation images of girl and women in media and advertising. The values and models of behaviour that were portrayed contribute to the perpetuation of inequalities and inferiority.
- Legislative measures to ban all the traditions and customs contrary to the rights of the child would create a meaningful deterrent and clearly contribute to changing attitude.
- The national legislation of the State Parties should clearly recognise the principle of equality before the law and forbid gender discrimination while providing for effective protection and remedies in case of non-respect.

- Law reforms should be undertaken in both the civil and penal spheres against those provisions which deprives the comprehensive protection of the Convention, e.g. Linking the age of criminal responsibility to the attainment of puberty.
- The situation of specific vulnerable group of girl children should be separately addressed as they are deprived of their childhood enjoyment and the traditional inferiority is further aggravated by the prevailing external situation.
- Girls below the age of 15 often did household works as adults which is not considered as a "real work". They should be freed from the vicious circle by providing equal chances, equal treatment and education.
- There is an urgent need for gathering information and gender dis-aggregated data in a comprehensive and integrated manner at the international, regional, national and local level with a view to assess the prevailing reality affecting girls identified the persisting problem which allows for the perpetuation of vulnerability. Without analysing the root causes of gender gaps, it would not be possible to develop appropriate strategies and programmes to eliminate gender disparities and empower girls and women.

The Convention on the Elimination of All Forms of Discrimination Against Women (CEDAW)[10]

The Convention on the Elimination of All Forms of Discrimination Against Women (CEDAW) is a landmark international agreement that affirms principles of fundamental human rights and equality for women around the world. CEDAW is a practical blueprint for each country to achieve progress for women and girls.

Around the world, CEDAW has been used to reduce sex trafficking, domestic violence, and female genital mutilation; ensure primary education for girls and vocational training for women; ensure the right to vote; and forced marriage and child marriage; improve health care services and save lives during pregnancy and child-birth; allow women to own and inherit property; and ensure the right to work and own a business without discrimination.

The rights of the girl child is ensured in CEDAW, in the following articles:

- Discrimination against women, denying or limiting as it does their equality of rights with men, is fundamentally unjust and constitutes an offence against human dignity.
- All appropriate measures shall be taken to educate public opinion and to direct national aspirations towards the eradication of prejudice and the abolition of customary and all other practices, which are based on the idea of the inferiority of women.

CEDAW Convention insists that the state parties have the obligation to ensure the equal rights of men and women to enjoy all economic, social, cultural, civil and political rights.

INTERNATIONAL LABOUR ORGANISATION: 1919

According to a special report on the girl child and labour by International Labour Organisation (ILO) more than 100 million girl children between the ages of 5 and 17 are engaged in child labour, out of which over 50% of them are in hazardous industries, and 20% of those are below twelve years old. It is hard to get correct statistical information about girl child labour since the kind of the work girls undertake is more invisible than that of boys. For example agricultural work, domestic work and working in home-based workshops. Many girls are engaged in active labour which is disguised as household chores. ILO shows that 10% of girls are engaged in "household chores" for more than 24 hours in a week which is twice as much as boys. One of the most gender specific forms of child labour is child prostitution. One of the projects the ILO engaged in is International Programme on the Elimination of Child Labour (IPEC)[11]

INTERNATIONAL PROGRAMME ON THE ELIMINATION OF CHILD LABOUR (IPEC): 1992

International Programme on the Elimination of Child Labour was started with the overall goal of the ordered elimination of child labour. India was the first country to join it in the same year with ILO. It has projects in 88 countries. It is the biggest single operational programme of the ILO.

Child Rights Information Network

IT is an International body that supports the UNCRC with the aim of the organization is to publish knowledge through research and investigations so as to provide this information to states so that they may fulfill their commitment to the UNCRC. It has 2189 member organizations.

Child Helpline International[12]

It is a global network of child helpline working on the issue of child protection. The vision of CHI is to create a world where children can express themselves through telecommunications, which gives them an individual voice and in turn allows for their participation in shaping their world and realizing their rights. CHI aims at responding to children in need of care and protection as well as voicing their concern to policy makers. As per Nov. of 2009 CHI has 107 full members, as well as is working with 26 countries to establish child helpline.

The new goals for 2007-10 are:

- Improve the child protection system,
- Increase the recognition of child voices,
- Establish an effective global network of child helplines, and
- Facilitate adequate response to all children in need of care and protection.

UN International Day of the Girl Child

On December 19, 2011, the United Nations General Assembly adopted a resolution to declare October 11 as the International Day of the Girl Child, establishing a day to recognize girls' rights and the unique challenges girls face around the world. The action follows a multi-year campaign by activists in Canada and the United States. In reserving a day for advocacy and action by and for girls, the UN has signaled its commitment to end gender stereotypes, discrimination, violence, and economic disparities that disproportionately affect girls.

The International Day of the Girl Child serves to recognize girls as a population that faces difficult challenges, including gender violence, early marriage, Child labour, and discrimination at work. The term "Girl Child" is commonly used abroad to distinguish the unique challenges faced by those under age 18 from those faced by women.

The issues surrounding a girl child have been discusses in national child policies and laws and addressed in a few programmes.[13]

- The National Policy for Children, 1974,
- The National Plan of Action for Children, 2005,
- The Pre-natal Diagnostic Techniques (Regulation and Prevention of Misuse) Act, 1994,
- The Immoral Traffic (Prevention) Act, 1986,
- The Juvenile Justice Act of 2000,
- Indian Penal Code.
- Balika Samriddhi Yojana. and
- Kishori Shakti Yojana.

CONCLUSION

Although the need for special recognition of child rights has been identified and implemented by the international community, this action has not gone far enough to adequately protect the girl-child against harmful traditional practices. The inadequacy of existing international protection for the girl-child is rooted in the failure to address her intersecting identities. Because the girl-child at all times experiences the world on the basis of her age, gender, race, class and other characteristics, the intersection of these identities must be considered in any law or policy involving her.

You should have God's blessing to have a girl baby. You should do good things for several generations to get that good will from God. I think everybody agrees to this view but many people are forced to think otherwise because of socio-economic situations. Media plays a critical role in framing personal opinions. Media should focus more positive light on women to turn this around. If everybody understands the significance of genesis of a girl child, we will have a better world.

Framework for action at the state and international level against gender inequality must begin by the member-states of the United Nations upholding international treaties and enforcing laws, especially for the prevention of gender-based violence. In this regard it is particularly important for all member-states to enforce the Convention on the Elimination of All Forms of Discrimination against Women (CEDAW) and its Optional Protocol, and the Convention on the Rights of the Child (CRC) and its two Optional Protocols, with funding and accountability mechanisms. The member states should also ensure that all citizens understand the provisions of the conventions of the CEDAW and CRC. Further, eradication of gender inequality and empowerment of the women and girl child is only possible through a framework for action which involves the grassroot structures of the society which includes the family and the community. The approach should be bottom up and not top bottom. The needs and issues should be identified at the local level and then through the local bodies the state and the international community should chip in resources as per the broad policy frameworks agreed upon. Only reaching the needy directly can help solve the problem and bring hope for girl child. Action should be to empower people at the ground level through various methods including training and education. Throwing bread crumbs here and there would not serve the purpose at all. Finally once again let me reemphasize the fact that education of girls is one of the most effective methods of girl child empowerment as well as national growth and development. Girl child education helps in protecting girls from discrimination and violence, helps in strengthening the family as a unit and helps in eradicating poverty, corruption and malpractices from the society.

Notes and References

1. Info Change News & Features, October 2004.
2. http://articles.economictimes.indiatimes.com/2011-03-31/news/29365989_1_ratio-males-girl-child
3. Census Report 2011
4. http://www.crin.org.
5. http://www.rise-of-womanhood.org/hope-for-girl-child.html
6. http://www.unicef.org
7. United Nations Convention on the Rights of the Child.
8. http://equalityinsight.wordpress.com. December 27, 2011.
9. Beijing Convention.
10. The Convention on the Elimination of All Forms of Discrimination Against Women.
11. International Programme on the Elimination of Child Labour.
12. http://www.childlineindia.org
13. http://pcw.gov.ph/index.php/laws-legislation-filipino-women/24-laws-girl-child

7

'Nine Gems' of Judicial Verdicts Towards Gender Justice

P.B. Pankaja

INTRODUCTION

'Gender justice' in its wider context always refers to gender neutrality but in its restricted sense it is popularly referred to 'exclusively women specific'. Attributing restricted sense to the term is the result of emergence of 'Feminism' and 'Human Rights Jurisprudence'. While feminist movement is a specific gender-related movement that throws light upon gender based discrimination and deprivation of women, their grievances, struggles, desires, lawful claims, agendas and hopes, the human rights jurisprudence calls for recognition of women as human beings first and equal human beings as next. Women's right to survival, sustenance and development are part and parcel of the regimes of both Feminism and Human rights jurisprudence. Gender justice is a call against asymmetrical power relationship within the family, both natal and matrimonial; in the society, at work place and in the hands of the State at large. Patriarchy has become deep-rooted institution of almost all human societies in the world which led to psychological disempowerment, economic dependence and cultural inequality of women whereby 'bias against women' has become a strong institutionalized attitude and practice.

Our *Suprema lex* guarantees multi-dimensional promises for the empowerment of women. Legislations are in plethora out of which some provide *dejure* equality and some manifest patent inequality. All law is not justice at times. The executive, in spite of its required constitutional commitment to gender justice, makes certain policies and programs which reflect gender bias or do not reach the target groups — the women. Judiciary activates such laws and channelizes such policies and programs through its verdicts, *obiter dicta* and effective guidelines. Judicial activism is not only restricted to legislative and executive premises, its sway is extended to even social practices founded upon un-codified customary laws wherein women are treated as secondary human beings living at the mercy of male species, subjugated and subordinated.

The present write up is an endeavor to highlight certain landmark judgments of the apex court and of some High Courts, randomly selected as 'nine gems' which adorn the judicial cap. Six out of nine gems relate to greasing the friction between the un-codified law of Muslims and constitutional goal of gender justice, one gem relates to highlighting legislative bias against women under Hindu law and the judiciary's endeavor to remedy it through its 'golden rule' of interpretation. The eighth gem is a testimony to the fact that at times a judicial verdict acts as a forerunner of legislation which activates the slumbering legislature to its task. The last but not the least gem highlights a destitute wife's right to reside in the same dwelling place even after desertion or divorce.

GEM 1 — ITWARI v. ASGHARI[1]

Popular Myth: Under Muslim law first wife has to compromise if husband opts to have a second wife.

Judicial ruling: Muslim husband taking a second wife cannot compel his first wife to give conjugal society if first wife seeks separate residence and maintenance. It was a case wherein Asghari, a Muslim wife filed an application for maintenance u/sec. 488 Cr.P.C. contending that she was living separately on the ground that her husband had taken a second wife and accused him of cruelty to her. Itwari, her husband filed a suit for Restitution of conjugal rights against her to come back and join him. The trial court decreeing the suit held that mere fact of husband's second marriage does not raise a presumption of cruelty. On wife's appeal, the first appellate court reversing the Restitution decree held that husband's petition was only to counterblast wife's claim for maintenance. Husband appealed to the High Court and argued that every Muslim has a right to take up to four wives under his personal law and the mere fact that he has taken a second wife was no proof of cruelty. He should not be deprived of his right to have conjugal society of all his wives.

The High Court observed that *the question involved in this case was not whether the husband had the right to take a second wife but whether husband can compel his first wife to live with him along with his second wife. RCR is an equitable relief and the court should weigh the balance of hardship to the parties and decide accordingly. If granted—it would result in hardship to the wife; if not granted—it would result in hardship to the husband. Whose hardship is more?* To decide this question, the court relied on Koran IV. 3. wherein it is said that *Muslim law permits polygamy but has never encouraged it. It was only a conditional permission which imposed a ceiling on conjugal greed of Muslim husbands. Though it recognizes legal right of the husband to have four wives at a time it does not follow that it denies first wife the right to live separately, who has to share her husband's consortium with another woman helplessly. Under Muslim law marriage is a civil contract and contract restraining a Muslim husband from entering into a second marriage is not void under S. 23 of the Indian Contract Act, which bans agreements in restraint of marriage.*

Quoting the Privy Council's decision in *Shamsunnisa Begum's* case, the court observed that *Indian law does not recognize various types of cruelty such as 'Muslim cruelty', 'Christian 'ruelty', 'Hindu cruelty' and so on. The test of cruelty is based on universal and humanitarian standards, i.e., to say the conduct of husband which would cause bodily or mental pain to the wife. Today, social conditions and habits among Indian Muslims have changed considerably and with it, the conscience of the Muslim community too. Today importing of a second wife into the household ordinarily means a stinging insult to the first. It leads to asking of awkward questions, the raising of unsympathetic eyebrows and the pointing of derisive fingers at the first wife who is automatically degraded by society. All this is likely to prey upon her mind and health if she is compelled to live with her husband under the altered circumstances.* Extending the logic, the court further observed that *if husband's plea of RCR is granted, even second wife will be put to mental agony* and hence on these justifications, the court held that *it would be inequitable to compel the first wife to live with the husband.*

Comment: Though this judgement is about more than half a century old of a High Court, it has a great precedental value. But it is doubtful that how many Muslim women, ignorant of this judgement, are still toiling in the matrimonial home under the misimpression that they did not have any say in the matter except to bear the brunt if husband takes a second, third or fourth wife claiming it to be his fundamental right to have multiple consortium even by compulsion.

GEM 2 — SHAMIM ARA v. ST. OF U.P. AND ANOTHER[2]

Popular myth: A Muslim husband can easily pronounce triple *talaq* on his wife and dissolve the marriage with immediate effect.

Judicial ruling: Triple *talaq* is to be regarded as single pronouncement of *talaq*. Triple *talaq* is invalid.

It is often said that as per Muslim law, a husband may divorce his wife whenever he desires without assigning any reason at his whims and fancies, even in jest or under compulsion or in a state of intoxication, without recourse to the court and even in the absence of his wife;[3] that even a mockery *talaq* can be regarded as a valid *talaq*. In any proceedings for maintenance u/s. 125 CrPC or in a suit for RCR by wife, if the husband takes a plea in his counter or written statement that he had already pronounced *talaq* on her long ago, that was held to be a valid *talaq* communicated to her validly. But the apex court drew a curtain to that proposition in *Shamim Ara's* case.

It was a case wherein the husband in his reply to wife's petition u/s. 125 CrPC for maintenance contended that he had divorced her by way of *talaq* pronounced in her absence on a particular date. When asked about its communication to her he contended that the present reply itself was communication to her. But the apex court viewed that *the talaq to be effective has to be 'pronounced'. The term 'pronounce' means to proclaim, to utter formally and to declare. A mere plea taken in the written statement of a talaq having been pronounced sometime in the past cannot by itself be treated as a valid talaq. Because knowledge of talaq materially alters the status of the wife. Her rights and liabilities flow from the date of talaq. There is a question of Iddat to be followed by her; her right to residence; her right to dower, etc.. How would this be possible if the husband pronounced talaq secretly and does not inform it to wife at all?* So saying the court held *the husband liable for payment of maintenance until the obligation comes to an end in accordance with valid law.*

Comment: This decision has become a good precedent and is followed in *Masroor Ahmed's*[4] and other cases also.

GEM 3 MASROOR AHMED v. STATE (NCT OF DELHI)[5]

Popular myth: A Muslim husband can pronounce *talaq* even in the absence of his wife and it becomes effective from immediate effect.

Judicial ruling: An un-communicated *talaq* is no *talaq*.

Under Muslim law, the commonest form of divorce is a unilateral declaration of pronouncement of *talaq* on the wife by the husband according to three forms, *Talaq Ahasan*, *Talaq Hasan* and *Talaq-ul-biddat*. There is no controversy with *Ahasan* and *Hasan*. But the *Talaq-ul-biddat*, popularly known as triple *talaq* has always attracted a lot of criticism by jurists, academicians and judiciary. In this case, due to matrimonial discord, wife was living away from her husband. The husband pronounced triple *talaq* on his wife but did not communicate to her. He did not mean it seriously and later filed suit for RCR asking for wife's conjugal society. The fact of pronouncing *talaq* was not revealed to the court also. Wife, unaware of *talaq* being pronounced, consented for RCR and went to stay with her husband. After a few days she came to know about triple *talaq* pronounced on her in her absence. So she filed a case against her husband for rape as there was no marriage at all between them during those few days. The husband pleaded not guilty as he did not mean it seriously. The court after referring to opinions of Muslim jurists and its earlier judgements observed: "*Triple talaq is widely accepted as bad in theology but valid in law. It was deprecated by Prophet Mohammed as sinful. It is not even considered as valid talaq by Shias. It was only a later innovation which might have served a purpose at a particular point of time in history, but if it is rooted out, such a move would not be contrary to any basic tenet of Islam or the Quran. Triple talaq has brought about extreme misery to the divorced women and even to the men who are left with no chance to undo the wrong. Hence, I would hold that a triple talaq be regarded as single pronouncement under Talaq Ahasan. This would enable the husband to have time to revoke the same...*"

Comment: Thus the relevancy of triple *talaq* is now diluted by equating it to the single pronouncement of *talaq* under *talaq Ahasan* which is revocable. Unless there is abstinence from sexual intercourse for a period of three months from the date of pronouncement, the marriage continues and the *talaq* lapses. In such a case there is no need to perform 'halala' since the marriage is not dissolved with single pronouncement of *talaq*. This judgement has of much value in the present day context wherein there are a few instances whereby Muslim boys resort to triple *talaq* through mail or through phone and later on repent and ask for clarification from *Ulemas* or *Imams* who uphold the *talaq* as irrevocable triple *talaq* through *fatwas*, unmindful of court's ruling. The binding nature of *fatwas* is always a matter of debate even among Muslims who are divided on this issue. How many Muslim women, even men for that matter, know about it?

GEM 4 — MST. RUKIA KHATUN v. ABDUL KHALIQUE LASKAR[6]

Popular myth: A Muslim husband can pronounce *talaq* arbitrarily at his own whims and fancies.

Judicial ruling: Muslim husband cannot pronounce *talaq* unless there is a valid reason and only if conciliation fails.

It is a popular fallacy that a Muslim husband enjoys, under the *Quranic* law, unbridled authority to liquidate the marriage without assigning any reason. Commentators on the Koran have rightly observed and it tallies with the law in some of the Muslim countries like Iraq and Pakistan that the husband must satisfy the court about the reasons for divorce.[7] In this case the Division Bench stated that *the correct law of talaq as ordained by Holy Quran is:*

(i) *That talaq must be for a reasonable cause;*
(ii) *That it must be preceded by an attempt of reconciliation between the husband and wife;*
(iii) *That two arbiters, one chosen by the wife from her family and the other by the husband from his must hear the dispute; and*
(iv) *That if their attempts fail, talaq may be effected.*

Thus a unilateral decision to talaq by husband is no more a valid talaq unless the above said procedure is followed. The logic behind is that though marriage under Muslim law is only a civil contract, yet the rights and responsibilities arising out of such a marriage are of great importance to the welfare of the humanity as a whole, that a great degree of sanctity is attached to it.

Comments: Though this decision is of High Court, it has set a significant precedent. A correct interpretation of Quran makes it clear that no law tolerates or perpetuates injustice to women.

GEM 5 — DANIAL LATIFI v. UNION OF INDIA[8]

Popular myth: In case of *talaq*, a Muslim husband has to maintain his wife only during *iddat* period.

Judicial ruling: A Muslim husband is liable not only to pay maintenance to his wife during *iddat* period but also to make a reasonable and fair provision for her future and such a settlement should be made on or before the *Iddat* period.

The ruling given in *Shah Bano's*[9] case became very popular wherein the Supreme Court reiterated its stand already taken in *Bai Tahira*[10] and *Fuzlunbi*[11]. It observed that *if the divorced wife is not able to maintain herself after the period of iddat, she is entitled to have recourse to S. 125 CrPC and such an application is not barred u/s. 127(3)(b) CrPC as the Code overrides the personal law of the parties.* The decision has created a lot of uproar among a section of Muslim community who thought that Muslim husbands were unnecessarily penalized. Hence they pressurized the parliament to bring in The Muslim women (Protection of Rights on Divorce) Act, 1986 to nullify *Shah Bano* judgement. Though the title of the Act specifies that the rights of the Muslim women on divorce are to be protected, Ss. 3 and 4 of the Act limit the obligation of the husband to *iddat* period only. To nullify the Act, *Daniel Latifi* case was filed. The Act was challenged as unconstitutional and un-islamic, having the potential of suffocating the Muslim women and degrading the secular fabric, one of the basic features of the Indian Constitution and excluding the application of S. 125 CrPC violates Arts. 14 and 21 of the Constitution. The Muslim Personal Law Board, supporting the Act, argued that the social ethos of the Muslim community has a wider network to take care of divorced Muslim women and they are not made dependants on their former husbands only.

The present judgement was a milestone wherein the apex court has interpreted the provisions of the Act in such a manner that it laid great emphasis on the words used in Ss. 3 and 4 of the Act. The words '*a fair and reasonable provision and maintenance is to be made and paid to the wife within iddat period*' was construed so as to mean that the husband has to make fair and reasonable provision for future and pay customary maintenance to the present and both should be provided on or before *iddat* period. She cannot be made to run from pillar to post in search of her relatives one after the other and later to the *Waqf* Board as a last resort because true *Islam* does not preach such an injustice to women. The constitutional validity of the Act was declared in affirmative on the ground that no legislature would mean gender injustice to women.

Comment: This decision can be regarded as a research document on Muslim law wherein the relevant verses of Quran are analysed in detail and arrived at the present construction. Through this verdict, it is made clear that the liability of the Muslim husband to his divorced wife arising u/s.3 of the Act to pay maintenance is not confined to *iddat* period but the incidental obligation to settle for her future a fair and reasonable amount is to be discharged within the completion of *iddat* period. It is also to be noted that the stand taken by the apex court in *Danial Latifi* is reaffirmed subsequently in *Iqbal Bano v. St. of UP*[12] and *Anr.* and *Shabana Bano v. Imran Khan*[13] wherein the ambiguities in the application of s. 125 CrPC for Muslim divorced women are removed and the provisions of 1986 Act are construed pro-actively. Now it is made clear that if a divorced Muslim woman files a petition for maintenance u/s. 125 CrPC it will be open to the court to treat it as a petition under the Muslim Women (Protection of Rights on Divorce) Act 1986.

GEM 6 — NOOR SABHA KHATOON v. MOHD. QUASIM[14]

Popular Myth: After passing of the Muslim Women (Protection of Rights on Divorce) Act 1986, on divorce, if the children are with their mother then the obligation of the husband to maintain the children is only up to their age of two years as per S. 3(1)(b)[15] of the Act.

Court ruling: Correct interpretation of S.3(1)(b) provides for grant of *additional* maintenance to the wife for the extra nourishment needed to her during lactation and fosterage.

A short but interesting question involved in this case was *whether the minor children who are in the custody of their mother who has been divorced by their father are entitled to maintenance u/s.125 CrPC till their minority or is their right restricted only for a period of two years mentioned u/s. 3(1)(b) of 1986 Act?*

The parties in this case were married according to Muslim rites but on certain disputes arising between them, wife was turned out of her matrimonial home along with her three minor children aged 6, 3 and 1 and a half year by the husband, who subsequently took a second wife. Wife claimed maintenance for herself and her minor children u/s. 125 CrPC. Husband denied his liability to his wife as it was restricted to *iddat* period only under Muslim law and to the first and the second child as they have crossed two years as per S. 3(1)(b) of the 1986, Act. After a protracted battle and varied orders from the lower courts the case came before the Supreme Court. The Apex court's observation is a commendable one which runs as follows: *From the preamble of the Act it is clear that the Act aims to protect the rights of the divorced Muslim women only and the Act was not enacted to regulate the obligations of a Muslim father to maintain his minor children unable to maintain themselves which continued to be governed with S. 125 CrPC. Title of S.3 of the Act specifically refers to the entitlement of woman only.*[16] *The clauses in the section also should refer to the woman only. As per S. 3(1)(b) if she herself maintains the children, a fair and reasonable provision and maintenance to be made and paid to 'her' by 'her husband' for a period of two years from the date of birth of her children. This is to be construed as an additional provision in addition to her entitlement u/s. 3(1)(a) for her additional nutrition required as a fostering or lactating mother. Hence, the obligation of a Muslim father, like Hindu father, to maintain his minor children u/s. 125CrPC is absolute and not affected by S. 3(1)(b) of the Act. It does not take away their independent rights guaranteed u/s.125 CrPC. Two provisions cover two different situations and there is no conflict between the two.*

Through this decision, the apex court has converted a legislation passed to nullify the judicial verdict in *Shah Bano* into a beneficial legislation in favour of divorced women who would otherwise be left to vagrancy along with their children while the men continue their blissful life devoid of all obligations towards their divorced wives and children.

GEM 7 — GITA HARIHARAN v. RESERVE BANK OF INDIA[17]

Popular Myth: As per S. 6(a) of Hindu minority and Guardianship Act, 1956[18] father is the first natural guardian and after him mother is the next natural guardian.

Judicial verdict: Mother can act as a natural guardian even if father is alive under certain conditions.

It is a very popular case reflecting judicial activism towards equal justice. In this case, the mother of a minor boy, with the consent of her husband, singed as a natural guardian in a Relief Bond for the purpose of investments. The Reserve Bank of India, relying on S. 6(a) of the Act questioned her authority to act as guardian when father was alive and asked the parents either to resubmit the application signed by father or to get a certificate of guardianship from the court of Law. On a petition filed by the mother challenging the constitutional validity of S. 6(a) on the touch stone of Arts. 14 and 15 of the Constitution of India the Apex court heard the petition along with a similar petition filed by one Vandana Shiva,[19] in a tug of war between her and her husband over the custody of her son, challenging the same provision of law under the Act. Hearing both the petitions the court observed that *the wording of S. 6 (a) of the Act 'the father and after him the mother', do give an impression that the mother can act as a guardian only after the life time of the father.* However, instead of striking down the provision as unconstitutional, the court resorted to construe it harmoniously in tune with the constitutional mandate of gender justice. It further observed that *the parliament could not have intended to transgress the constitutional limits while making this enactment and could not have ignored it. Hence, the word 'after' need not necessarily mean 'after the life time' of the father but ' in the absence of'. 'In the absence of' again means 'in case father is not in the charge of actual affairs of the minor, either because of indifference or by mutual consent or because he is staying away from the mother and the child', in all these situations the father can be considered as absent and mother can act as a guardian in such cases.*

Comment: In this case the court by following the principle of *Ut res magis valeat quam pereat*[20] and harmonious construction of S. 4 and S. 6(a) of the Act tried to contribute for equal gender justice. However, it is to be noticed that the court did not do full justice to mother by making her an equal guardian in case where such situations do not exist. In spite of this lacuna, after this landmark judgement governments, banks and other institutions started requiring the consent of 'parent' instead of father or mother, recognizing the fact, either willingly or under court's direction, that father is not a preferred guardian.

GEM 8 — VISHAKA AND OTHERS v. STATE OF RAJASTHAN[21]

Popular myth: Women in employment are left unprotected without the employer's obligation to make working environment safe for her.

Judicial verdict: In case of any type of sexual harassment of a woman at work place, the primary responsibility lies on the employer either as a perpetrator or as a defaulter.

The famous *Vishaka's* case has revolutionized the concept of safe working environment as a fundamental right of a working woman. The observations made by the Apex court in this case are worth mentioning. *Sexual harassment at work place, shortly called as SHW, is a violation of the Right to Gender Equality guaranteed under Arts. 14, 15 and 16, Freedom to work under Art. 19 (1)(g) and Right to privacy under Art. 21 of the Constitution...... The spirit of international conventions can be imbibed into the domestic law through an effective legislation.* Lamenting on the lacuna existing in the legal system in this area, the court issued Guidelines and declared that till a law is made by the Parliament to prevent SHW, the guidelines issued by the court would be the law. It also suggested creation of adequate machinery within the workplace to look in to the matter such as complaints committee, compliance committee, special counselor, modifications in service rules, Industrial standing orders, etc.

Comment: In this case the right against SHW has been raised to the level of Fundamental Right. In pursuant to this decision, the government is persuaded to enact a law and after a lot of deliberations it has prepared The protection against Sexual Harassment of Women Bill 2005. It is on the anvil.

GEM 9 — B.P. ACHALA ANAND v. S. APPI REDDY[22]

Popular notion: A deserted wife loses her right to stay in the matrimonial home.

Judicial verdict: A deserted wife's right to stay in her matrimonial home is effective not only against her husband but also against the landlord.

Wife's right to reside in the dwelling place which stands in the husband's name or in the name of his employer or the landlord emerged from the decade of 1980s. The Apex court in this case affirmed and endorsed the legal principles upheld by various High Courts[23] and said: *Where a husband who was a statutory tenant of the matrimonial home, deserted his wife and left the house, the landlord could not turn her out as long as she paid the rent. Wife's right is effective not only against her husband but also against the landlord.... A suitable amendment in the legislation is called for. And so long as that is not done, we, responding to the demands of social and gender justice, need to mould the relief and do justice by exercising our jurisdiction under Art. 142 of the Constitution.* Speaking on the power of judicial law making, the court commented: *Unusual situations posing issues for resolution is an opportunity for innovation.*

Comment: Through this decision the Apex court has instilled a ray of hope in destituted women and suggested for a law to fill the legislative lacuna. It served as a forerunner to the incorporation of right to residence under Domestic violence Act 2005.

CONCLUSION

Thus, judiciary through its dynamism and commitment to safeguard the interest of women has rendered significant judgements that go a long way to ameliorate the conditions of women, to get themselves empowered and to contribute for the familial, societal and national prosperity. They are adorning the crown of Indian judiciary as valuable gems.

NOTES AND REFERENCES

1. AIR 1960 ALL 684.
2. AIR 2002 SC 3551.
3. Saiyed Rashid Ahmad *v.* Mt. Anisa Khatun.
4. Masroor Ahmed *v.* State (NCT of Delhi) 2008 (103) DRJ 137 (Del).
5. *Ibid.*
6. (1981) Gauhati Law Reports.
7. Krishna Iyer J., in *Yousuf Rowthar* v. *Sowramma* (AIR 1971 Ker 261).
8. (2001) 7 SCC 740.
9. Mohd. Ahmed Khan *v.* Shah Bano Begum (AIR 1985 SC 945).
10. Bai Tahira *v.* Ali Hussain [(1979) 2 SCC 316].
11. Fuzlunbi *v.* K. Khader Vali [(1980) 4 SCC 125].
12. AIR 2007 SC 2215-2218.
13. [(2010) I SCC 666].
14. AIR 1997 SC 3280.
15. S. 3. *Mahr or other properties of Muslim woman to be given to her at the time of divorce:* (1)...(a)...(b) where she herself maintains the children born to her before or after her divorce, a reasonable and fair provision and maintenance to be made and paid to her by her former husband for a period of two years from the respective dates of birth of such children.
16. *Ibid.*
17. (1999) 2 SCC 228.
18. S. 6: The natural guardians of a Hindu minor ... are: (a) in the case of a boy or an unmarried girl—the father, and after him, the mother:...
19. Vandana Shiva *v.* Bandhopadhyaya, AIR 1999 SC 1149.
20. In case of possibility of two constructions, one rendering the provision unconstitutional and the other rendering it constitutioal, the court should prefer the second construction to give effect to the provision.
21. AIR 1997 SC 922.
22. AIR 2005 SC 986.
23. Abdul Rahim *v.* Padma, (AIR 1982 Bom. 341) and Mala Viswanathan *v.* P. Visvanathan, [II (2003) DMC 809 (DB) Cal] as cited by Flavia Agnes, *Hindu conjugality: Transition from sacrament to Contractual obligation*, Redefining Family Law in India (Routledge,Tolstoy House, New Delhi, 2008) pp. 252-55.

8

Gender Mainstreaming in Legal Policy for Gender Justice

D.B. Krishna Kumari

INTRODUCTION

The gender roles framework focuses on the household unit as a system for allocating resources among the family members rather than as a cohesive and co-operative group that shares a common production and consumption system. Social relation analysis and empowerment approach are complimentary to achieve gender equality. Gender mainstreaming is a deliberate effort in providing visibility and support to women's contribution rather than making women to benefit equality gender neutral development interventions. Gender mainstreaming requires a focus on results to improve well being of women.

UNIFEM emphasized on women's human rights and the ultimate goal of equality can be achieved by mainstreaming gender in all legal implications. The division of work, based on sex differentiation has given rise to two broad occupations, namely, female-oriented and male-oriented to power which are allocated to men whereas womenhood is associated with soft, gentle, tender and home-bound occupations.

To overcome such inequalities effective legal implications were essential with gender perspective. Thus gender analysis of the Indian Penal Code, reconceptualization of laws, judicial activism and effective enforcement of law, women-friendly amendments to the laws, etc. were need of the day to reduce gender injustice in the family and society.

An attempt is made in this paper to find out how the gender construction in society is responsible for gender injustices and non-legal implications? Secondly, what type of legal enforcement mechanism is essential to avoid gender imbalance thereby to protect women? Thirdly, to identify the relevant legal policies that are essential for gender mainstreaming to achieve gender equality and justice.

ANALYSIS OF CASES ON PUBLIC OUTRAGE AND ATTACKS ON GIRLS

The Guwahati incident has done nothing to stem the flow of similar incidents being reported from across the country. The repeated coverage and telecasting of the incident on television channels has encouraged others to do such culprit. It is quite evident as the usage of modern media expanded where repeated footage of such crimes on woman and girl reported with sensationalizing the case influenced others as such several incidents occurs.

A similar case was also happened at Mangalore in Karnataka on 28th July 2012, a mob belonging to the Hindu Jagaran Vedika decided that a group of boys and girls enjoying a birthday party were attending a "rave" event. The local television channels with earners, with groups of men entered into the venue of the party and they dragged, hit and molested the women. The whole issue was captured on film where we can see the pathetic shot of several girls cowering on a bed, trying to cover their faces and bodies with pillows while the cameras continue to film. Even after the police intervened, the cameras did not switchoff and kept trying to literally "uncover" the women as they left.

Another incident at Bhoovanapadu beach, a popular tourist spot in Srikakulam District, Andhra Pradesh, a gang of five young men pounced on a couple seeking a private moment. The man was beaten up while the woman, a 20 year college girl has her clothes ripped off. The men had pinned her to the ground, had takenoff her gold ornaments and were getting ready to record what would follow on their mobile phones when the police arrived.

The horror story at Mandya, Karnataka, a 19 year old garment worker was thrown out of a moving train when she tried to resist a gang of men who were harassing her. She is now in a hospital with multiple injuries, having fallen 25 feet from on to a rocky riverbed. She said none of the other women in compartment intervened even though they saw the men harassing and offering her money for sex.

All these incidents occurred and reported across the country in the month of July 2012.

Inspite of feminist movements, the woman and girl child have more access to rights but they are not exercising in the public spaces because those were violated by the powerful class of the society. It is ashamed to say that the mob not involved to stop the acts or combat of such culprit. Their indifference has influenced them to prolong and encouraged the incidents.

GENDER ISSUES INVOLVED IN VIOLENCE AGAINST WOMEN

It was well known that the gender-based violence is clearly dependent on unequal power relations between men and women. Using the life cycle approach at every stage there is a discrimination and violence against girl child and woman. Violence is the result of the complex interplay of individual relationship, social, cultural and environmental factors. Power inequalities between women and men and the masculine culture are the major sources of this violence. Violence against women is not an isolated or contingent problem, but one with deep structural roots whose definitive solution will call for an ongoing effort from society as a whole. Violence against women is a social phenomenon of many and varied dimensions. It is the expression of a social order based on inequality, resulted with the assignment of different roles to women and men on the grounds of their sex and differential treatment for male role as 'superior'. Violence, an expression of gender inequality, is therefore a means to which many men recur to maintain their privileges by subjugating women, with devastating effects for the victims.

Violence against women is also a human rights issue. Therefore, development aims at securing and maintaining women's basic rights to social peace and security. Violence and the fear of violence is profoundly disabling to women, inhibiting or preventing their full participation in development. Further, violence against women should also be viewed as one of the major crucial social mechanisms by which they are forced into subordinate position. It is considered a major threat to ensuring gender equality and empowerment of women and keeps women within the ambit of socially accepted decision-makers. It is also a preventive measure for defying male authority and interference.

GENDER ANALYSIS OF THE INDIAN PENAL CODE

It is to say that India does not have laws dealing with violence against women. But the existing provisions related to such violence in the Indian Penal Code (IPC) are antiquated–framed way back in 1860 and completely out of sync with the times. Kriti Singh, Supreme Court Advocate and Former Member, Law Commission stated that "The existing laws related to rape, molestation and eve teasing are flawed and do not reflect the reality and manner in which women experience sexual assault".

The 172nd Law Commission report recommended changes to the existing IPC provisions in 2000 dealing with rape, molestation and other forms of sexual assault. Based on it, the Government of India constituted High Powered Committee to prepare a draft on Criminal Law (Amendment bill) in 2010, which focused on social realities, included new provisions, proposed higher penalties, ultimately aimed for women empowerment. Gender injustice resulting from the patriarchal nature of the law has led to active discourses for reconceptualisation and reformulation of the law. The National Commission for Women has proposed enactment of a comprehensive code on criminal laws relating to women and had nationwide consultations on its advisability.

All laws need conceptual scrutiny but criminal law needs it most. Criminal law in India for far too long has ensured law and order by maintaining *status quo* among various groups in the State. As in other societies, men as a group in India have enjoyed a better social and political status compared to women. Gender-friendly definition of violence like rape, molestation and stalking in the existing IPC has not only resulted in abysmally no conviction rate but has also ensured that in cases where offenders are caught, they get away with a very lenient punishment.

In India, the division of work based on sex differentiation has given rise to two broad occupations, namely female-oriented and male-oriented occupations related to power (physical, economic, political and even intellectual) which are allocated to men whereas womanhood is associated with soft, gentle, tender and home-bound occupations. It is also important to remember the distinction in the usage of 'he' by the IPC in contrast with, 'man' and 'woman'. The general explanation in the IPC states that the pronoun 'he' and its derivatives are used for any person whether male and female. Removal of such gender bias in language should be replaced with gender natural terms.

GENDER MAINSTREAMING LEGAL POLICY

Effective legal implications were to be articulated from gender perspective to overcome various discriminations, oppressions and powerlessness among girl child and woman. It is the responsibility of the judiciary it has to act as "protectors and keepers of the law" and reduce gaps in legal policy of the land. The following were some of the issues to be taken into consideration:

1. Gender-friendly Laws to deal with Modern or Newer forms of Crimes

The latest developments of aggression against women such as date rape, honour killing, acid attacks, stalking, cyber stalking, gang rape in the public place, incest etc. Under the existing legislations in Indian Penal Code related to rape and sexual assault cases have been found appallingly inadequate in dealing with such cases.

2. Introspection of Existing Laws

Mainstreaming gender in the Indian Penal Code (IPC) in the form of reconceptualization of existing laws, women-friendly amendments to laws, proper definition of crimes etc. were essential to sustain gender justice in the family and society.

3. Enforcement of Legal System

The effective execution of laws in the legal system, judicial activism and systematic enforcement of judgments should act as cognizant of gender-based needs and rights which can realize gender equality and removal of gender conflict (powerlessness and powerfulness). It also results in non-violation of human rights and sustains freedom of woman and girl child.

Analysis of few cases and special laws of the predicament that women face may bring the importance of mainstream gender in all laws and its enforcement. The law of the land must be strengthened so that it will not work as determent unless the law enforcing machinery actually enforces the law. Further it is also equally important of gender-based revision of existing laws for women's protection.

The following cases clearly points out the inherent loop holes that are existed in the execution of law or protection of women's rights in the society:

> A minor girl who was molested by former Haryana DGP during the 1990's, fed up with the harassment that followed, the girl committed suicide while the officer got away with a light punishment, that too several years after the incident was reported. The rape of the two nuns in Gajraula, a town in Uttar Pradesh in 1992, was so poorly handled by the police and other authorities that it took the intervention of Central Bureau of Investigation (CBI) to finally settlement of the case. Bhanwari Devi, a village social worker in Rajasthan was brutally raped by five people (Jawans) for intervening in a child marriage case that led to the formulation of Vishakha guidelines on prevention of sexual harassment at work place. Roop Kanwar was burnt to death on her husband's funeral pyre. This led to State intervention and prohibition against this horrendous act was brought about due to public outcry. The courts recognized Madhu Kishwar's right to inherit as part of the legal system's provision of justice. In Pakistan, a young, 18 year old, Mukhataran Bibi was raped at the instigation of a tribunal which allowed revenge by humiliating a girl. In Mathura, a young girl was raped while at the police station. The very keepers of the law became the violators of the law they have sworn to defend.

4. Victims were in the Various Circle of Violation of Rights

When a victim is molested, her rights are crusted into oblivion by social and traditional fears. Hiding the atrocity on woman for fear of shame because marriage of that person can become a problem. As a result, there was no courage and initiation to report the case in police station. Police may also threaten the victim and make indecent comments and some times character assassination was the common phenomena. Again the law presidencies do not help in justice being mated out to the one who is seeking it.

Judges also biased usually they take decades of time to give their judgments and they are not gender centric. To break this type of vicious circle of violations, the stakeholders of law including media should take certains strategic steps to safeguard the law and reduce the violations at different stages of enforcement of Law and facilitate the following needs:

- Motivate all the stakeholders to formulate gender inclusive laws.
- Develop women-friendly attitudes among the lawyers, police and medical personnel.
  1. Identify the existing loopholes in the laws and judgments accordingly necessary action for the future has to take.
  2. Concentrate on gender-based procedural changes in the laws and effective enforcement of laws.
  3. Sustainability of gender justice to protect future victims.
  4. Generate the motto of freedom, fraternity and equality not only in society even in work place.
  5. Procedural Changes and Execution of Law.

The following were the important issues to be implemented in the execution of law:

1. Law protectors should accept oral testimonies of the victims and treat them with seriousness.
2. Testimony should be given in the absence of the perpetrator.
3. Police should aware of gender disparity and take care in the collecting of the evidence and importance to gender justice equally for all.
4. Women police and women cells should support and undertake counseling of the victims who have come to file the FIR.
5. Medical personnel should intervene immediately to the victims of rape, burn and molestation cases and safeguard them.
6. Women-friendly perspective in handling the victims and certain ethics in protection of law should be taken by everyone concerned.
7. Women should have a speedy trial, fast trac courts and helplines.
8. Strict prohibition of humiliation or harassment during the process or filing of a FIR, medical examination or trial or any other related action.

9. Justice should be given based on the merits of a case and compensation should be made in deserving cases.
10. Medical helpline, counseling and rehabilitation should be made available for the victims and similarly to the family, co-employees and close friends as and when needed.

The stakeholders should implement and follow certain procedural changes in the execution of law from gender perspective in the protection of women victims and violation of law. Above all, the severity of the violence against women should articulate mainstreaming gender in different levels for its need-based interventions.

Women and law have a very close relationship and they have to meet the strategic needs, holistic and full coverage of the perpetrators resulted in biased legal system. Therefore, in drafting specific laws for women, sufficient care should be taken to avoid gender conflicts or powerlessness and reduce over domination in the family and society.

A new UN agency in its first report titled 'Progress of the World's Women: In Pursuit of Justice", stated that "the laws that exist on paper, do not translate into equality and justice". Systematic targeting of women for brutal sexual violence is a hallmark of modern conflicts. Balanced, well informed and unbiased judicial decision-making is an essential part of ensuring that women who go to court will get justice. Further "it is also recommended support to women's legal organization, implementing the gender sensitive law reforms, putting women on the frontline of law enforcement and increasing their access to courts and truth commission during and after conflict".

The following stakeholders should undertake such responsibility to combat violence against women and implement multi-dimension approach from gender perspective with effective policy interventions.

CONCLUTION

Inspite of different socio-legal supportive mechanisms that evolved for the protection of women against violence in the country, still their rights are violated and they are not free from gender discrimination and gender stereotypes. National Policy for Empowerment of Women, Government of India, 2001, aptly pointed out, "The effective implementation of legislation should be promoted by involving civil society and community with appropriate changes in legislations". Violence against Women, its incidence, prevention, investigation, detection and prosecution will be regularly reviewed at all Crime Review forums and Conferences at the Central, State and District levels. Recognized, local, voluntary organizations will be authorized to lodge complaints and facilitate registration, investigations and legal proceedings related to violence and atrocities against girls and women.

Gender mainstreaming the legal policy with women-friendly laws, revision of Indian Penal Code, introspection of existing laws, effective enforcement of legal system, procedural changes and execution of laws, control violation of victim's rights etc. will change existing scenario of women's position. Combating the ideology of patriarchy facilitating oppression and suppression of women in the country is a felt-need to advance women's development and empowerment. Therefore, a holistic approach for the combating gender violence through active commitment and co-operation of all stakeholders such as legal personnel, judiciary, police, medicos, NGOs and public will arrest the violation of human rights at law in the country. The gender mainstreaming for government in partnership with those stakeholders will enable them to attain gender equality and gender justice through policy making, planning and implementing of the different activities in the society.

References

Abraham, T. (Ed.) (2002), Women and the Politics of Violence. New Delhi: Shakti Books.

Advani Poornima (2001), Report of the Regional Workshop on Gender and Law Enforcement, organized by National Commission for Women, Chandigarh, Feb. 23-24.

Jaisingh, Indira (ed.) (2001), Law of Domestic Violence: AUsers Manual for Women, Delhi, Universal.

Kathey Davis, Mary Evans and Judith Lorber (2006), (ed.), Handbook of Gender and Women's Studies, Sage Publications, New Delhi.

Mahbub UL Haq (2000). Human Development Centre, Human Development in South Asia, 2000: The Gender Questions, Oxtord University Press. National Crime Records Bureau (2010), Government of India.

National Crime Records Bureau (2011), Government of India.

Population Reference Bureau (2000), Conveying Concerns: Women Report on Gender-based Violence, Washington DC.

Shankthi, K. (2005), Women in India: Retrospect and Prospect, Anmol Publications Pvt. Ltd, New Delhi.

UNDP (1995), Human Development Report.

UNDP (2000), Human Development Report.
UNDP (2011), Human Development Report.
Veena Poonacha and Neeta Raymon (2002), Prevention of Sexual Harassment in Workplaces/Education Institutions: An Action Research Project, Research Centre for Women's Studies.
Viswanathan, Renuka (2000), Measuring Development, Human Rights and Domestic Violence: Experiences from an Indian State.

9

Rights of the Girl Child and Related to Legal Provisions in India

N. Victoria

INTRODUCTION

The Constitution of India offers all citizens, including children, certain basic Fundamental Rights, the right to life and liberty, the right to equality, right to freedom of speech and expression, right against exploitation, right to freedom of religion, right to conserve culture and the right to constitutional remedies for the enforcement of Fundamental rights. Further, the Directive Principles of State Policy directs the State to ensure that all Children are provided with services and opportunities to grow and develop in a safe and secure environment.

The Constitution guarantees equality and prohibits discrimination on the ground of sex. The Constitution guarantees the right to equality, Article 14, rights to life, Article 21, prohibits discrimination and empowers the state to make special provisions for the girl child Article 15. The State has formulated a number of legislation such as the Child Marriage Restraint Act 1929, Immoral Traffic Prevention Act 1956, the Child Labor (Prohibition and Regulations Act) and the Juvenile Justice (Care and Protection of

Children) Act, 2000. In addition, a number of policies and plans i.e., National Policy for Children 1974, National Policy on Education, National Policy on Child Labor, National Charter for Children, 2004 and National Plan of Action for Children, 2005, the Discriminatory provisions of law are being progressively reviewed. The National Commission for Women, the Department of women and Child Development and the Parliamentary Committee on empowerment of women have reviewed various laws and recommended amendments to many of the laws with the objective of promoting equality and to amend discriminatory provisions. Despite the Constitution mandate of equal legal status for the girl child. The same is yet to realized. The *de-jure* laws have not been translated into de-facto situation for various reasons such as illiteracy, social practices, prejudices, cultural norms based on patriarchal values, poor representation of women in policy-making poverty, regional disparity in development, lack of access and opportunity to information and resources, etc.

In incorporating Fundamental Rights in Part III of the constitution of India and Directive Principles of State Policy in Part IV, the Constitution-makers were influenced by the just adopted Universal Declaration of Human Rights (UDHR). "All human. beings are born free and equal in dignity and rights". The proclaims the right to life, liberty and security of person a right essential to the enjoyment of all other rights. However, the fact is that even these basic human rights are denied to the girl child and India has a long way to go before the human rights of the girl child are enforced.

The Convention on the Rights of the Child (CRC) recognizes that "States Parties shall respect and ensure the rights set forth in the present convention to each child within their jurisdiction without discrimination of any kind, irrespective of the child's or his or her parent's or legal guardian's race, colour, sex, language, religion, political or other opinion, national, ethnic or social origin, property, disability, birth or status".

The reasons for the discrepancy include, among other things, harmful attitudes and practices, such as preferences for sons — which results in female infanticide and prenatal sex selection, early marriage, including child marriage, violence against women, sexual exploitation, sexual abuse, discrimination against girls in food allocation and other practices related to health and well-being. The girl child is discriminated even before her birth in the form of foeticide and after birth in the form of infanticide, and numerous other forms of violence and parental neglect.

RIGHT TO EDUCATION A FUNDAMENTAL RIGHT

The Fundamental Right to Education has been incorporated in our Constitution under Article 21A, on April 1, 2010. From now onwards all the children in the age group of 6-14 years will be provided 8 years of elementary education in an appropriate classroom in the vicinity of his/her neighbourhood. The cost of facilitating school education to a child will be borne by the State. The government will be responsible for the enrollment and regular attendance of children. All schools will have to prescribe to norms and standards laid out in the Act and no school that does not fulfill these standards within 3 years will be allowed to function. Unrecognized private schools operating in the country will have to apply for recognition, failing which they will be penalized to the tune of Rs. 1 lakh and if they still continue to function will be liable to pay Rs. 10,000 per day as fine.

Article 21A was inserted into the Constitution of India. Article 21A provides that "The State shall provide free and compulsory education to all children of the age of six to fourteen years in such manner as the State may, by law, determine."

The further inserted Article 51A(k) making it a fundamental duty on part of a "parent or guardian to provide opportunities for education to his child or, as the case may be ward between the age of six and fourteen years."

Thus, the right to free and compulsory education is the fundamental right of every child between six and fourteen years of age as guaranteed under the Constitution. It is further, the fundamental duty of every parent or guardian to provide opportunities for education of their child or ward between six and fourteen years of age[1].

The Right of Children to Free and Compulsory Education Act, 2009

An act passed by the parliament in 2009 completely known as right of children to free and compulsory act, 2009 was notified by the parliament on 27 August 2009. The purpose of this act was to make education a right for all children until they complete the age of 14 years. It was decided by the members of parliament to make RTE Act at elementary level one of the fundamental right. For this purpose

India joined a group of 135 countries in making RTE. The new law makes it obligatory on part of the state governments and local bodies to ensure that every child gets education in a school in the neighbourhood. Its implementation will directly benefit close to one core children who do not go to schools at present. These children, who have either dropped out from schools or have Implementation Act: Under the 86th constitutional amendment , 2002 right of children to free and compulsory education act, 2009 in the Article 21-A of the Indian constitution inserted RTE as one of the Fundamental Right by special majority of both the houses of parliament. The act came into force from 1st April 2010. Prime Minister Manmohan Singh announced the operationalisation of the Act. Children, who had either dropped out of schools or never been to any educational institution, will get elementary education. "*The Right to Education Act* came into force from 1st April 2010."

Main features of Right to Education Act

- Free and compulsory education to all children of India in the six to 14 age group.
- No child shall be held back, expelled, or required to pass a board examination until completion of elementary education.
- A child who completes elementary education shall be awarded a certificate. Calls for a fixed student-teacher ratio.
- Will apply to all of India except Jammu and Kashmir. Provides for 25 percent reservation for economically disadvantaged communities in admission to Class One in all private schools mandates improvement in quality of education.
- School teachers will need adequate professional degree within five years or else will lose Job.
- School infrastructure (where there is problem) to be improved in three years, else recognition cancelled.
- Financial burden will be shared between state and central government.

Concern of Quality Education

One of the primary objectives of Right of Children Free and Compulsory Education Act, 2009 is improving quality education. The quality of elementary education, particularly in government schools, is a matter of serious concern. The quality of school education depends on various variables which includes physical infrastructure, method of teaching, learning environment, type of books, qualification of teachers, number of teachers, attendance of teachers and students and so on.

Ensuring 25 percent Reservation

The RTE Act, 2009 clause 12 (1) (c) mandates for private schools to admit quarter of their class strength from weaker section and disadvantaged groups. The constitutional validity of this clause was challenged in the apex court of country. However on 12 April 2012, a bench of Chief Justice S.H. Kapadia, Justice K.S. Radhakrishnan and Swatanter Kumar upheld the constitutional validity of the Act. The Supreme Court today upheld the Constitutional validity of landmark Right To Education Act (RTE), providing for reservation of 25 percent seats for poor children in all government, private-aided and unaided schools but not in minority institutions.

ENABLING EDUCATION FOR THE GIRL CHILD

The need to encourage all girls to enrol in school and to retain them in the school system is imperative as education not only improves the worth and self-esteem of the girl child but also enables her to become an economically productive woman and delays her marriage age. Community Vigilance Committees should be formed at village level and the members should ensure that every girl in the village is enrolled and regularly goes to school. Mid-day meals should be made compulsory for girls irrespective of the stage of their school education. This has a two-fold effect—on the one hand it encourages the child to remain in school and secondly it provides the girl with a nourishing meal.

An important reason for girls dropping out of school is the lack of proper toilet and sanitary facilities. High priority is therefore needed to be accorded to providing separate girls' toilet with proper water and sanitation facilities. Efforts through Department of Education should be made to increase the number of female teachers at all levels so as to encourage girl child to continue in school in a safer environment. Further, Bridge schools with quality education package should be provided to girl children, especially street children, child labourers, seasonal migrants, who may have not been in formal education system. These bridge schools should ultimately lead to their integration in the formal system.

Pre-school education is very important input not only for 0-6 years old but also for the older children as it serves as the motivating factor for the girl child to enrol in school. For this purpose, Training of Anganwadi workers and regular teachers at pre-school levels as well in regular school is required. Special training also needs to be given for early detection of mental disability among girl children and appropriate interventions that are needed to address their educational requirements. Additionally, parents and families of such children should be educated and provided with coping mechanisms to enable them to take care and support the girl child. Special incentive/ scholarships and recognition should be provided to motivate girls and help them to continue their education, especially those who succeed in education extra-curricular activities, etc. The proposed Conditional Transfer Scheme has a separate Cash and non cash transfer component to induce enrolment of girls in school and subsequently for their retention at different stages—primary, elementary and secondary.

There are a number of logistic constraints, which restrict girls from attending schools, especially after they have crossed the primary stage. These include distance from school and lack of girl friendly-facilities in school buildings. Efforts should be made to enrol and retain girls in school by reducing distance of school from home as far as possible. There is need to provide safe transport to girls who have to travel considerable distances. In this context, the proposed Conditional Transfer Scheme, can examine the possibility of providing bicycles to girls for traveling to school to young girls so that they need not depend on irregular public transport services. Also, if there are no elementary schools or secondary schools in the vicinity, Department of Education may undertake alternative schooling system, like National Programme for Education of Girls for Elementary Education, which can take care of their schooling needs till such time an elementary school is made available. More residential schools on the lines of Kasturba Gandhi Balika Vidyalaya, and hostels should be provided for girls to facilitate their continuation in education.

ABOLITION OF CHILD MARRIAGE

The Child Marriage Restraint Act, 1929 (CMRA) provides for punishment to those who have allowed, contracted, performed or have been involved in a child marriage. The amendments to Child Marriage Restraint Act (CMRA) is under preparation by the MWCD and the amended bill is likely to be called the 'Prohibition of Child Marriage Bill' with emphasis on 'prohibition' instead of just 'prevention' . The legislation to be successful however should include provisions for declaring child marriages null and void and also impose stringent punishments on all parties which have supported the child marriage. Compulsory registration of marriages is a significant deterrent to child marriages. The Government should ensure that this Registration is brought into force and implemented effectively to disallow child marriages. The local panchayats should register all marriages taking place in their jurisdiction and thus keep a close vigil on occurrences of child marriages. Every Panchayat should put up a notice to the effect that child marriages are illegal and indicate the consequences that will result if such marriages take place[2].

IMMORAL TRAFFIC PREVENTION ACT, 1986

In 1950 the Government of India ratified the International Convention for the Suppression of Immoral Traffic in Persons and the Exploitation of the Prostitution of others. In 1956, India passed the Suppression of Immoral Traffic in Women and Girls Act, 1956 (SITA). The act was further amended and changed in 1986, resulting in the Immoral Traffic Prevention Act also know as PITA. PITA only discusses trafficking in relation to prostitution and not in relation to other purposes of trafficking such as domestic work, child labour, organ harvesting, etc. The following is an outline of the provisions in this law that pertains to children below the age of 18.

Section five of the act states that if a person procures, induces or takes a child for the purpose of prostitution then the prison sentence is a minimum of seven years but can be extended to life. If a person if found with a child it is assumed that he has detained that child there for the purpose of sexual intercourse or any person committing prostitution in public extend with a child and hence shall be punishable to seven years in prison up to life imprisonment, or a term which may extend to ten years and also a maximum fine of one lakh rupees. In 2006, the Ministry of Women and Child Development proposed an amendment bill that has yet to be passed. The amendment does not really concern any of the provisions related to the child but has many important consequences for the right of women sex workers[3].

GIRL CHILD ABUSE, EXPLOITATION AND VIOLENCE

The efforts to prevent girl child abuse and violence calls for strengthening and strict enforcement of laws for rape, sexual harassment, trafficking, domestic violence, dowry and other related issues. A major lacuna in assessing the magnitude and spread of various types of violence against girls is the absence of proper gender disaggregated reporting mechanisms. It is essential to put such a system in place with proper networking and inbuilt tracking systems. Community Vigilance Groups along with Self-Help Groups and Youth Groups should ensure that girl children in their community are protected against abuse, violence and exploitation. To ensure that the above groups carry out the work efficiently, sensitization and training should be conducted on regular basis. Open and frank discussions and discourses on issues related to abuse, exploitation and violence against girl child should be freely allowed to sensitize the general public.

Child-friendly police stations should be constituted in all districts through the setting up of women's police stations. The Police Stations should have a team of policewomen, social workers and counselors to attend to the needs of the girl child victim. Well thought out Rehabilitation packages need to be designed with specific modules for specific types of abuse! violence perpetuated so that the victim receives the correct and appropriate rehabilitation required to be successfully reintegrated back into society. Family counseling and services too need to be provided to families of girls affected by abuse and exploitation so that they can provide care and support to the victim.[4]

SURVIVAL OF THE GIRL CHILD AND HER RIGHT TO BE BORN PREVENTION OF FEMALE FESTICIDE AND INFANTICIDE

The survival of the girl child and her right to be born, and to be an informed, secure and productive participating member of the community and society will necessarily have to be multidimensional in nature with legislative, preventive, advocacy and programmatic input. The discriminatory treatment meted to the girl child is largely an outcome of the traditional perspectives of society towards the girl child which is reflective of the growing incidence of crime and violence against her—a phenomenon that starts even before she takes birth through female feticide. Thus, the problem of the girl child and her being unwanted begins even before she is born with growth in sex selective abortions, i.e. female foeticide. She is not even allowed to be born to start enjoying all her rights. In an effort to combat sex-selective abortions, the government of India passed legislation in 1996 banning prenatal sex determination through ultrasound. However, this law has done little to change the disturbing trend of missing girl.

- Female feticide should be treated as a crime and not just a social evil and therefore the State must take primarily corrective, preventive and punitive action to address the crime.
- Magistrates, DMs/CEOs, Divisional Commissioners should be held accountable for performances, lapses in enforcing the law.
- Enhancement of punishment for all violations of PNDT Act. There should be a firm crack down on offenders with exemplary punishments.
- Correctives should include suspension and/or cancellation of license, seizure and confiscation of equipment, closure of clinics, public censure of doctors and clinics, public notification of such corrective actions taken.
- State Medical Council should take action to suspend/ deregister errant doctors and give wide publicity to this.
- A system of telescoping of offences can be formulated with punishment becoming more stringent with the number of times offences are committed.
- As foeticide is murder of the unborn child, it should be examined whether it can be treated as a crime under IPC and brought under the jurisdiction of Sessions Court.
- A website could be developed to disseminate to wider audiences and flag the names of black-listed organizations/ clinics/doctors.
- There must be better mandatory record-keeping, and obligation to submit full information required under Form F. The clinic should be suspended in any instance of default, until the default is corrected in conformity with legal requirements. Public notification of such suspensions should be made.

A system of incentives can be formulated (as in the case of drugs and narcotics seizures) for tip-offs on clinics which are indulging in sex determination[5].

WELFARE AND DEVELOPMENT OF ADOLESENT GIRLS

Adolescents also have physical and biological needs at this stage of their development, it is important to take care of their psycho-social needs and encourage them to develop their self-esteem and self confidence. Counseling centers for adolescents should be opened in all schools and information centers at every block for adolescents. Balika Sanghas could be formed in every village of the country. The Balika Sanghas play a role of catalysts in creating an environment and becoming the support group for empowerment of girls. The aim should be to raise the profile of the girls and support them in becoming change agents for themselves, their peers and the community, in general. Efforts should also be made to converge programmers I schemes of various different Departments and service providers from Government and Non-Government Organisations. Efforts should also be made to involve the family of adolescents and community as a whole.

The Ministry in collaboration with reputed institutions and NGOs should undertake training and awareness programmes for adolescent girls on crucial issues of reproductive system, changes during the adolescent phase and sensitization to oppressive social systems, social realities and their rights. Vocational training and skill development keeping newly emerging areas in mind should be imparted to adolescent girls as part of their education independent[6].

CHILD TARGETED SCHEMES AND PROGRAMMES (BSY)

The Balika Samriddhi Yojana started in 1997 is an important initiative of the government to raise the status of the girl child. The scheme's aims at changing the negative attitude of families and communities towards the girl child, to increase enrolment and retention of girls in schools, to raise the marriage age of girls and to create income opportunities and activities. A series of incentives are incorporated into the Yojana, such as a gift of Rs. 500 to the mother on delivery of a baby girl and the condition of an annual scholarship for the girl child education.

In 1999-2000 the scheme was changed to benefit the girl child. Hence now the girl child can receive, a post-birth grant amount of Rs. 500. Part of the money given to the girl child at birth or in scholarships can be put aside for paying the premium on an insurance policy in the name of the girl child under the Bhagyashri Balika Kalyan Bima Yojna (BBKBY). Under this scheme the girl child can withdraw the scholarship amount and interest when she turns 18. If she marries or dies before she is eighteen the amount incurred in interest bearing account will be withdrawn[7].

KISHORI SHAKTI YOJANA (KSY)

Taking into consideration the extension of benefits under Janasri Bhima Yojana (JBY) Scheme to eligible family members wherever the girl child is covered by GCPS, the premium of Rs. 100 per annum already collected with effect from 2005 under JBY shall be adjusted towards future premium payable by those girl child. Further, the premium of Rs. 100 per annum shall not be collected from such members covered under JBY with effect from 2008.

KSY aims at empowering adolescent girls so that they may become responsible citizens. It looks at all aspects of adolescent girl development. The large objective of the scheme is to advance the nutritional, health and development status of adolescent girls, support increasing knowledge of health, hygiene, nutrition and family care, and to integrate them with opportunities for learning life skills, going back to school, helping girls grow to understand their society and become prolific members of the society[8].

INDIA PENAL CODE AND CHILD-RELATED OFFENSES

Apart from the various acts concerning children means Boy/ Girl. The Indian Penal Code (IPC) also has a list of offences against children. According to the sections 82 and 83 of the IPC a child who commits a crime and is below the age of seven is not considered to have committed a crime. A child who is between the ages of seven and twelve and is deemed to have immature understanding about the consequences of his/her actions is also considered incapable of committing a crime.

Sections 315 and 316 IPC discusses the offence of foeticide and infanticide. If a person commits an act with the intention of preventing the child from being born alive or an act that results in the death of the child after birth, that person is committing foeticide/ infanticide as long as they do not do it in the interest of the mother's health or life. If a person does an act that amounts to culpable death which results in the quick death of an unborn child, he will be charged with culpable homicide.

Section 305 IPC states that it is a crime for any person to abet the suicide of a child, i.e. a person who has not completed eighteen years of age.

Section 317 IPC states that is it a crime against children, if their mother or father expose or leave a child in a place with the intention of abandonment. This does not prevent the law from pursuing further if the abandonment results in the death of the child. The parents would then be charged with culpable homicide or murder.

There are a number of sections in the IPC that discuss kidnapping and abduction.

Section 361 IPC states that if a female minor of not yet eighteen is taken from their lawful guardians without their consent it is termed kidnapping from lawful guardianship.

Section 363-A IPC states, it is a crime to kidnap or maim a minor for the purpose or employment of begging. If a person if found employing a minor for begging, and that person is not the legal guardian of the child, it is assumed that the child has been kidnapped for the purpose of employment in begging.

Section 366A IPC specially outlines such a crime being committed against a minor girl who has not attained eighteen years of age. Section 367 IPC states it is a crime to kidnap a person in order to cause them grievous hurt, place them in slavery, or subject them to the unnatural lust of a person.

Sexual offences against children are also covered in the IPC. Section 372 IPC discusses the selling of a child (below the age of eighteen) for the purpose of prostitution or to illicit intercourse with any person, or knowing that it is likely that the child is being sold for such a purpose. Section 3721PC states it is a crime to buy a child for the purpose of prostitution or to illicit sex from any person.

Section 376 IPC discusses the offence of rape. Under this section a man who rapes his wife, who is not below twelve years old is given a lesser punishment. The section also discusses special circumstances of rape such as rape committed by a civil servant or police man, rape of a pregnant woman, gang rape or rape of a child below the age of twelve[9].

CONCLUSION

The reason for gross-violation of the rights of the girl is in the absence of a social norm in favor of her survival, dignity and education. And also be a campaign against child labour and an argument for its total abolition in emphasizing on abolition of child labor in 'hazardous' industry alone girls are left out. The middle classes must abide by the law and not employ girls as domestic servants. They should know that they are violating the constitution and its provisions for right to education in giving employing girls. They have to give a lead as protagonists of child rights. There could be pressure built to rescue girls from child labor, child trafficking and early marriage.

From the study findings it is abundantly clear that efforts at gender equality and gender justice must start with equality for the girl child. All barriers must therefore be eliminated to enable girls without exception to develop their full potential and skills through equal access to education and training, nutrition, physical and mental health care and related information. To eliminate all forms of discrimination against the girl child and the root causes of son preference, that result in harmful and unethical practices like female infanticide and sex selection before birth. To increase public awareness of the value of the girl child and at the same time strengthen the self-image, self-esteem and status of the girl child. To improve the welfare of the girl child, especially in regards to health, nutrition and education. Elimination of girl child labor and protection the girl child from economic exploitation and from performing any work that is likely to be hazardous or to interfere with her education, or to be harmful to her health or physical, mental, spiritual, moral or social development. Eradicate violence against the girl child i.e., female infanticide and prenatal sex selection, sexual abuse, sexual exploitation, child prostitution and child pornography. Promote the girl child's awareness of and participation in social, economic and political life.

Notes and References

1. Dr. J.N. Pandey The Constitutional Law of India, 47th Edition, page no. 294.
2. Prohibition of Child Marriage Act, 2006.
3. Immoral Traffic Prevention Act, 986.
4. Study on Child Abuse India 2007 and Ministry of Women and Child Development, Government of India.
5. Pre-Conception and Pre-Natal Diagnostic Techniques Act, 1994.
6. ICDS General Scheme.
7. The Scheme of Balika Samridhi Yojana was launched by Government of India w.e.f. 15-8-97.
8. National Mechanism Child Targeted Schemes and Programmes.
9. Indian Penal Code (45 of 1960).

References

www.google.com
The Indian Constitution.
Prohibition of Child Marriage Act, 2006.
The immoral Traffic (Prevention) Amendment Bill, No. 47 of 2006.
Study on Child Abuse in India 2007 and Ministry of Women and Child Development Government of India.
Pre-Conception & Pre-Natal Diagnostic Techniques Act, 1994.
ICDS General Scheme.
The Scheme of Balika Samridhi Yojana was launched by Govt. of India w.e.f. 15-8-97.
National Mechanism Child Targeted Schemes and Programmes.
Indian Penal Code (45 of 1960).

10

Special Provisions for the Protection of Women against Sexual Offences in India

V. SUNITHA

INTRODUCTION

Women in Indian society have been the victims of ill-treatment, humiliation, torture and exploitation. In the ancient India women held a high place of respect in the society as mentioned in Rig-Veda. Volumes can be written about the status of our women and their heroic deeds from the Vedic-period to the modern times. The problem of violence against women is not new. A woman's life lies between pleasure at one end and danger at another end[1]. Many evil customs and traditions stepped in which enslaved the women and tied them to the boundaries of the house[2]. The spread of social evils like dowry deaths, child marriage, domestic violence, rape, sexual harassment, exploitation of women workers are rampant in different parts of India. Humiliation, rape, kidnapping, molestation, dowry death, torture, wife-beating, etc. have grown up over the years. Virginity is valued by man, yet it is man who violates it and commits rape. When violence is committed at home it becomes domestic violence. Domestic violence may involve different means such as hitting, kicking, beating and restraining, throwing objects. In broad terms, it includes threats, sexual abuse, emotional abuse, controlling or domineering, Intimidation, stalking, passive/covert abuse and economic deprivation, rape, abduction, kidnapping, murder, etc.

THE OFFENCE OF RAPE AGAINST WOMEN IN INDIA

Among the states Madhya Pradesh has reported the highest number of rape cases (2,998) accounting for 14% of all such cases reported in the country but if one look at the figures of incest rape (i.e., rape by someone in the family) Chhattisgarh reported the highest number in all (107). Incidentally, incest rape cases have increased by 30.7% from 309 cases in 2008 to 404 cases in 2009 compared to 0.3% decrease in overall rapc cases[3]. Besides Delhi, the other cities which reported a large number of rape cases are Mumbai (182), Bhopal (117), Jabalpur (76), Jaipur (69) and Pune (67).

Incidentally most of the rapes were committed by the offenders who knew the victims. Overall 21.21 lakh cases in 2008 a marginal increase. Among the cities Delhi, Bangalore and Mumbai accounted for 13.2%, 9.4% and 9.1% respectively of the total crimes. Uttar Pradesh toped the crime rate in the country in 2010 according to the latest statistics released by the National Crime Report Bureau[4]. The state registered 33.9% of the crime reported in 2010 followed by Andhra Pradesh (12%), Tamil Nadu (10.4%) according to the National Crime Report Bureau Report for 2010. Madhya Pradesh recorded the highest number of rates while Andhra Pradesh registered the highest number of crimes against women which included sexual harassment.

LEGAL/SPECIAL PROVISIONS FOR WOMEN

Protection of Women from Domestic Violence Act, 2005: This Act protects women from any act/conduct/omission/commission that harms, injures or potential to harm is to be considered as domestic violence. It protects the women from physical, sexual, emotional, verbal, psychological, economic abuse[4]. Protection of Women against Sexual Harassment at Workplace Bill, 2010: On November 4, 2010, the Government introduced protection of Women against Sexual Harassment at Workplace Bill, 2010, which aims at protecting the women at workplace not only to women employee but also to female clients, customer, students and research scholars in colleges and universities patients in hospitals. The Bill was passed in Lok Sabah on 3.9.2012.

INDIAN PENAL CODE (IPC)

The Indian Penal Code 1860 provides certain provisions for the protection of women from sexual abuses. Punishment for kidnap and abduction (sec. 366): This section provides that whoever kidnaps or abducts any woman with an intent that she may be compelled or knowing it to be likely that she will be compelled to marry any person against her will or in order that she may be forced or seduced to illicit intercourse shall be punished with imprisonment of either description for a term which may extent to 10 years and shall also be liable to fine[5] punishment for Rape (sec. 376): whoever commits rape shall be punished with imprisonment of either description for a term which shall not be less than 7 years but which may be for life or for life or for a term which may extend to 10 years and shall also be liable to fine[6].

The Criminal Law (Amendment), 2013 Act has expressly recognised certain acts as offences. The offences like sexual harassment, voyeurism and stalking acid attack have been incorporated into the Indian Penal Code. Sexual harassment (sec. 354A)—Any person who commits physical contact and advances involves unwelcome and explicit sexual overtures; oral demand or request for sexual favours; or making sexually coloured remarks; or forcibly showing pornography; or any other unwelcome physical, verbal or non-verbal conduct of sexual nature shall punished with rigorous imprisonment up to 5 years, or with fine, or with both.

Voyeurism (354C) watching or capturing a woman in 'private act', which includes an act of watching carried out in a place which, in the circumstances would reasonably be expected to provide privacy, and where the victim's genitals, buttocks or breasts are exposed or covered only in underwear; or the victim is using a lavatory; or the person is doing a sexual act that is not of a kind ordinarily done in public, in the case of first conviction imprisonment not less than one year, but which may extend to three years, and shall also be liable to fine, and be punished on a second or subsequent conviction, with imprisonment of either description for a term which shall not be less than three years, but which may extend to seven years, and shall also be liable to fine[7].

THE CONSTITUTION OF INDIA

The Constitution of India protects women by providing special provisions. Article 14, right to equality, Article 15(3) lays down special provisions for women and children. Under Art. 14 Supreme Court of India lays down certain guidelines to prevent sexual harassment of working women in landmark judgment *Priyanka* v. *State of Rajasthan*[8]. It includes that gender equality includes protection from sexual harassment and right to work with dignity.

NATIONAL COMMISION FOR WOMEN

Under sec 10(1) of the National Commission for Women Act, 1994 provides the functions of the commission namely[9] : (a) investigate and examine all matters relating to the safeguards provided for women under the constitution and other laws, (b) call for special studies or investigations into specific problems or situations arising out of discrimination and atrocities against women and identify the constraints so as to recommend strategies for the removal[10].

CONCLUSION

The legislature has passes many laws to keep pace with the changing time and to meet the demands of women in India. Implementation of these laws in an effective manner obeying not merely the letter but also the spirit of such laws will certainly improve the conditions of the women.

Notes and References

1. Aruna Goel, Violence and Protective Measures for Women Development and Empowerment, New Delhi, Deep and Deep Publications, 2004.
2. Violence against Women and Children—Issues and Concerns, By Awadhesh Kumar Singh and Jayanta Choudhury, New Delhi, Serials Publications, 2012.
3. www.crimesagainst women.com
4. http://www.ndtv.com/article/cheat-sheet/recommendations-of-the-justice-verma-committee-...2/1/2013.
5. India, Ministry of Home Affairs, National Crime Records Bureau, Crime in India, 2011, p. 79.
6. Y.V. Chandra Chud and V.R. Manohar, Indian Penal Code.
7. *Ibid.*
8. J.N. Pandey, Constitutional Law of India, Central Law Agency, 2011 ed., p. 213.
9. Dr. Dalbir Bharthi, Women and the Law, APH Publishing Corporation, 2008.
10. Ram Ahuja, Violence Against Women, p. 3.

11

History of Prostitution and Trafficking Laws in India

K. Sudha and T.Y. Nirmala Devi

Prostitution is an age-old social institution. The genealogy of trafficking can also be traced along with prostitution through the annals of history. This is a research paper which traces the history of prostitution and trafficking laws. A study of modern law pertaining to prostitution and trafficking would be incomplete without tracing the history of this institution. A characteristic feature of our laws related to marriage and prostitution is that the native Vedic laws and the British tenets are blended and they flow together. The institution of prostitution in India enfolds within itself the devadasi system, another unique feature of Indian society.

As in other parts of the world, prostitution was prevalent in India from a very early period. It is mentioned in the Rigveda[1] and various Smrithis, ancient religious scriptures. Gautama, a Smrithikara, also refers to prostitutes[2]. In the Mahabharata[3] and the Arthasastra courtesans are described as an established institution. Kautilya, a famous political and economic thinker during the Mauryan empire, recommends appointment of a superintendent of prostitutes to watch over their activities and look after their welfare.

The prostitutes also paid regular tax to the king, attended his court and rendered him personal service.[4]

In the Jatakas, a collection of Buddhist stories written in the ancient period, there are numerous references to prostitutes indicating that they were tolerated and even esteemed to a certain degree. The fees paid to them were exceedingly high.[5] However, Manu, prominent among the Smrithikaras, was very stern in the matter. He forbids a Brahmana from taking food offered by the prostitute and goes on to say that those who take such food are excluded from the higher worlds.[6] He also condemns the food offered by such persons who subsist on the income of prostitutes. He denounces them strongly and says that they are worse than even a slaughterhouse.[7] He regards them as a social evil stating that the King is required to punish the 'clever harlots'. Manu recommends very simple penance for even killing them.[8] Gautama says that for killing a woman who subsists by 'harlotry' no Prayaschitta is necessary, simply eight handfuls of corn may be gifted.[9] Post-mortem offerings too are denied to them.

Manu refers to the case of such men who make money by allowing their wives to act as prostitutes and says that people holding conversation with such women are not to be punished but are to pay only a small amount as a fine.[10] Ram Mohan Das, an eminent sociologist states that Manu had a very low opinion of such women. He states that the patriarchal double standards of allowing the institution to prevail while at the same time looking down at these women as 'fallen women' and calling them 'harlots' is reflected in Manu's Philosophy.[11]

But despite such severe condemnation during that period, the institution of prostitution persisted and laws had to be made with regard to them also. Yajnavalkya, another prominent Smrithikara, lays down that if a prostitute after getting a fee, refuses to receive the customer she shall pay twice the amount of the fee and the same shall be imposed on a man who does not pay her after having had intercourse with her.[12] Matsya Purana, one of the ancient scriptures, dilates upon the duties of the prostitutes and the special clauses of law applicable to them.[13]

The Kamasutras define a *ganika* as a vesya (prostitute) who is accomplished and proficient in the 64 kalas.[14] Though the word *ganika* at first denoted all classes of prostitutes in general, it later came to be applied to the courtesan class only, and sometimes it was the best among them who received this appellation.[15] The *ganikas* were the castaways of society. In almost all the Samhitas, ancient scriptures, all decent people are forbidden to partake of the cooked food of a *ganika* and a *gana*, though the latter was apparently not so detestable as the former in other respects. *Gana* meant a body corporate or the body politic and in its wider sense might have signified any party or a club especially in the towns, while the *ganika* denoted itself as the property of the *gana*. The Vishnu Samhita[16] ordains a seven days fast with only a diet of milk for a man or woman who takes the food of a *gana, ganika*, a thief and a professional musician.

The Mitakhsara[17] states that the Skanda Purana, ancient scriptures, regards the prostitutes as the fifth caste beyond the four recognised ones. It adds that such courtesans who are not maintained exclusively by any particular person do not incur any sin if they have intercourse with men of the same or the superior caste. The king punishes neither them nor the men having connection with them.[18] It is ironical that even these 'Panchamas' were the castaways like the untouchables. While the former provided sexual services to the *gana* the latter provided them labour.

The lawgivers condemned pimps and procurers in the most vehement terms. Vasistha[19] lays down a strict rule that no one should seek hospitality under the roof and food from the hands of a man who tolerates a paramour of his wife for sordid gain or sells his daughter for immoral purposes.[20] Yajnavalkya endorses this section by adding pimps to it and all people who live on the earnings of the prostitutes.[21] Gautama predicts horrible consequences in this life and thereafter for those who force their legally married wives into prostitution.[22]

From this it is evident that trafficking was prevalent at the time, though not on such an extensive scale as in the present era. Vishnu and several others hold the firm view that it is an unpardonable sin to act the procurer or the go between, to entice a girl away from home and force her into the life of a prostitute and live on those earnings. A majority of the legislators never wanted however, to withhold from the prostitutes rights that they were entitled to enjoy as human beings.

Yajnavalkya formulated clear-cut laws in respect of prostitutes.[23] If a prostitute promised to entertain a man in her room and takes her proper fees in advance, but subsequently refuses intercourse, she must return the full money from her own purse as well as compensation. In case she has made an oral contract but accepted no money, she will have to pay the compensation only. If, on the other hand, the visitor after settling the price and paying it in advance, is unwilling to have intercourse with her, he will not be eligible for the return of his money.[24]

Promiscuous intercourse has been greatly circumscribed since the days of the early Epics. The lawgivers were confronted with this growing 'menace' and tried their best to frame laws to cope with it. During the five centuries preceding the Christian era, clandestine and public prostitution had grown into a well-established institution and could not be curbed. While tracing the history of prostitution in the Indian context, prominent historians S.N. Sinha and N.K. Basu state: "Brahmin legislators of the kings, nevertheless, in order to preserve the moral integrity of the higher castes tried their heart and soul to dissuade the delinquents from off the dangerous path and correct their pernicious habits, not through the award of heavy sentences, but by proper ethical teachings and a system of penance and auto-purification in a spiritual manner."[25] The penance often consisted of fasting for one or several days only with water or milk diet and gift of a milch-cow to the family priest; while the auto-purification physically manifested itself in the subject's swallowing of the holy Panchagavya (i.e. cow's milk, cow's curd, cow's clarified butter, cow's dung and urine mixed together).

Most lawgivers, therefore, were quite severe in their efforts at maintaining chastity in the body politic, but made little efforts towards penalising prostitution. It was far from their mind to cause it to disappear from the civil life of Aryan society; they must have accepted it as a necessary and incurable evil so as to obviate greater ones.[26] According to Basu and Sinha: "The Brahmin sages did not disdain to come to the aide of the secular authorities and suggest to the latter how to restrain the evil within its proper boundaries and dissimulate it to the eyes of the decent people. They reasoned out that in trying to suppress this social sore, they would only compromise the security of the social life. But, on the contrary, with a relentless zeal they sought to destroy the existing causes of prostitution and prescribed exemplary penalties for the pimps and lenons."[27] Prajapatya prescribed a rather hard form of penance for the sin of intercourse with a 'prostitute'.[28] Basu and Sinha point out that this 'utopian' legislation never fully attained its end and that prostitution further strengthened since the time of the early Epics.[29]

RELIGION AND PROSTITUTION

In the latter half of the Puranic age, and close on the heels of the Greek influence in India, diverse gods within their wooden, metal or stone images were brought into being and temples were erected all over the country to shelter these images.[30] The priests, stone-cutters, brick-layers, sculptors, carpenters and masons thus found themselves busy from one end of the year to the other round these temples which held out to them and their succeeding generations a most promising future. Devoted people from all parts of the country flocked there in season and out of season, particularly on the 'holy days'. As these temples became a hub of activity even women in prostitution settled near them. The temple priests could not stop the women in prostitution from gradually settling there in large numbers. The visible leniency or unremitting non-chalance of the priests gave the women in prostitution enough latitude to practise their 'business' freely in and outside the temple compound.

Gradually a compromise, as it were, was affected between religion and prostitution, the latter being in some sort sanctified thereby. Schopenhauer in his "Metaphysics of Sexual Life" has analysed: "The identity of religion and sexual perceptions explain the frequent transformations of one into the other, and the continuous association between the two. A sexual emotion will often function vicariously for a religious emotion, in part or wholly. The unusually interesting history of the complicated and remarkable sexual phenomenon it renders clear to us individual process of their kind and certain peculiarities of the racial psychology; and thereby we are led to understand the powerful after-effects of the phenomenon in the customs, the morals and the conventions of our time, and we are enlightened as to the role still played by the religio-sexual factor in the life of many men even of our day."[31]

It was in these ways that legal prostitution thrust out as an offshoot towards the boundary walls of the temples to revive religious prostitution. As this religious-legal prostitution grew near the temples, other 'chaste' women could not enter the temples freely. Keeping probably this in view the women in prostitution who lived near the holy places were in course of time debarred from entering the temple compound except at a certain fixed hour of the day, leaving out a chosen few who wielded a great influence with the presiding priest.[32] This system, we have reasons to presume, ruled in almost all the temples of Northern India sometime during the

Puranic period to be suppressed in course of time to a great extent; while in Southern India it was refined and amended with the progress of time to yield place to the usage of 'Devadasi'. In Northern India, however, the growing demands for morality about the holy places could never expatriate the prostitutes.[33]

GENEALOGY OF DEVADASI

Tracing the genealogy of the temple dancer shows that as a 'nityasumangali', an ever auspicious woman, the devadasi was expected to deal with the 'dangerous divine', a role that was soon overshadowed by her artistic performances in the temples and in the court.[34] The textual authority of the tradition of temple dancing is somewhat uncertain. There are no known direct references to dancing in the temple in the oldest books of the theory, the Natyashastra and the Abhinaya Darpana. The first mention of temple dancing is in the 11th century collection of stories, the Kathasagara. Only in the 13th century did the Natyashastra become legitimised as Veda or holy knowledge.[35]

Inscriptional evidence from medieval Karnataka is more revealing. Even before the 11th century, when temple girls came to have specific duties assigned to them, there is mention of the word *sule* (meaning prostitute) in inscriptions. Only after the 11th century, a time when the temple as an institution was expanding did the word *patra (*meaning singing or dancing girl) gradually attach to them.[36]

Whatever the tortuous historical process by which *lasya* (signifying dance) became "the art of lust", by the late 19th century, the devadasi tradition was a decidedly matrilineal one. The young dedicated girl underwent rigorous training in Nritya and Gita under a male guru, for which she enjoyed donations, including land grants, made to her personally or to the temple, frequently by upper caste women themselves.[37] Her strict professionalism, says Amrit Srinivasan, made her an adjunct to conservative domestic society, not its 'ravager', an assertion borne out by the number of female donors who supported her work.[38] Indeed, the devadasi's legal rights were unusual for women under Hindu law, since she was able to adopt daughters, and pass property on to her female descendants.

Janaki Nair, an eminent historian, says that the power enjoyed by devadasis must not be exaggerated. Despite their relative autonomy, they nevertheless remained firmly under the control of those men within the political economy of the temple: the priest, guru and patron. The sexual services, however, were embedded within the wider cultural sphere of symbolic and material exchanges in the temple.[39] As a key institution in the formation of social communities in pre-colonial South India, temple was a site where both symbolic and material resources were redistributed, rendering public, stable and culturally appropriate exchanges at the level of politics and economics.

REGULATION OF PROSTITUTION AND TRAFFICKING BY THE BRITISH EMPIRE

The modern law of prostitution and trafficking in India draws its content nonetheless from the British tenets also. The debate that took place in Britain about regulation of prostitution has significance in assessing the Indian regulatory measures. Feminists of the 19th century have tried to decipher issues related to prostitution and female sexuality in myriad voices. Their theoretical presumptions had contributed to the moulding of prostitution laws of those times. To understand the regulation of prostitution in colonial India familiarity with the British approach towards it is very essential.

The late-Victorian England during 1870s-1890 had witnessed an upsurge of a strong social purity movement. The 1880s was a period of low profit, high unemployment, severe cyclical depression and a chronic housing shortage. This economic instability, says Lucy Bland, a feminist of repute, combined with political developments (the rise of socialism and the immigration into the East End of London of foreign anarchists) generated a deep fear amongst the propertied classes of a working class uprising.[40] But it was not just overtly political beliefs and activities, which were seen as a threat; immoral behaviour, too, was viewed as potentially subversive. Further, the desire for moral reform was present even in the pursuit of what might appear to us today as predominantly material reform. For example, the concern to improve working class housing partly related to the belief that overcrowding encouraged incest and juvenile prostitution.[41]

Through legislation and philanthropy, many efforts were made to encourage the working class into a middle class 'decency'. While the 'respectable working classes' were wooed, the casual poor - the 'dangerous classes'—were policed more coercively, and their behavior, including their leisure pursuits, was subjected to greater intervention.[42] This led to the rise of the social purity movement.

Mrs. Laura Ormiston Chant, a social purity feminist, was a protagonist of this movement. She protested against the renewal of licenses by the Empire to music halls where prostitutes came in search of clients. Chant, a member of the National Vigilance Association, insisted: "I am no puritan. We don't want to lessen the amusements...but we will have them decent. They will not be as highways of ruin to the young, licensed opportunities for the vicious."[43] By 'decent' she meant entertainment that was 'respectable' and family centered, so that the husband could take his wife there without the fear that they could be confronted with a 'prostitute'.

Not all feminists applauded Chant's action. Josephine Butler was one among them. A 'repressive' response to the moral matters from feminists was of particular concern to Butler. "I continue to protest that I do not believe that any real reform will ever be reached by outward repression."[44] Much to Butler's concern a number of feminists, once apparently *laissez-faire* and anti-statists in matters of sexuality and morality, were now, in the 1880s and 1890s, adopting a more 'repressive' stance and were taking to closing brothels, clearing the streets of prostitutes and attempting to 'clean up' indecent pursuits, from literature to music halls.

Parallel to the social purity movement, a protest against the repressive measures taken up by the Empire started in the 1870s itself. The focus was on the abolition of the Contagious Diseases Acts. Even Butler championed the cause. The legislation had been introduced in the 1860s to regulate prostitution in the hope of countering venereal disease amongst the army and the navy. The Acts introduced into certain military depots the forced inspection, detention and treatment of women who were suspected of being women in prostitution. But in 1870s, opposition to the Acts had sprung up in the form of a coalition of middle-class evangelicals, working-class radicals and active groups of feminists headed by Butler. The Acts were eventually repealed in 1886.

Even though the Contagious Diseases Acts were repealed, a group of feminists including Josephine Butler, Elizabeth Wolstenholm Elmy, a veteran feminist and a repealer, were still concerned about repressive actions against the prostitutes. Their primary concern was the attempts made by the National Vigilance Association, to enforce certain clauses of the Criminal Law Amendment Act concerning brothels.[45] The Act aimed to raise the age of consent and reform the law on sexual assault. Most feminists supported these measures, but the Bills also contained various repressive clauses relating to soliciting and brothels. Brothel keeping and the procurement of women for prostitution were outlawed under the Act. Landlords could be held responsible under the Act if they knowingly let out houses for the purpose of prostitution. Rising pressure on such landlords from vigilance groups led to a wariness about letting property to 'suspect' women (such a label would apply to most women living without men). This created a housing problem not only for women in prostitution living in lodging-houses brothels, but also for any women living with other women, and even women living on their own, although the latter did not constitute a 'brothel'.[46]

These measures had a two-fold effect on the lives of the women in prostitution. Many of the women in prostitution were forced to set up houses with pimps, or, as they were called 'bullies', to provide a cover for their work. Pimps were only too eager to provide the 'protection'.[47] Meanwhile, women were being thrown out into the streets with nowhere to go. Some of these women were being subsequently sent to prison on charges of vagrancy. Incidentally, the upper class brothels, the 'fashionable houses' as it were, remained virtually untouched.

Ms. Lucy Wilson, the editor of the Journal of Vigilance Association for the Defense of Personal Rights states: "Forcible interference with the voluntary vice of adult persons, when it is not without external injury to others, never had done any good and never will."[48] Elizabeth Wolstenholme Elmy in a letter to the journal quotes French repealer Ives Guyots' sharp recognition of the double moral standard at work:

> "Would the men of England tolerate the inspection of their habits by police, and the suppression of their houses, if police morality was dissatisfied with their conduct?"[49]

Elmy asked 'those old fellow workers':

> "Have you protested against arbitrary arrest and examination of women as 'unconstitutional and unjust' (when campaigning against the Contagious Diseases Acts) solely because they were inspected in the name of public health? Do such things become constitutional and just because they are done in the name of public morals? ...in the name of public morality and social purity our mistaken friends will have brought us back to the cruel oppression of women which they denounced and resisted when enforced in the alleged interests of the public health."[50]

In sharp contrast to these criticisms, the National Vigilance Association's journal 'The Vigilance Record' was full of appreciation of the 'good work' done by the Vigilance groups in closing brothels.[51] The NVA was embarrassed when 90 women in prostitution unwilling to be 'led to the slaughter' marched through the London streets in protest, four abreast, singing as they went. The Vigilance Record was shocked: 'a very bad sight was witnessed'.[52]

Dr Elizabeth Blackwell, another active member of the NVA felt that prostitutes if not caught in time, became 'demons', 'human tigers' that delight in destruction and torture.[53] She believed that: "The tenderest compassion may be shown to the poor creature who ceases to be a prostitute... But do nothing to raise the condition of prostitutes as such, any more than you would try to improve the condition of murderers and thieves."[54]

Lucy Bland, a feminist lawyer, tries to evaluate why the feminist repealers of those times tried to push in repressive actions against the women in prostitution.[55] "One of the reasons was that more and more 'respectable' women were entering into the public domain. The term 'public woman' meant the same as the term 'street walker'; both implied that the public world excluded respectable women. It was reserved for men and those women who 'immorally' serviced them. Feminists then, wanted the streets and other public places to be safe for women, both literally and symbolically; for women to be able to venture into such places without being labelled 'immoral' which necessarily acted as a constraint upon their freedom of movement. Breaking down the barriers of that constraint was obviously part of that agenda.[56]

The feminists of the late 19th century in Britain were preoccupied with their work within local governments and philanthropy. Carol Smart, a noted feminist, states that their work at local governments was one extension of women's home influence and extending their domesticating and 'civilising' role into the wider world. Women active in local government thought of themselves as engaging in municipal housekeeping.[57] Thus, these women raised issues related to morality. They tried to impose middle class norms of domesticity. Donzelot has analysed this as 'familialist strategy' intervening to control women and children's sexual and social behavior and to remake working class culture.[58]

Bland states that these attitudes tended to pervade the actions of those feminists involved in social purity campaigning. The desire to administer 'protective surveillance' was likely to be 'repressive' in its implications. It was crucially related to the dominant ideas about female sexuality. She also states that Josephine Butler and Elizabeth Wolstenholme Elmy may have been horrified by their former colleagues' repressive actions, but most Butlerites and repressive moralists shared an attitude towards female sexuality that had 'protective surveillance' within its logic.

Judith Walkowitz describes feminists' responses to girls' that they came across during their philanthropic work: "Butlerites ...registered the same feelings of repugnance and ambivalence toward unrepentant prostitutes. For them as well as for more repressive moralists, the desire to protect young girls thinly masked coercive impulses to control their voluntary sexual impulses".[59]

The debate between the Butlerites and the repressive moralists extended to issues related to the personal rights of the victims of this 'vice'. The Personal Rights Association, highly critical of the NVA's repressive actions, objected especially to its attack not on the instigators of 'criminal vice' but on the 'helpless victims'. They felt that the repression of immorality by crushing its helpless victims was miscalled morality and that it represented nothing better than outward indecency.

But Laura Chant felt: "A great deal of well meant nonsense is talked about the 'liberty of the subject', whenever there is effort to clear the streets. Some good people seem to be zealous in defending the victims from injustice that it seems as if they were in danger of forgetting the vice is in itself a colossal injustice, an infringement of the liberty of the subject."[60] Bland analyses the work done by the feminists of various hues and cries: "These women cannot be dismissed as simply 'prying prudes' or interfering busybodies, however undesirable the means to their feminist ends may seem to us today. It is worth recognizing that in our approach to current issues of pornography, prostitution and sex industry many of the same dilemmas and difficulties remain as to how to use the law and how to take issue with beliefs and practices, which we, as feminists, find unacceptable. As in the past, there is no one feminist answer to these problems.[61]

These feminist responses to the regulation of prostitution help in evaluating these regulations and also to assess their impact on the body politic that includes women at large and sex workers in particular. The contemporary debate on prostitution and trafficking caught the imagination of the rest of the world also, especially in the British colonies.

THE PURITY CAMPAIGN AND THE EMPIRE

The twentieth century international campaign to control prostitution was essentially British inspired, colonial India being no exception to it. The first attempt to close down indigenous brothels in the Empire was made by General Sir Charles Napier in 1845 in Karachi. Ronald Hyam, a sociologist, observes that the Purity Campaign that was exported overseas had also initially started with the intention to regulate prostitution but ended up with the demand for complete abolition of the practice.[62] The British Government accepted this demand and decided to implement it even in the Empire.

The early years of the 20th century witnessed the closure of the brothels throughout the world. The 'tolerated' brothels of Colombo had been closed in 1912. A clean up campaign had begun in Hong Kong and the licensed brothels in the city were closed in 1934. Other powers were moving too. The Netherlands closed its Indonesian tolerated brothels in 1911 and abolished regulated ones in 1913. The Meigi government in Japan was in a fix due to the pressure built up by the international community. It was worried about the incompatibility between a westernizing image and its easy traditional sexual patterns. From 1888, the Japanese were considering an end to licensed prostitution altogether. Licensed prostitution in Japan was finally abolished in 1957. The French, Portuguese and the Thais were regulationists. China was already prohibitionist and rigorous in its application. The licensed brothel in Shanghai was shut in 1934. Communists everywhere were puritanical in the matter. The unregulated brothels of Shanghai were completely shut down in 1954 when Mao-tse-tung was at the helm of affairs. But Shanghai's persistent boy brothels were a principal source of embarrassment that prostitution gave to Communist ideology.[63]

Egypt somehow escaped the big clear up despite Montgomery's efforts. Brothels were tolerated throughout Malaya until 1927. In 1929 brothels were made illegal over there.

Ronald Hyam observes that as empires came to an end, some newly independent regimes initially saw a future in sexually motivated tourism. According to him, even such proceedings in the end succumbed to the backlash of puritanical international interdiction.[64]

TRAFFICKING AND EFFORTS TO REGULATE IT BY THE INTERNATIONAL COMMUNITY

It was often alleged in the mid nineteenth century that there was 'white slave' traffic in under-age British girls to the Continent. But little was heard of 'white slavery' emanating from Britain. Hyam believes that in international prostitution Britain was essentially a customer than a supplier. Unlike the French, the British Empire builders never took their own 'prostitutes' with them. Their presence was thought to be a source of embarrassment. Indeed, any British woman in prostitution found in India or elsewhere was sent home. The French, Italians, Central European Jews and Russians fed international prostitution. Above all there were the Chinese and Japanese.

Japanese brothels were renowned the world over for their excellent management, technical proficiency, cleanliness and quietness. The Japanese maintained a vast network of prostitution extending from Kyushu, north to Siberia and south to Cape Town, with Singapore, Mauritius and Australia as major terminus. The Chinese did a not inconsiderable trade in little girls to the United States. There was also a definite and long standing trade in small boys to Indonesia. In the geography of white slavery the main route was from Europe to Latin America especially to Brazil, Argentina and Uruguay. Buenos Aires was a beehive. But there was also a major supply line running to North Africa, Egypt and Constantinople. This line, especially after the opening of the Suez Canal in 1869 led to Bombay, Colombo, Saigon, Hong Kong and Shanghai. The Russians had their own export line to Manchuria and North China. The Italians had a direct line to the goldfields of Western Australia. New York was always a major city in the network, with a westward supply line via San Francisco to Hong Kong and Shanghai and further branches to Singapore or to the Philippines. The Southern route from New York linked up Texas, New Orleans (the greatest brothel city of all times), Cuba, Panama and ultimately Cape Town and Johannesburg.

Hyam states that the organisers of this international traffic were officially regarded with extreme disgust, but they were by any standards resourceful entrepreneurs. Husband and wife teams were typical, one a pimp, the other a brothel madam.

The outstanding characteristics of these sexual entrepreneurs were their mobility, their readiness to diversify and their ruthless professionalism. Movement was essential to the whole business. Customers needed new faces, and so the maintenance of a chain of brothels along a well-established passing on route was essential.[65] There was an elaborate informed organization efficiently run on the best entrepreneurial lines. The nodal distributive points were Buenos Aires, New York, Alexandria, Constantinople, Hong Kong and Shanghai. The whole international network relied heavily on technological advance: on cables and canals (Suez Canal and railway link from Lourneco Marques to Johannesburg).

These were the findings of an inquiry held by the League of Nations between 1924 and 1927. The inquiry was held in 28 countries, 112 cities and conducted 6500 interviews.

The international community responded to these activities from time to time. In 1889 there was a London Congress on the 'white slave traffic'. In 1910 a similar convention declared procuring to be an offence. The League of Nations inherited this emerging pattern of international cooperation. A 1921 Convention increased the age of protection in trafficking and extended it to boys. In an International Convention held in 1933 procuration was made an offence even for a consenting adult female. Individual countries were under pressure to abolish regulated prostitution. The League was convinced that the mere existence of tolerated brothels encouraged the growth of prostitution. Hence, as discussed earlier, various countries took the initiative for the abolition of prostitution.

DEVADASI SYSTEM AND SOCIAL PURITY MOVEMENT IN COLONIAL INDIA

It is against this backdrop that one has to understand the modern history of law in respect of prostitution and trafficking. Though the roots of modern law in India lie in the Vedic culture, it has been superimposed by the western principles of justice. The contemporary social purity debate found its echo here and was picked up by counterparts in India. Feminist repealers and repressive moralists of all shades were found even in India. However, the debate revolved mainly around the devadasi system, not prostitution in general. Devadasi, a term that literally means maid or servant of god, refers to the practice among certain communities in India of dedicating their daughter to the service of the temple deity (in South India usually to the Goddess Yellamma). The girl is 'married' to the goddess and in case of those married to the Goddess Yellamma, the symbol of this is a little necklace of white and red beads tied around her neck. A ceremony is held to mark the dedication and the girl has to then earn her living by dancing and singing in praise of the goddess. Over time, the system underwent a change and the women (from the era of the Vijayanagar empire) started serving kings and emperors and gradually over the years, powerful men from various strata of society. Although the custom is now illegal, in Karnataka and other States where the practice persists, women who are dedicated to the Goddess Yellammma when very young, are often sold into prostitution. Activists say only 15 per cent of the total women dedicated enter prostitution but there are sizeable number of devadasis in the brothels of India.

The devadasi system found social acceptance as well as State approval in colonial India. It was a time when the colonial rulers were grappling with codification of penal laws. During this period there was a debate whether a devadasi could be charged of prostitution. Prostitution was a classified offence under Sec 372 and 373 of I.P.C. Uma Chakravarthy, an eminent sociologist, says that the Vedic dasi found no place in the colonial scheme.[66] Kalpana Kannabiran, a feminist sociologist, states that charging a devadasi with prostitution should be seen as an attempt by the colonial government to resolve its own contradictions in bringing the entire Indian population within its own ambit either through a process of exclusion (through the criminalisation of social practice) or through co-option via marriage reform.[67]

Kalpana feels that predictably, the most unacceptable part of social organisation of this group in the eyes of the British was the legitimate multiple sexual relationships the women entered into.[68] The only way the devadasi could be 'fixed' within the colonial scheme was by shifting her out of the religious sphere to the 'secular' sphere where she could be charged with an offence. But prostitution was a charge that could not be easily proved because colonial and 'native' conceptions of prostitution differed. Indians did not consider it as deviant behavior. Framing this charge, therefore, was not as simple as the British perhaps anticipated.

Early in the history of the British penal law this charge was framed by accusing the women not of prostitution but of the disposal or procurement of a minor for purposes of prostitution. That this charge could be framed at all was because adoption of female children was customary among devadasis.

Judicial Responses

The unqualified equation of the devadasi with the 'prostitute' caused considerable tension within the judiciary. The 'native' judges forced the colonial government to recognise and address its violation of the principles of jurisprudence on which it built its entire judicial system and to admit of its biases.[69] They further stated that as Hindu law generally recognised adoption as a way of ensuring continuity of the lineage, 'it should therefore not in the case of dancing girls to be confounded with prostitution which is neither its essential condition nor necessary consequence but an incident due to social influence'[70]

In *Queen Empress* v. *Ramamma* (1889)[71] Ramabai, the daughter of parents who belong to the 'Bhogam or dancing class' was given in adoption to an aunt of her father. This aunt had been convicted four years earlier by the Sessions judge for adopting a girl belonging to another community and for using her for prostitution in her minority. In Ramabai's case, however, it was argued that she could not be convicted because the child belonged to the Bhogam caste even prior to the adoption.

Justice Muthuswami Iyer felt this argument violated the 'universal principles of jurisprudence'. He argued that the law could not differentiate between minors on the basis of caste. At one level Iyer was really contesting the authority of the British forcing problematic interpretations on Indian society. On yet another trajectory, this was a line of argument that asserted the civil rights of prostitutes.[72]

The entire judiciary, however, was consistent in its perception of this institution as an 'unfortunate' and 'undesirable' reality. The disagreement was on the manner and degree of intervention that the judiciary could engage in. Almost without exception English judges were insistent on pressing charges of immorality and moral depravity, while Indian judges, more sympathetic to the reality, hoped that the 'mind' of the community would change.

The Indian judges further asserted that the devadasi was entitled to civil rights and hence had a right to adopt a daughter if she chose to and to offer the girl a choice between her mother's profession and marriage when the time came.[73]

DEVADASI ABOLITION MOVEMENT FOR SOCIAL PURITY

The response of the colonial judicature to the devadasi question corresponded with the movement for social reform that gained momentum. Kalpana says that the moral strength of the community was defined in terms of the sexual morality of its women.[74] Efforts at reform in the Madras Presidency started in the 1830's. These efforts developed into an organised movement under the leadership of Kandukuri Veeresilingam. His thrust was primarily towards the rearticulation of the moral question, directed not only towards issues of sexual relationships and questions of conjugality, but also towards health, hygiene, education, religious practices and corruption in administration. Reform movements almost exclusively focused on women's emancipation. In this climate of reform, the devadasi question was articulated in two identifiable phases, the first originating in the Telugu areas of the Presidency, and the second in the Tamil areas. Simultaneously, the devadasi abolition movement got triggered-off in the Mysore area also.

First Phase

The protagonist of the Devadasi movement was Raghupathi Venkataratnam Naidu (1862-1939). He started the movement for social purity in the 1880s. It was the time when the Purity Campaign had caught the imagination of England and America and was assuming the dimensions of a mass movement. Between 1881 and 1910, the anti-nautch agitation had spread all over Andhra. Public opinion forced the government to consider the question of 'nautch' reform seriously. Despite public support the colonial government was not in a position to take any conclusive steps towards abolishing the devadasi system.

While the colonial judicature had since 1861 been attempting unsuccessfully, no doubt, to criminalise the devadasi practice by confounding it with prostitution and penalising individual women, it now became necessary for the government to take a stand on the legality of the devadasi practice.[75] Kalpana Kannabiran observes that this was decidedly more problematic than dealing with the issue from one case to the next, given the history of the colonial government's complicity with Brahmin orthodoxy, the rise of the nationalist movement which in the Presidency had a predominantly Brahmin composition, and the fact that devadasi abolition was an important item on the agenda of the non-Brahmin movement.[76] It therefore remained as an unresolved issue and legal abolition had to wait till 1947 for the nationalist movement.

Anti-Nautch Movement

Nautch is actually a Hindi term connoting dance. The anti-nautch movement is well depicted in 'Kanyasulkam', a famous Telugu play written by Gurazada Appa Rao. The first edition of 'Kanyasulkam' was published in 1897. In the play, the writer etches out a scene in which an interesting conversation takes place between Madhuravani, a *vesya* belonging to Vijayanagaram and Soujanya Rao Panthulu, a prototype of Kandukuri Veeresilingam Panthulu. Madhuravani enters Soujanya Rao's bedroom in the wee hours, in the guise of a stranger, to pass on information very valuable to him. Soujanya Rao takes pride in being an anti-nautch protagonist. Madhuravani asks him how dancing girls could survive if people stopped visiting their houses. Rao replies that the girls could do so by getting married or obtaining an education and taking up some profession thereby leading an 'honourable' life. Madhuravani taunts Rao asking him: "would you marry a *vesya*?" She finally reveals her identity and strikes a deal with him. Madhuravani says she is not interested in his offer of a thousand rupees but would part with the information that is of importance to him and his clients if Rao gives her one kiss. Rao initially winces at the idea but agrees since he badly needs the information she possesses. When he gets down to keeping his end of the bargain, Madhuravani backs off saying her mother had told her not to 'spoil' 'good' people. Subsequently, Rao gives her a copy of the Bhagvatgeeta as a gift saying she would find in Lord Krishna a good friend. To this Madhuravani asks him: "Would Lord Krishna befriend a prostitute"? Rao replies that the Almighty made no distinctions of caste. She then wonders: "But isn't Lord Krishna an anti-nautch"?! Rao realises she is being mischievous and Madhuravani takes leave of him.

With remarkable insight, great wit and unique creativity, Gurazada manages to bring out elements of the dilemmas present in the anti-nautch movement. The predicament of the *vesyas* and the puritanical and moralist presumptions of the social reformers get played out in a subtle manner between Madhuravani and Soujanya Rao. These were genuine concerns that affected the lives of women in prostitution in the Andhra region. A concert by women belonging to the Bhogam or Kalavanthula community during the marriage ceremonies was treated as auspicious. A ban was imposed due to the pressure brought about by the anti-nautch agitation. In the 1930s Communist leaders like C.V.K. Rao arranged marriages for Kalavanthulu and Bhogam women. Men belonging to these communities also arranged such marriages. Puvvula Suribabu was one of them. Organizations like Divgnan Samajam and Brahma Samajam worked for the betterment of these women as did Durgabai Deshmukh, a prominent social reformer. Once a ban was slapped on the performances of Bhogam and Kalavanthulu women, some of them took to acting in the theatre and movies. Those who were not so resourceful, opted for prostitution.

Kondapalli Koteswaramma, an octogenarian woman's activist, recollects an incident during the Indian freedom struggle. At the time, women donated ornaments to M.K. Gandhi for the cause of the struggle. Addressing a meeting at Kakinada, a port town of Andhra, Gandhi was initially reluctant to accept donations offered by the women in prostitution. This was because he felt that these women had earned their valuables by employing immoral methods. Moreover, how could the freedom movement receive donations from 'prostitutes'! However, Balusu Sambamurthy, a veteran freedom fighter and several others, tried to convince Gandhi to change his opinion. Later, Gandhi concurred with them and appreciated the efforts of these women as a useful contribution to the freedom struggle. He went on to accept the gold offered by the women.

Second Phase

In the second phase of the movement in the 1920s, Muthulakshmi Reddi, a medical doctor and legislator was to rapidly become the undisputed leader of the movement seeking abolition of the devadasi system. There were basically three trends evident at the time. Muthulakshmi represented the first trend. The caste associations, who were also abolitionists, represented the second trend. The third were the retentionists. In seeking to abolish the devadasi system Muthulakshmi was explicitly following in the footsteps of Josephine Butler whose campaign against prostitution in England was self-admittedly her chief source of inspiration.

This reform was for Muthulakshmi only the first step in a much larger endeavour: "Once the Bill is made into an Act and the sanction of the temple to such a practice is taken away, this caste will naturally and spontaneously disappear from our midst. Then we will have to deal with a wider question of the international problem of prostitution and protection of young women and children from the indecent attacks of men, which I feel will be an easier task."[77] When Muthulakshmi met with opposition from a section of devadasis her reaction was that they were only a 'set of prostitutes who have been set up by their keepers'. She urged the government 'not to pay heed to such protests from a most objectionable class of people in society'. This superior self-perception and the separation of self from the objects of reform were again not something that was peculiar to Muthulakshmi alone. Rather, it seems characteristic of middle and upper class women in the late 19th and early 20th centuries, who took up the cause of women's emancipation in the West and India. Although advancing a radical critique of prostitution, they were ambivalent about women in prostitution and the right of women from the lower classes to control their own sexuality.[78]

Anandhi, a sociologist, states that while Muthulakshmi Reddi, the 'progressive' nationalist as well as certain caste associations defended the Devadasi Abolition Bill, the 'conservative' nationalists like S. Satyamurthy opposed the bill.[79] In 1931, C. Rajagopalachari, President of the Tamil Nadu Congress Committee wrote to Muthulakshmi Reddy stating that he was burdened with other matters and had no time to take up the question of devadasis. In 1937, when the Indian National Congress entered the Madras legislature, Rajagopalachari as the Chief Minister of Madras Presidency showed great reluctance to place the bill before the Legislative Assembly. Muthulakshmi noted that Rajagopalachari was not much in favour of abolition of this 'pernicious' practice.[80] Later, when the bill was under discussion, the 'conservatives', within the Congress Party organised a Devadasi Conference in Tanjavur district to oppose the bill.

Anandhi observes that S. Satyamurthy of the Madras Congress represented the quintessential conservative opinion. He was so committed to the cause of perpetuating the devadasi system that he argued that devadasi families should dedicate at least one girl to the Hindu temples instead of many.[81] Satyamurthy felt that the devadasi system needed to be protected because it was essentially part of the indigenous Hindu/national culture. He cautioned the protagonists of abolition that if the system were abolished, the non-Brahmins would demand scrapping of the temple priests (who were Brahmins).[82]

It is noteworthy that in 1929 when Muthulakshmi Reddy introduced an amendment to the Madras Hindu Religious Endowment Act of 1926 to completely dispense with the services of the devadasis in all temples and also to enfranchise them to hold inam lands without the obligation of providing services to the temples, Satyamurthy, raised a series of objections in the Legislative Assembly and even persuaded Reddy to introduce a separate bill, so that the non-Brahmins did not put forth demands such as dispensing of temple 'archakas' of the Brahmin caste. His interest was to delay the bill as long as possible.[83] Significantly, Satyamurthy's argument was challenged by a section of the devadasis themselves. For instance, the meeting of devadasis at Mayuram town condemned Satyamurthy's reluctance and noted that he was more worried about the position of Brahmin priests and not the welfare of devadasis. Importantly, they also pointed out that his logic of preserving the devadasi system, as part of an ancient religious tradition, was similar to the logic underpinning Sati as religious tradition.[84]

Another group of people, who participated throughout the debate on devadasi abolition, were the associations of those castes from which devadasis were, by and large, drawn such as Sengundars and Isai Vellalars of Tamil Nadu. While they passed resolutions in their associations in support of the Devadasi Abolition Bill, they denounced devadasi as a dishonour to their castes and as an impediment to their progress as caste groups.[85] In their efforts to erase the identification of their castes with the devadasis and to assist their so-called caste honour, these caste associations vehemently supported the Devadasi Abolition Bill. In other words, they were concerned only with the self-image of their castes. According to them, while the idealized chaste Hindu women represented the 'honour' of the caste, the devadasis stood for the caste's dishonour. Thus, here too devadasis were stereotyped and essentialised as unchaste to represent concerns other than their own.[86]

The third group of abolitionists was closely associated with the non-Brahmin movement that was picking up momentum at that time. Ramamirtham Ammaiyar, a remarkable woman by all accounts, led this group. Her political career began in the Congress which she left later. It is probable that she left the Congress because of the insensitive attitude of local leaders towards the devadasis and other problems related to women. She joined the Self-respect Movement founded by E.V. Ramasamy Naicker. Ramamirthammal herself was a devadasi, emerging as an organic intellectual of that community. Her belief was that religion and god (both terms by implication Aryan and Brahmin) created caste differences, untouchability, enforced widowhood and prostitution that was practiced under the guise of euphemism. The devadasis, she said were mere instruments of their treachery.[87]

According to her, the tensions within the traditional Hindu family between the women and their mothers-in-law and sisters-in-law and the conventionalism that exists between husbands and wives, forced the husbands into easier and more relaxed relationships with dasis.[88] The solution to the dasi question would be reached, she felt, if the strains of marriage were loosened to accommodate a greater ease in conjugal relationships.

Apart from supporting and campaigning for the bill introduced by Muthulakshmi Reddy, Ramamirthammal also organised inter-caste marriages and marriages of consent for the 'dasis' in order to retrieve them from their so-called services to Hindu temples. In an article Ramamirthammal lashes out at the devadasi system saying: "My strong opinion is that from the ancient times, the temple priests, the kings and the landlords ...in the name of art, had encouraged particular communities to indulge in prostitution. These days, more than the Kumbhakonam Shastris (the Brahmin priests of orthodox Kumbhakonam town), Satyamurthy Shastri (the Congress leader) has been making noise about preserving devadasi custom ...our women have been suppressed in all spheres. The legitimisation of the suppression given through religion and 'shastras' is evident in the manner in which women have been assigned the role of prostitutes."[89]

Ramamirthammal did not stop with the devadasi system, but raised her voice against other institutions of women's oppression like child marriage, widowhood, religious rituals and Hinduism itself. As a political activist, she identifies 'dasi' system with the prevailing class inequities and demands abolition of both; 'the zamindari and mirasdari systems are to be abolished immediately, since they have perpetuated the devadasi system and other forms of sexual exploitation.'

To sum up, 'conservatives' on the one hand, and the 'progressives' and the caste associations on the other, took diametrically opposite positions on the question of devadasi abolition. All their discourses shared a common feature. Their real concern, while they spoke about devadasis, was not the welfare of the women in question but issues other than those concerning the devadasis. The devadasis were a mere trope for them to address these other issues. While alluding to the devadasis, the 'conservatives' really were holding forth on indigenous culture, the 'progressives' spelt out how Hindu womanhood ought to be, and the caste associations emphasised caste honour. The debate as a whole denied the devadasis their role as subjects, and thus, their own consciousness. Ramamirthammal's approach seems to be a radical departure from these three trends.

MOVEMENT AGAINST DEVADASI ABOLITION

There were many devadasis who opposed abolition. They formed into groups to oppose the proposed bill tabled by Muthulakshmi Reddy in the Legislative Assembly. Twenty-eight devadasis of Periyakanchivaram formed a Sangam and sent the following appeal to the law member of the Madras Legislative Council: "We condemn Dr Muthulakshmi Reddy's Bill. There is no connection between our ancient and noble practice of Pottukkattal and the disgraceful profession of prostitution. We appeal to the government not to enforce any law that destroys our rights."[90]

T. Doraikannammal, the Secretary of the Madras Presidency Devadasi Association was of the opinion that instead of looking at social evils and thinking of effective ways of stemming prostitution, a blind judicial system was being put into the service of the men of the Isai Vellalar community who had a vested interest in dispensing with and discrediting of devadasis.[91]

The Madras Rudra Kanni Kai Sangam, an active anti-abolition body, issued a statement saying: "the people who propose the Bill offer the lame excuse that Isai Vellalar themselves support it. But Isai Vellalars are men born of Rudra Kannikas. It is strange that they are supporting the Bill. We will soon see that selfishness prompts them to support the Bill. The women of this class have the sole right to property and the right to funeral honours ... It is a fact that in this world men always had a selfish motive. The men of this class wanted to have the right to property and therefore they bite hands that feeds them."[92]

Yet another anti-abolitionist says: "No healthy social conditions can be founded on inequality and injustice. Without male chastity female chastity is impossible."[93]

THE MYSORE EXPERIENCE

The devadasi debate contoured around the same issues in Mysore as were raised in the Tamil and Andhra regions. The opposition to devadasi system's abolition was stronger among the devadasis in Mysore compared to the other parts. The Mysore officials tried to undermine the dancing girls by denying them services in the temples, thus depriving them economic sustenance.

Restrictions on devadasis began in Mysore in late 19th century. The Committee on Women's Rights under Hindu Law proudly claimed that Mysore had won early distinction for removing devadasis from all Muzrai (State supported) institutions. The historian Janaki Nair observes that officials in the Mysore of the late 1800s began to see themselves as the seed-bearers of a reformed Indian tradition, a 'modern' social order better able to resist the derogatory attitudes of the colonial power to that tradition.[94]

In 1892 Srinivasacharyulu the Muzrai Secretary was presented with a bill of Rs. 12/5/4 payment for the services of Ramamani who had performed tafe (singing and dancing) services at the rath (car) festival of a temple in Chikkaballapur. He reluctantly agreed to pay, saying that such tafe services were an unnecessary waste of money that could be better spent on 'improving sanitation'. Promising to issue a circular outlining the legitimate services of devadasis in temples, Srinivasacharyulu categorically asserted that they did not include tafe or dancing. Though he did not issue a circular as promised in 1898 during the revision of the tasdik pattis (apportionment of revenues) of the Nanjangud and Melkote temples, he directed that tafe women should not be admitted to any kind of duty in the two temples, and although they may continue to be paid while they were alive, their posts were not to be filled after their demise.[95]

This was not something that could be implemented without the resistance of those affected. The devadasis of Nanjagud, Kittasani, Nanjsani, Kalyanasani and six other women appealed against this decision in a petition to the Maharaja of Mysore. The petition to the Maharaja cited the authority of the shastras (Veda Bharata Shastra, Agamashastra) and Sampradaya (customary practice) to remind the sovereign of his duties to protect hereditary occupations such as theirs. Unlike the Brahmins, they said, who had chattrams and mutts (free boarding houses and monasteries) to take care of their needs, devadasis had only their artistic skills with which to render service to God and earn their livelihoods. The petitions emphasised the sovereign's duty to protect customary practices and duties ordained by the scriptures.

The Mysore officials sought a reference to the shastras and entrusted the job to the agamiks (priests conversant with temple rituals). Citing several scriptures, the agamiks stated that devadasis did not have specific services to render in the temple, which included singing and dancing before the deity. They concluded their comment with the rather ambiguous remark that this was what the shastras said but the government should do whatever was appropriate.[96]

The government opted for abolition. The new measures that had been applied to the two large temples were extended to all Muzrai institutions in Mysore.

Janaki Nair believes that "the gradual erosion of the material support for the artistic abilities of the devadasis resulted in her decline as a professional dancer. Instead she became a proletarianised sex-worker with nothing to trade but her sexual services. As such, she was now a threat, rather than an adjunct, to the patriarchal household. Through the suppression of the polyvalent roles of the devadasis, the Mysore authorities had begun drawing the lines between respectable and disrespectable female sexuality, a distinction that was consonant with the dominant nationalist discourse."[97]

She adds: "the acts of Mysore officials led to the gradual proleterianisation of unorganised, subaltern female sex-worker. The attack on the livelihood of the devadasis signalled the decline of a pre-capitalist form of work embedded in a religio-cultural formation which was not entirely commodified."[98]

The distinction between 'respectable' and 'disrespectable' women was reinforced by the imperatives of the imperial military machine in India. In Bangalore, as elsewhere, the military authorities made arrangements for the sexual needs of a larger number of lower class British 'subalterns who lacked the material sources for marriage and were considered lacking the moral resources for sexual abstinence'.[99] Such arrangements produced their own problems, since the military authorities claimed that the very women who helped British soldiers to maintain their virility, threatened that virility with venereal disease. In Bangalore, between 1833 and 1837, the annual proportion of venereal disease cases amongst European troops ranged from 32 to 45 percent.[100]

To combat the spread of venereal disease an elaborate regime involving both military and medical authorities were instituted, including the setting up of 'lock hospitals' where women in prostitution were confined until they were declared free of infection. The lock hospital system was tried intermittently and with varying degrees of success in the cantonments of India in the early 19th century. It was replaced by the even more invasive Contagious Diseases Act of 1868, which provided for compulsory regulation of brothels and women in prostitution, periodic medical examinations and compulsory treatment of women in prostitution found infected. Given the medical developments of the time, such a punitive regime was more feasible than a preventive one. The colonial application of the Contagious Diseases Acts is a replica of similar laws passed in Britain. Such is the homogenising effect of colonisation on the cultures it encounters with.

By the beginning of the First World War there was a shift in the policy adopted by the authorities. An enormous increase in the incidence of venereal disease prompted the first steps towards introduction of therapeutic measures for men, in addition to the punitive measures for women. This meant a reordering of priorities and redoubled efforts of a different nature. The first moves were made towards controlling the promiscuity of soldiers through propaganda, and arrangements were made for the supply of a preventive ointment, a distinct shift from a punitive to a therapeutic regime

Janaki Nair, observes: "The institution of measures such as putting the Bangalore city area out of bounds for European troops, provision of facilities for demonstrating the evils of venereal and other sexually transmitted diseases, rather than increasing the surveillance of the women, was an admission of defeat at controlling the 'roaming prostitute. The military concluded in 1925 that prostitution would always exist and that no man would willingly contract venereal disease, so every effort was to be made to teach soldiers preventive measures and to control the quantity of drink available to the troops."[101]

The exigencies of the imperial military presence in India produced a new proletarian 'sex-worker' who, unlike the devadasi, did not embody any superior artistic skills and as a result, possessed none of the cultural or symbolic capital that could be deployed in the emerging economic configurations of colonial India. Unlike other proletarians, however, the sex-worker was just selling her services, since as Carole Pateman points out, "the prostitute cannot sell her sexual services alone; what she sells is her body".[102]

Beginning in the early 20th century, however, efforts were also made by some voluntary agencies such as the City Progress Committee and the Temperate and Social Purity Committee, (later called the Association of Moral and Social Hygiene), to reform the 'traffic in women'. It was due to their efforts that a private bill was introduced in the Mysore Legislative Council and the Representative Assembly in the early 1930's, which was designed to regulate prostitution. The discussions on the bill in both the houses evoked the figure of the women-as-victim, possessing no agency, not even the dangerous sexuality of the devadasi or the military station's sex-worker. She was a figure who had to be rescued from the 'evil of commercialised vice'. In this discussion, the question of 'Indian tradition', which had been completely absent from the military discourse, assumed a central role. The ideal of a 'traffic-in-women' was a recognition that prostitution was a trade in sex objects, but also a recognition that it was the trade that was objectionable rather than the commodification of women as such.[103]

The bill was passed in the houses and became law in 1937, but what is most interesting is that both opponents and supporters of the bill framed their arguments in terms of wider societal, even national interests. D.S. Mallappa, while introducing the bill in the Legislature Council, said that the 'morality of the country was going down', a sentiment echoed by Ramachandra Rao Scindhia when he states: "VD is one of the causes for the degeneration of the nation". As part of the effort for national renewal, the traffic in women had to be curbed.

The strongest plank amongst those opposing the bill, however, was that it would result in young women being rescued by missionaries for the ulterior purpose of conversion to Christianity. C.V. Gundappa put it quite bluntly in his intervention on the bill: "My own reading of the motive behind this bill is the impatience and great anxiety of certain fine souls and certain highly evolved souls to establish the Kingdom of Christ in our midst."[104]

For opponents of the bill, if the choice was between the evil designs of the missionaries and the evils of trafficking in women, the latter was preferable. In the words of N.G. Sanjivaiah "prostitution formed a regular limb of Hindu society from times immemorial" and, furthermore, that there was a greater danger to enforcing such a law because 'by abolishing prostitution altogether the safety of the family women might possibly be endangered'[105]. The sanctity of the family, the institution that the nationalists had modernized, but nevertheless invested with the responsibility of preserving Indian tradition, could not be guaranteed without the parallel figure of the 'disrespectable' public women.[106]

Lata Mani, a sociologist, remarks: "it was the tradition rather than the women herself which formed the centre of the debates. In the decades between the first move against devadasi in 1892 and the passage of the Suppression of Immoral Traffic in Women and Girls Act (SITA hereafter) in 1937, we may plot the series of transitions which resulted in the complete proleterianisation of sex-work: from dangerous non-wife to wilful perpetrator of disease; from the active sexuality of the devadasi and cantonment sex worker to voiceless victim who had to be rescued by the institution of marriage; from one whose life work was embedded in a religio-cultural sphere to one who was the embodiment of vice".[107]

A singular absence in these discussions on prostitution, women and Indian tradition, was the voice of the women herself. She had been promised new freedoms in the name of modernity, but remained marginalised in the emerging nationalist patriarchal order. Her critique of the administrative and legislative agenda of reform of sexuality in this period nevertheless did exist: sometimes through an appeal to a different conception of 'tradition' (as in the case of the devadasi) or else in seeking routes to escape from the categories that were being produced by the increasing criminalisation of sex-work.[108]

This then was the backdrop against which the SITA was passed.

REGULATION OF TRAFFICKING AND PROSTITUTION IN THE POST-INDEPENDENCE PERIOD

In the post-independence era also regulation of trafficking and prostitution was initiated at the instance of pressure built up by the international community. The voice of the subaltern sex worker has not been the epicentre of the debate. The major concern of policy-makers was largely related to the nation state's obligation of conformity to international instruments. These instruments initially addressed the problem of White Slave Trafficking. Though some of the international agreements and conventions took place prior to independence, India had expressed its allegiance to the will of the International Community and respect to its sentiments.

International Instruments

The League of Nations in 1937, through a draft resolution took up this issue. Later, a UN Convention to suppress the traffic in persons and against the practice of prostitution was signed at New York (U.S.A.) by several nations including India on May 9, 1950. Other international instruments on the issue are as follows:

1. International Agreement of 18 May, 1904 for the Suppression of White Slave Traffic, as amended by the Protocol approved by the General Assembly of the United Nations on the December 1948.
2. International Convention of the 4 May, 1910 for the Suppression of White Slave Traffic, as amended by the above mentioned Protocol.

3. International Convention of 30 September, 1921, for the Suppression of the Traffic in Women and Children, as amended by the Protocol approved by the General Assembly of the United Nations on 20 October 1947.
4. International Convention of 11 October 1933 for the Suppression of Traffic in Women of Full Age, as amended by the aforesaid Protocol.
5. Convention for the Suppression of Traffic in Human Beings and Exploitation of Children, 1950. India is a signatory to this Convention.
6. Convention on the Rights of the Girl Child, 1990. India has also signed this Convention. Section 18 of this Convention recognises the child's right to protection from sexual exploitation and abuse including prostitution.

The fact that the law on prostitution was passed for compliance of international obligations is evident from the objects and reasons stated in the Suppression of Immoral Traffic in Women and Girls Bill. This Bill No. 58 of 1954 was published in Government of India, Extraordinary, Part 2, and Section 2, dated December 20, 1954. The objects and reasons of the bill are reproduced below:

1. In 1930, the Government of India ratified an International Convention for the Suppression of Immoral Traffic in Persons and the Exploitation of the Prostitution of Others. Under Article 23 of the Convention, traffic in human beings is prohibited and any contravention of the prohibition is an offence punishable by law. Under Art. 35, such a law has to be passed by Parliament as soon as may be, after the commencement of the Constitution.
2. Legislation on the subject of Suppression of Immoral Traffic does exist in a few States but the laws are neither uniform nor do they go far enough. In the remaining States there is no bar on the subject at all.
3. In the circumstances, it is necessary and desirable that a Central law should be passed which will not only secure uniformity but would be sufficiently deterrent for the purpose. But a special feature of the Bill is that it provides that no person or authority other than the State Government shall establish or maintain any protective home except under a license issued by the State

Government. This will check the establishment of homes that are really dens for prostitution.

The law was passed keeping only a commitment to the international comity in view. The preferences and wishes of the women in prostitution did not fall within the purview of legislative intent.

CONCLUSION

All these social, political and historical aspects have led to the drafting of the 1956 Act on trafficking. From the Vedic '*ganika*' to the contemporary 'sex worker', woman engaged in commercial sex have been an enigma to society at large and the law in particular. They have been subjects of pity, sympathy, contempt, reproach or even remorse depending on the situation prevailing at that particular time. The debate meandering along the contours laid down in the Vedas, Manusmrithi, and Yajnavalkyasmrithi has firmly entrenched such women in the public domain and brought them into the gaze of the law. Though social and legal control mechanisms have not been homogeneous with change in times, they have spelt out in clear terms how contemporary society perceives the issue.

When one goes down memory lane, as it were, to seek out the unique relation between law and history, we see that these laws themselves act as mileposts to understand the political economy and socio-cultural ethos of that society. The law on prostitution and trafficking also reflects the social, economic, political and cultural web woven around these women. While the Vedas and the Mahabharatha accord prostitution the status of an institution, Kautilya tries to bring it into the economy by imposition of tax on this institution. That society accorded social acceptance to the institution is evident from the fact that it was found to be tax worthy. It also points out to the fact that the politics of sexuality are determined by economic considerations obtaining at the time. The Manusmrithi, Kamasutras and the Samhithas ordain the Brahmin community not to get socially entangled with these women and circumscribe the social perimeters for the women involved in prostitution. This social ostracism indicates the alienation of this community and its denigrated status in the hierarchy of the caste system. The legal control over this institution was regulatory in nature laying the limits of interaction for the clientele. Public health and public morality were not causes of concern then. The social morality of the time accepted the sustenance of this institution. The primary concern was that this institution should not dilute the rigid rules of the caste system. The Brahmin sages framed the rules of the 'game'. Clearly, caste-based and gender-based norms went hand in hand.

The reinforcement of the Vedic tenets is reflected in the later period during the emergence and working of the devadasi system. Both the nurturing and destruction of the devadasi system were not gone into with the welfare of the devadasi in mind. The concerns of the retentionists or reformists lay elsewhere. Retentionists like Satyamurthy, the caste organisations or the well-meaning social purists like Dr Muthulakshmi Reddy took stands that were tangential to the interests of devadasis. Neither Muthulakshmi nor her British counterparts like Josephine Butler could sense the essential predicament of women engaged in prostitution. Domestication of the public arena seemed to be their primary concern. In the whole debate spearheaded by the social purists, trafficking does not figure at all.

The initial steps taken by the international community in respect of the prostitution question were also inspired by the British outrage against white slave traffic. They were more concerned about the protection of the white race much like the Brahmin sages were about perpetuation of the caste system. It was only at a later stage that trafficking altogether was condemned. Trafficking emerged as a global phenomenon and remedies were sought at the international level. Significantly, what was absent throughout all the efforts to stall trafficking was an articulation of the voices of the women involved in prostitution. The focus of the international community revolved around delegitimising and deregulating prostitution. Since the welfare of the women was the basic objective, they should also have been included as a party to the whole endeavour. This did not happen. Making them mute witnesses would serve no purpose. Trafficking in women cannot be contained without the consent and cooperation of the women involved in prostitution. The laws on suppressing trafficking were also passed due to mounting international pressure rather than taking due cognizance of the needs and sensitivities of the women in question. This is the backdrop against which The Suppression of Immoral Traffic in Women and Girls Act, 1956 was passed.

Notes and References

1. R.V.1.167.4, Quoted by Das, Ram Mohan, Women in Manu's Philosophy, ABS Pub., 27, 1st Floor, Modern Market, Nehru Garden Road, Jalandhar, 1st Ed, 1993, p. 127.

2. Gaut. XXII.27, Quoted by Das, Ram Mohan , p. 128. A Smrithikara is the author of a Smrithi.
3. Mbh.1.115.39, Quoted by Das, Ram Mohan , p. 128. It is an epic.
4. Kaut, 11.27.124-125, Quoted by Das, Ram Mohan, *Supra* Note 1, p. 129.
5. Encyclopedia of Religion & Ethics, Vol. X, p. 406, *Supra* Note 1, p. 129.
6. Manu, IV, 209, 219, Quoted by Das, Ram Mohan, *Supra* Note 1, p. 130.
7. Manu, IV. 84,85, *ibid.*
8. *Ibid,* IX. 259, 138, p. 130
9. Gaut, XXII. 27, Quoted by Das Ram Mohan, Supra Note 1, p. 128.
10. Manu, VIII. 262-263, Quoted by Das, Ram Mohan, *Supra* Note 1, p. 130.
11. *Supra* Note 1, p. 129.
12. Yajnavalkya Samhita, Ch. I, 293, Quoted by Das, Ram Mohan, *Supra* Note 1, p. 131.
13. Matsya Purana, Ch. LXX, Quoted by Das, Ram Mohan, *Supra* Note 1, p. 128.
14. Kamasutra, 1.3.20, Quoted by Das, Ram Mohan, *Supra* Note 1, p. 129.
15. Chakladar, H.C., "Social Life in Ancient India", p. 198, Quoted by Das, Ram Mohan, *Supra* Note 1, p. 131.
16. Smrithi written by Vishnu, a prominent Smrithikara.
17. A school of thought propounded by Yagnavalkya.
18. Yajnavalkya Samhita II.290. Quoted by Das, Ram Mohan, *Supra* Note 1, p. 131.
19. A Smrithikara.
20. Vasistha, 14, Quoted by Das, Ram Mohan, *Supra* Note 1, p. 130.
21. Yajnavalkya, I, 160-167, Quoted by Das, Ram Mohan, *Supra* Note 1, p. 131.
22. Gautama, 7, Quoted by Das, Ram Mohan, *Supra* Note 1, p. 128.
23. Yajnavalkya, II, 235, Quoted by Das, Ram Mohan, *Supra* Note 1, p. 131.
24. *Ibid.*, 236, Quoted by Das, Ram Mohan, *Supra* Note 1, p. 131.
25. Sinha, S.N. and Basu, N.K., The History of Marriage and Prostitution (Vedas to Vatsyayana), Khama Pub. 21-D, Nivedite Enclave, A6, Paschim Vihar, ND-110063, 1st Ed., 1992; p. 110.
26. *Ibid.*, p. 111.
27. Sinha, S.N. and Basu, N.K., *Supra* Note 25, p. 111.
28. Samvarta, 161, Sinha, S.N. & Basu, N.K. *Supra* Note 25, p. 114.
29. Sinha & Basu, *Ibid.*, p.114.
30. Sinha & Basu, *Ibid.*, p. 132.
31. Quoted by Sinha & Basu, *Supra* Note 25, p. 114.
32. *Ibid.*, 133.
33. *Ibid.*, p. 134.
34. Janaki Nair, "From Devadasi Reform to SITA: Reforming sex worker in Mysore State -1892-1937", NLSJ—Feminism & Law, 1993, p. 85.
35. Gayathri Chakravorty Spivak, "Feminism and Decolonisation", 3:3 Differences 153 (1991), quoted by Janaki Nair, *Supra* Note 34, p. 9.
36. Aloka Parasher and Usha Naik, "Temple Girls of Medieval Karnataka" 23:1 *Indian Economic and Social History Review* 63, 66-67 (1986).
37. Amrit Srinivasan, "Reform and Revival: the Devadasi and her Dance", 20:44 EPW 1869(1985).

38. *Ibid.*
39. Janaki Nair, *Supra* Note 34, p. 85.
40. Lucy Bland, "Feminist Vigilants of late-Victorian England", Regulating Womanhood—Historical Essays on Marriage, Motherhood & Sexuality, Ed. By Carol Smart, Routlege Pub. 11, New Fetterlane, London, 1st. Ed., 1992, p. 35.
41. *Ibid.*
42. *Ibid.*
43. Laura Chant, The Vigilance Record, October 1894, Quoted by Lucy Bland, *Supra* Note 40, p. 37.
44. Josephine Butler, 1894, Personal letter, Lucy Bland, *Supra* Note 40, p. 35.
45. Lucy Bland, *Ibid.*, p. 37.
46. Lucy Bland, *Supra* Note 40, p. 37.
47. Lucy Wilson, 1886, quoted by Lucy Bland, *Ibid.*, p. 39.
48. Wolstenholme Elmy, 1886, quoted by Lucy Bland, *Ibid.*, p. 39.
49. *Ibid.*
50. Lucy Bland , *Supra* Note 40, p. 40.
51. The Vigilance Record, 15 April 1887. Quoted by Lucy Bland, p. 40.
52. The Vigilance Record, July 1888, Quoted by Lucy Bland, p. 41.
53. Blackwell, 1887:35, Quoted by Lucy Bland, p. 17.
54. *Ibid.*, 17.
55. Bland, *Ibid.*, p. 43.
56. The Pioneer, August 1887, Quoted by Lucy Bland, *Supra* Note 40, p. 40.
57. Bland, *Supra* Note 40, p. 44.
58. Donzelot, 1979. Quoted by Bland, *ibid*, p. 47.
59. *Ibid.*
60. Chant, 1902:129, Quoted by Lucy Bland, *Supra* Note 40, p. 40.
61. Bland, *Ibid.*, p. 52.
62. Ronald Hyam, Empire and Sexuality—The British Experience, Manchester University Press, Oxford Road, Manchester, M139 PLUK, 1st Ed., 1991, p. 149.
63. Ronald Hyam, *Supra* Note 62, p. 151.
64. *Ibid.*, p. 152.
65. Ronald Hyam, *Supra* Note 62, p. 146.
66. Chakravarthi Uma, "Whatever Happened to the Vedic Dasi? Orientalism, Nationalism and a Script of the past", in K. Sangari and S. Vaid (editors), Recasting Women: Essays in Colonial History, Rutgers University Press, New Jersey, 1990.
67. Kalpana Kannabiran, "Judiciary, Social Reform and Debate on 'Religious Prostitution' in Colonial India", *EPW*, Oct. 28, 1995, p. 60.
68. *Ibid.*
69. Kalpana Kannabiran, *Supra* Note 67, p. 62.
70. *Ibid.*
71. Quoted by Kalpana Kannabiran, *Ibid.*, p. 60.
72. *Ibid.*, p. 62.
73. Kalpana Kannabiran, *Supra* Note 67, p. 62.
74. *Ibid.*, p 63.
75. Kalpana Kannabiran, *Supra* Note 67, p. 62.

76. *Ibid.*
77. Kalpana Kannabiran, *Supra* Note 67, p. 62.
78. *Ibid.*, p. 62.
79. Anandhi S., "Representing Devadasis 'Dasi Mosavalai' as a Radical Text", *EPW*, 26,1991, p. 739.
80. Anandhi, S, *Supra* Note 79, p. 740.
81. *Ibid.*
82. *Ibid.*
83. *Ibid.*
84. Anandhi S., *Supra* Note 79, 740.
85. *Ibid.*
86. *Ibid.*
87. *Ibid.*
88. Anandhi S., *Supra* Note 79.
89. *Ibid.*
90. Anandhi, S., *Supra* Note 79, p. 742.
91. *Ibid.*
92. *Ibid.*, p. 741.
93. *Ibid.*
94. Janaki Nair, Supra Note 34, p. 82.
95. *Ibid*, p. 83
96. Janaki Nair, *Supra* Note 34, p. 87.
97. *Ibid.*, p. 90.
98. *Ibid.*, p 88.
99. *Ibid.*
100. Janaki Nair, *Supra* Note 34.
101. Janaki Nair, *Supra* Note 34, p. 91.
102. Carole Pateman, "Defending Prostitution: Charges Against Ericson" 93 Ethics 561, 562 (April 1983).
103. Janaki Nair, *Supra* Note 34, p. 93.
104. Proceedings of the Legislative Council, 18 December, 1935 at 177.
105. Janaki Nair, *Supra* Note 34, p 93.
106. *Ibid.*, p. 93.
107. Lata Mani, "Contentious Traditions: The Debate on Sati in Colonial India" in K. Sangari and S. Vaid (editors), Recasting Women: Essays in Colonial History, Rutgers University Press, New Jersey, 1990. p. 118.
108. Janaki Nair, *Supra* Note 34, p. 94.

12

Marital Violence

A Societal Evil

K. Sita Manikyam

"Where women are honored, the gods are delighted."

INTRODUCTION

The co-existence of two fades of human species is beyond comprehension and challenge and co existence is for living and not necessarily for live-in. Marriage is a voluntary, consensual amalgamation of not only minds/bodies but also two hearts. It implies the partial surrender of individual autonomy in favor of exercise of dominance by the opposite party to take control of a definite situation; it is parasitic and mutual rewarding. India is a country with rich heritage and culture to keep up the family and institution of marriage had been critically tormented by the spouse under the veil of marriage. Right from the beginning, marital violence is taken in a lighter view by taking lacunas in laws treat marital rape not as crime, wife is only given remedy to live with pain or leave with pain in both the ways women is a sufferer and hence most of the Indian women bare all the violence and take it as their fate. The present paper focuses on the position of women as a wife and her protection against violence by the spouse.

CONCEPT OF MARRIAGE IN INDIAN SOCIETY

Marriage (also called matrimony or wedlock) is a social union or legal contract between spouses that establishes rights and obligations between them, between them and their children, and between them and their in-laws.[1] The definition of marriage varies according to different cultures, but it is principally an institution in which interpersonal relationships, usually intimate and sexual, are acknowledged. When defined broadly, marriage is considered a cultural universal. In many cultures, marriage is formalized via a wedding ceremony. In terms of legal recognition, most sovereign states and other jurisdictions limit marriage to opposite-sex couples or two persons of opposite gender in the gender binary, and a diminishing number of these permit polygamy, child marriages, and forced marriages. In modern times, a growing number of countries and other jurisdictions have lifted bans on and have established legal recognition for same-sex marriage,[2] inter-racial marriage, and interfaith marriage. In some cultures, marriage is recommended or compulsory before pursuing any sexual activity.

MARRIAGE UNDER HINDU PHILOSOPHY

Among Hindus marriage is treated as sacrament and wife is a divine institution given by Gods. One should not think that one has obtained her by choice[3], her unity with her husband is established by the Vedas[4] , further Manu said I, hold your hand for saubhagya (good luck)that you may grow old with your Husband, you are given to me by the just, the creator, the wise and by the learned people[5], wife is treated as Ardhangini' half is she of the husband that is wife'[6], Manu declared mutual fidelity between husband and wife is highest dharma, further they must see that there is no differences between them, and that they remain faithful to each other.wife is treated as source of dharma, artha, kama, moksha[7] wife is not merely grihapatni but also dharmapatni and sahadharmini.

UNDER MUSLIM PHILOSOPHY

Muslims have, from the beginning of Islam, regarded their marriage as a contract for legalization of sexual intercourse and procreation of children it is not sacramental but purely a civil contract[8] but J. Krishna Iyer concurs with the view in his paper, Reform of the Muslim personal law, he said, The impression that a muslim marriage is a mere contract is not, therefore, sufficiently solemn or sacred is another fallacy of the Hindu and Western student".[9]

Under Christianity : Christian marriage being sacramental and indissoluble parties to the marriage is treated as 'ministers of sacrament' the trite saying marriages are made in heaven what God hath joined together, no man put it asunder. According to Augustine, all human institutions were essentially sinful but some were redeemed by the grace of God, marriage was such institution, and if man and woman, parties to the marriage choose wrongly, they should take their cross on their back gladly as a duty owned to God.[10]

Among Parsis : Marriage is considered to be a ceremony of 'ashirwad' literally means blessings—it is a prayer or extortion to the parties to observe their marital obligations.[11]

Among Jews: They treat marriage as a written contract called kutuba, which makes their union essentially union of families.[12] Under Indian society marriage is always treated as high and important institution with norms and morals of living together, mutually, voluntarily, giving respect to each other and enjoy the life with dignity, happiness and strict conjugal fidelity.

Unveiling Marital Relationships-Violence by the Partner

Violence against women: Violence against women has been recognized as a significant worldwide human rights issue and public health problem. Violence against women is partly a result of gender relations that assumes men to be superior to women. Given the subordinate status of women, much of gender violence is considered normal and enjoys social sanction.[13] Manifestations of violence include physical aggression, such as blows of varying intensity, burns, attempted hanging, sexual abuse and rape, psychological violence through insults, humiliation, coercion, blackmail, economic or emotional threats, and control over speech and actions. In extreme, but not unknown cases.

According to Strauss "Violence is an act where there is the high potential of causing injury". In the opinion of Margaret Violence as "the unsanctioned damage to person or property". Violence is a behavior in which a more powerful person takes advantage of and abuses a less powerful one. Violence is horrifying in that it enables the strong to establish profitable relations with those who are weak, without expending any energy on. These expressions of violence take place in a man-woman relationship within the family, state and society. Usually, domestic aggression towards women and girls, due to various reasons remain hidden.

Cultural and social factors are interlinked with the development and propagation of violent behavior. With different processes of socialization that men and women undergo, men take up stereotyped gender roles of domination and control, whereas women take up that of submission, dependence and respect for authority. A female child grows up with a constant sense of being weak and in need, of protection, whether physical, social or economic. This helplessness has led to her exploitation at almost every stage of life.[14] The epitome of Indian culture in dharma sasthra women should be treated with great honour and in western way need to be respected and protected. Among all special responsibility is given to spouse i.e., husband as the husband and wife relationship is treated as one body and soul.

Violence against woman is a routine affair in most of Indian families in one way or other. The violence, harassment against women is more in domestic than outside the family. According to the National Crime Record Bureau (NCRB) in 2012 total no. of dowry death cases booked in states is 8092 and percentage is 98.29% and violence and cruelty of huband and in-laws is 104454 with percentage of 98.05%.[15]

VIOLENCE AGAINST WIFE

The violence by spouse can be classified as:

1. Physical violence
2. Sexual violence
3. Psychological violence

Physical Violence

Physical violence is the intentional use of physical force with a potential for causing injury, harm, disability or death example hitting, shoving ,biting, restraint, kicking, etc. The study shows the percentage of women who have experienced physical violence at any time since the age of 15 years—ever and in the previous 12 months—by background characteristics. Thirty-four percent of all women age 15-49 have experienced violence at any time since the age of 15. Nineteen percent of women age 15-49 have experienced violence in the 12 months preceding the survey. Notably, the majority (56 percent) of women who have ever experienced violence since the age of 15 have experienced violence in the 12 months preceding the survey of women who experienced any violence in the past 12 months, one in five reported that they experienced the violence often, and the remainder said that they experienced it sometimes.[16]

Sexual Violence

Marriage is not a morally imposition condition but facilitator factor in favour of future generation. Though family life is not totally based on the conjugal life of the couple yet it is an accelerating an adhesive solution. With the various factors men with their egotistic behavior lead to marital rape, also known as spousal rape is non-consensual sex in which the perpetrator is the victim's spouse. It is a form of partner rape, of domestic violence, and of sexual abuse. It can be equally, if not more, emotionally and physically damaging than rape by a stranger. Rape by a spouse, partner or ex-partner is more often associated with physical violence. A nine-nation study within the European Union found that current or ex-partners were the perpetrators of around 25% of all sexual assaults, and that violence was more common in assaults by ex-partners (50% of the time) and partners (40%) than in assaults by strangers or recent acquaintances (25%)[17].

Attributing the effects of marital rape in research is problematic as it is nearly impossible to find a large enough sample of spouses to study who have experienced sexual violence but have not also been physically assaulted by their spouse[18]. While rape by a stranger is highly traumatic, it is typically a one-time event and is clearly understood as rape. In the case of rape by a spouse or long-term sexual partner, the history of the relationship affects the victim's reactions. There is research showing that marital rape can be more emotionally and physically damaging than rape by a stranger.[19] Marital rape may occur as part of an abusive relationship. Trauma from the rape adds to the effect of other abusive acts or abusive and demeaning talk. Furthermore, marital rape is rarely a one-time event, but a repeated if not frequent occurrence[20]. Whether it takes place once or is part of an established pattern of domestic violence, trauma from rape has serious long-term consequences for victims regardless of whether the assault is prosecuted or not. Act to sodomy or cruelty and injury to the private parts are taken in lighter ways most of the woman will not entertain a thought to talk about it. Sexual violence may be rape, sodomy, sadism, injury to the private parts.

Psychological Violence

Involves emotional violence to the victim caused by acts, threats of acts or coercive tactics which include humiliating wife, deliberately doing something to make wife feel diminished or embarrassed, it is considered psychological violence when there has been prior physical or sexual violence or prior threat of physical or sexual violence.[21]

Legal protection available to wife: Physical, Sexual violence and psychological violence is treated to be a mistake or fault on the part of wife and included as a ground for divorce under all personal laws like:

1. Sec. 13(2), ii of Hindu Marriage Act, 1956
2. Under Sec. 27(1A)(i) of Special Marriage Act
3. Sec. 2, vii of Dissolution of Muslim Marriage Act
4. Sec. 10(2) of Divorce Act, 1869
5. Sec. 32(a) of Parsi Marriage and Divorce Act, 1936, That the husband is guilty of rape, sodomy and bestiality
6. Under Domestic Violence Act, 2005 made all the violence may it be physical, emotional verbal, sexual is treated as violence and remedy available to the wife is either claim for compensation, maintenance
7. Under Sec. 498A of Indian penal code can file petition against husband and convict him.

CONCLUSION

Need of the hour: India is a country with rich heritage and culture to keep up the family and institution of marriage had been critically tormented by the spouse under the veil of marriage. Right from the beginning, marital violence is taken in a lighter view by taking lacunas in laws treat marital rape not as crime, wife is only given remedy to live with pain or leave with pain-in both the ways woman is a sufferer and hence most of the Indian women bare all the violence and take it as their fate.

The great boon for Indian society is family system which will be stand only with maintaining family relationships. In order to protect martial sanctity, need of the hour is to create awareness of Gender sensitization right from the childhood, Educate responsibility of male child to protect women and treat them with honor. And Social workers have to encourage women for the financial stability.

Notes and References

1. Haviland, William A.; Prins, Harald, E.L.; McBride, Bunny; Walrath, Dana (2011). *Cultural Anthropology: The Human Challenge* (13th ed.). Cengage Learning. ISBN 978-0-495-81178-7. *"A nonethnocentric definition of marriage is a culturally sanctioned union between two or more people that establishes certain rights and obligations between the people, between them and their children, and between them and their in-laws."*
2. http://blogs.kqed.org/lowdown/2013/07/15/nations-that-have-legalized-same-sex-marriage/
3. Manu Smrithi IX, 95.
4. Manu Smrithi IX, 96.
5. Manu Smrithi VII, 227.
6. Taittiriya Samhita, III, 1, 2, 57.
7. Mahabharat Anu Parva, 46, 1-13.
8. Sharma Charan Sircar, Mohammadean Law, (Tagore Law Lectures, 1873), 30.
9. Islamic Law in Modern India, p. 23.
10. Friedman, Law in a changing Society, 1970, p. 174.
11. See Sec. 3(b) of Parsi Marriage and Divorce Act, 1936.
12. Benjamin *v.* Benjamin AIR 1926 Bombay 169.
13. Abused Women's Perspectives on the Criminal Justice System's Response to Domestic Violence by Paula C. Barata, A Dissertation Submitted to the Faculty of Graduate Studies and Research Through the Department of Psychology In Partial Fulfillment of the Requirements for the Degree of Doctor of Philosophy at the University of Windsor, Windsor, Ontario, Canada 2004 © 2004 Paula C. Barata.
14. Interrogating Violence, Uncovering Silences: Investigating Marital Violence in India By Sreeparna Chattopadhyay Advisor: David Ikertzer B.A., St. Xavier's College, Bombay University, 2001 A.M., Brown University, 2003A.
15. *National Family Health Survey, 2005-06 (NFHS-3), India Reports,* ncrb.gov.in/ý.
16. *National Family Health Survey, 2005-06 (NFHS-3) India Reports,* Domestic Violence, 497.
17. Burman, M.; J. Lovett, L. Kelly (2009). *Different systems, similar outcomes? Tracking attrition in reported rape cases in eleven countries*. London: Child and Woman Abuse Studies Unit, London Metropolitan University, p. 106.
18. Bernice, *et al.*, The Relative Effects of Intimate Partner Physical and Sexual Violence on Post-Traumatic Stress Disorder Symptomatology, Violence and Victims, 2003 February; 18, Vol. 1, p. 87.
19. "Marital Rape" RAIN, Retrieved 9 May 2013.
20. "Marital Rape". Hiddenhurt.co.uk. 2007-06-17. Retrieved 2012-05-14.
21. Bhattacharya, Rink, 2004, Behind closed doors: Domestic violence in India, New Delhi, Sage Publications.

13

Rights of Girl Child

T. KEERTHI

INTRODUCTION

In a civilized society, the importance of child welfare cannot be underestimated because the welfare of the entire community, its growth and development, depends on the health and well-being of its children. Children are "Supremely important national asset", but the girl child is seen as an economic drain as her marriage and dowry, crushes her family under huge burden of debts. Despite the legal emancipation of women in India, the traditional bias regarding female children has not undergone a change

Manu, the arch law-giver of the Hindu religion stipulated: women should never be free, "A woman must be dependent upon her father in childhood, upon her husband in young and upon her sons in old age, she should never be free".

The Practice of female foeticide has been reported quite less in the under developed (Particularly Tribal) regions in comparison to the developed regions in India. However, the practice of dowry is slowly sliding gradually into the tribal culture also.

Reformers, by the end of 19th century came to style marriages involving bride wealth as "selling of girls". Arya Samaj and the Singh

Sabha reformers of various hues in Punjab tried to protect their high-born status and social privilege by controlling women's sexuality[1].

GOVERNMENTAL POLICIES

1. *National population policy*: In relation to female foeticide, there is a worrying fact that population control, worsens the situations. Couples determined to have only the two children will see that they get their "Share" of boys. Through the new population policy of the Government of India does not talk of two-child norm. The two-child norm will widen the inequality gap among the people, as the disincentives would disproportionately impact on the already deprived population. It would provide an impetus for an increase in sex selective abortions and female foeticide, worsening the alarming decline in the child sex ratio noticed in the 2001 census.
2. *National abortion policy*: MTP Act, 1971 permits abortion only in certain cases (Socio-medical grounds) and disallowed those which are based on gender. The Government being concerned only with its family planning programs. "Target" is thus a willing party to this legalized female focticide.

STUDIES ON SEX RATIOS

Several studies have been conducted on the sex ratio in the country. They provide useful insight into the linkages between various factors (like regional development, female labour participation, education, birth order, religion, etc.) and the sex ratio. The results of these studies could be utilized in the development of strategy to check the menace of female foeticide.

(I) *Female Labour Participation and Sex Ratio*: The economic contribution made to the family by a woman through her participation in the workforce is a significant factor that contributes to the viability of the girl child. Miller finds a strong correlation between female labour participation rates and juvenile sex ratios in India. Where female labour participation is high (as in some southern States) there is always a high preservation of female life and where female labour participation is low (as in north India) female children may or may not be preserved.[2]

(II) *Birth Order and Sex Ratio*: There has been observed a negative correlation between birth order and sex ratio. A study done by the Christian Medical Association of India (CMAL) shows that in Delhi, the sex ratio at birth (SRB) for third children, when both earlier children are females, is a shocking 219 girls for every 1000 boys born. The Study analyzed trends in hospital deliveries in Delhi.

(III) *Religion and Sex Ratio*: The 'First Report on Religion Data, 2001', collected during Census 2001, brings to light the persistent bias among communities against the girl-child and clarifies that region plays a greater role than religion in overall development indicators. Although the population growth rate among both Hindus and Muslims fell significantly between 1991 and 2001, the most alarming revelation of Census 2001 was the declining child sex ratio within the age-group 0-6 years. More disturbing is the continuing bias shown by prosperous communities towards the girl-child.[3]

(IV) *Literacy and Sex Ratio*: The 'First Report on Religion Data, 2001', collected during Census 2001, questions the popular belief that literacy rates have a direct bearing on population, and that literate people are less prone to gender bias. Although this may be true in some cases, as with Muslims having one of the lowest literacy rates (59.1%) and the highest population growth rates, the same logic does not hold true among the Jain community that has the highest literacy rate (94.1%) but a low child sex ratio. The report is quick to point out that Tamil Nadu, despite its low literacy rate, has been able to keep a check on its fertility rate.[4]

There is a difference between the impact of male and female education or literacy on gender bias in child survival. Education or literacy of men had no impact on gender bias or increased female disadvantage. Female education has long been advocated to promote declines in fertility and child mortality. However, the relationship between maternal education and gender bias can be positive or negative depending on region, parity or contextual details. A Positive relationship may exist either because educated women more efficiently withhold high quality care from less desired children, or because they have lower fertility, which is accompanied by greater gender bias since parents have narrower latitude to ensure the desired number of sons.[5]

LITERACY EDUCATION AND GENDER BIAS

It is clear from the above studies that in the Indian context, the impact of education on the gender bias is not clear-cut. There are other factors involved which are analysed in the study mentioned below. The study focused on trends of estimated sex ratios at birth (SRB) and sex ratios of child mortality risk in India.[6]

CONCLUSION AND SUGGESTIONS

Since the bias against the girl child is based on economic consideration, the solution too will have to be economic, turning the girl child from an economic liability into an economic asset in the most effective way of tackling the problem. Thus, developments augur well for the cause of female foeticide/infanticide. Independence and assertiveness of women and the parent's concern for their daughters might initiate a new beginning for the girl child in India. The situation will improve only when mothers themselves treat their children with equality. The future for sure is that of equality of respect, equality of opportunity, equality of honour and equality of life for all.

NOTES AND REFERENCES

1. Article of Girl Child. The Saga of Female Foeticide in India—Ashok K. Jain.
2. B. Miller, The Endangered Sex: Neglect of Female Children in Rural North India, OUP, New Delhi, p. 117 (1997), in S.C. Singh, "Pre-Natal Diagnosis and Female Foeticide", *Unreported Judgments Journal*, pp. 7-8 (2002)(1).
3. "Disappearing Girl Child", available at http://WWW.infochangeinida-org.
4. *Ibid.*
5. *Ibid.*
6. *Ibid.*

14

Internalizing International Human Rights in the Domestic Law

With Special Reference to Women Rights in India—A Critical Analysis

R. SRINIVASAN

INTRODUCTION

Life, Liberty, Equality and Dignity are the basic tenets of human rights. It evolved at the global level and is internalized by the Legislature and harmonized by the judiciary at the domestic level. India suffered under the imperialistic yoke for centuries. All the existing Criminal laws are based on British legal system. Hence, it declared human rights as its cardinal principle to the protected at all costs. Being the largest democracy with a heterogeneous population makes this aspect even more important and difficult. Therefore, corresponding to the developments of human rights at the global level, India periodically attempts to internalize such laws into the domestic system either by amending the Constitution or through legislative enactments. In spite of that, there is persisting gap between the evolving global laws and the existing laws relating to women rights. Global human rights are far ahead of national human rights. In this context, this research attempts to analyze the role of the Supreme Court in assimilating internalizing and harmonizing the global laws in order to minimize the gap. In this research work certain questions crop up, which are sought to be answered.

"All human beings are born free and equal in dignity and rights," said Irving Kristol.[1] In the same breath he also stated that "democracy doesn't guarantee equality of conditions, it only guarantees equality of opportunity." The UN Charter prohibits discrimination in the name of sex, and stated in Article 1, "the promotion and encouragement of respect for human rights and for fundamental freedom for all without discrimination as to sex." Article 8 of the UN Charter states that, "The United Nations shall place no restrictions on the eligibility of men and women to participate in any capacity and under conditions of equality in its principle and subsidiary organs." Under Article 13(1)(b) of UN Charter, gender equality for women is guaranteed and it is the first ever international instrument to proclaim gender justice as fundamental human rights.

The list of formal international legal instruments on women's right is very impressive in the international arena after 1945. It started from the inauguration of the Universal Declaration of Human Rights (UDHR), 1948, which guarantees the right of every individual not to be discriminated against on the basis of sex among other things. From the declaration of UDHR, 1948 to 1966 when international covenants were made, there were numerous international instruments sponsored by the United Nations. These include the *Convention on the Political Rights of Women*, New York, 31st March, 1953; the *Convention on the Nationality of Married Women*, New York, 20th February, 1957; and the *Convention on Consent to Marriage, Minimum Age for Marriage and Registration of Marriages*, New York, 10th December, 1962. Articles 2 and 3 of the *International Covenants on Civil and Political Rights* (ICCPR)[2] rightly assures that, "All persons are equal before the law and are entitled without any discrimination to the equal protection of the law. In this respect, the law prohibits discrimination and guarantees all persons equal and effective protection against discrimination on any ground such as sex."[3] *International Covenant on Economic, Social and Cultural Rights*, 1966 provides that "the State party undertakes to respect and to ensure all individuals within its territory and subject to its jurisdiction the rights recognized in the covenant without any discrimination and other optional protocols laid stress on equality between men and women."[4] All these international instruments prohibit the discrimination of women.

The first exclusive human rights instrument concerning women was the *Convention on Trafficking in Women, 1949* sponsored by UN, followed by *Supplementary Convention on Abolition of Slavery, the Slave trade and Institutions and Practices similar to slavery, 1956, the Convention against Torture and other Cruel, Inhumane and Degrading Treatment or Punishment, 1984* and above all *Convention on the Elimination of All forms of Discrimination against Women (*CEDAW*), 1979.* Other *International Labour Organization* (ILO) Conventions have also referred to the gender equality and the need for special action to provide justice to women. It also urged national constitutions and laws to be made to adopt the international human rights language on women towards entrenchment of implementation.[5]

The *Mexico Plan for Action* (1975), the *Nairobi Forward Looking Strategies* (1985) and *Covenant on Elimination of Discrimination against Women,* 1981 (CEDAW) adopted by the General Assembly, 1979 have come to be recognized as International Bill of Rights for Women. It was ratified by India in 1993. The Covenant prohibits all restrictions on women and work towards empowering of women, her right and freedom—civil, political, economic, social and cultural. The Preamble of CEDAW convinced that "the full and complete development of a country, the welfare of the women and the cause of peace require the maximum participation of women on equal terms with men in all fields".

The equality of women was reaffirmed in the *Second World Conference on Human Rights at Vienna in June 1993* (*Vienna Human Rights Declaration*), *Cairo Programme of Action*, the *Millennium development goals and World Summit and in the Fourth World Conference on Women held in Beijing (Beijing Declaration) in 1995* as well as "Beijing +5" follow-up in June, 2000. These developments together represent significant progress in the struggle by women rights activists, who have been working at local, regional, national and international levels to recognize women's rights under human rights in international law. Indeed, this recognition is a tribute to the great success of the Beijing Conference. But it is regrettable to note that after decades of omission the subject of the worldwide occurrence of violence against women was seriously recognized by the United Nations.

Indian women faced a paradoxical situation. On the one hand, they were highly venerated like mother earth and on the other subjected to immense hardship both physical and mental, due to innumerable social practices. The Constitution of India guarantees the concept of 'equality' and 'non-discrimination'. Part III, Fundamental Rights ensures different rights for women's equality under Article 14;[6] special protection under Article 15(4);[7] and the right against exploitation under Articles 23 & 24 which includes the rights of girl children,[8]. Apart from that, directive principles provide adequate means of livelihood and equal pay for equal work for both sexes. Under Article 39(a), the State has to make just and humane conditions of work and maternity relief and Articles 42, 51A(e) imposes fundamental duties. It requires every citizen to renounce practices derogatory to the dignity of women. Articles 243(D) (3) and 243 (T)(3)[9] ensures reservation of seats in every Panchayat and Municipality for women. Since 1950, the Parliament of India has enacted a sizeable number of legislations for protecting the rights of women.[10] The Indian Penal Code has also provided provisions for dealing with offences against women. Apart from these legislative protections, the Government of India constituted two commissions in 1993: the National Commission on Women (NCW) and the National Human Rights Commission (NHRC). The Commission's task is to study human rights violations against women and forward the report periodically to the Government of India. The Indian Government is committed to bring parity between sexes in all walks of life and to eradicate discrimination in all its manifestation.

RESEARCH METHODOLOGY

It is an *ex-post facto* research. The cases decided by the Supreme Court from 1950 to 2009 related to human rights have been taken for analysis. It is a doctrinaire research. The process of interpretation by the judiciary is analyzed. However, in this research work, the role of the Supreme Court in harmonizing the international human rights law into domestic law has been explored, analyzed and formulated only through the cases already decided by the Supreme Court.[11] The doctrine human right has been analyzed in the context of interpretation and construction of the Constitution and Statutes by the Supreme Court.

There are various stages in this research:

Firstly, Supreme Court judgments in which one or more international human rights instruments mentioned are explored;

Secondly, such explored cases are arranged chronologically and classified into four groups, which constitute four phases namely, from 1950 to 1966, i.e., from the commencement of the Constitution to the year of enactment of ICCPR and ICESCR, the Second phase from 1966 to 1979, i.e. after the enactment of ICCPR and ICESCR to the year of ratification of these two instruments by India;

The Third phase commenced from 1979 i.e. after the ratification of the two covenants and before the enactment of Protection of Human Rights Act, 1993;

The Fourth phase commences from the enactment of Protection of Human Rights Act, 1993 to 2009;

Fifthly, all the above classified cases are further classified into 'Reference' and 'Expansion'. If the Supreme Court mentioned international human rights instruments in its judgements and used such instruments for the purpose of expanding domestic human rights in the light of international human rights such cases are referred as 'expansion' and other cases are mentioned as 'reference'.

For the purpose of the present study harmonization takes place in two dimensions. In the first dimension it is mere reference of referring the international instruments. In the second dimension after referring international instruments the rights available in international instruments are expanded into the domestic rights. As if they are part of the law of the land. It is also to be noted that in all dimensions of expansion references are available. Notwithstanding overlapping of cases which have reference and expansion, an attempt is made to classify cases that are categorized as 'reference' and 'expansion'.

Trend analysis is used to critically analyze the role of the Supreme Court during various phases of harmonization. For trend analysis, the content analysis technique is applied. In this research for the purpose of exploring and identifying various Supreme Court decisions on human rights 'Google' search engine is used along with <manupatra.com> which has published cases decided by the Supreme Court on various subjects besides High Court cases. With the help of <manupatra.com> content analysis technique is applied to find out the number of judgments delivered by Supreme Court under the heading "Human Rights". Then following the chronological classification, the distribution of cases from 1950 to 2011 has been listed out. Similar techniques were applied to find out the number of cases which contain international human rights instruments like "Universal Declaration of Human Rights" and they have been enumerated on the basis of the above chronological classification. The same method is applied to find out the distribution of cases wherein "International Covenant on Civil and Political Rights" and "International Covenant on Economic, Social and Cultural Rights" are applied. Besides this quantitative analysis, the qualitative analysis of the Supreme Court judgments delivered on various human rights cases is also listed and analyzed under the heading 'Reference' and 'Expansion".

Harmonization

The role played by the Supreme Court in harmonizing the International Human Rights Law with the Domestic Law relating to women is analyzed under the following four phases.

First Phase

This phase was the formative period for the Supreme Court of India and it analyzed the concepts of equality and non-discrimination relating to women in a limited scope as the sexually weak and vulnerable group of the society. In this aspect, though the Court did not rely on the international human rights instruments directly, it observed that "Sex is a sound classification and although there can be no discrimination in general in that ground the Constitution itself provides for special provisions in the case of women and children by clause (3) of Article 15. Articles 14 and 15 thus read together validate the last sentence of Section 497 IPC which prohibits women from being punished as an abettor of the offence of adultery."[12] The provisions of UN Charter and UDHR instruments on equality and non-discrimination did not play a significant role in the domestic law, but it is found that the Court started to apply the 'human rights' angle in the domestic law relating to women's equality. Hence, there was no assimilation and harmonization of international laws on women's rights into the domestic sphere during this phase.

Second Phase

This is a significant phase for the development of women empowerment in the international sphere. In 1966, International Covenants urged the world countries to take appropriate steps for protecting women from inequality and discrimination. The Fifth Five Year Plan (1974-78) in India saw a marked shift in the approach of women's issue from welfare to development. During this period

India attended the *International Convention on Civil and Political Rights, Convention on Elimination of All forms of Discrimination against Women in 1979* (CEDAW), and ratified the *Mexico Plan of Action, 1975*. Despite all the positive developments in the international arena, there was no respite in the brutality and violence against women. The declaration of emergency changed the outlook of the Supreme Court from a docile and adjusting third organ of the State to a highly activistic Court pulling up the other organ for their failure. This phase is noted for many women centric laws, but cases relating to women's rights and other issues did not come to the Supreme Court.

Third Phase

This phase saw a gender sensitized judiciary swinging into action to provide equality for women. The *Shah Bano case*[13] saw the Supreme Court playing an active role to bring uniform personal laws for women, irrespective of religion to attain gender equality as guaranteed by Uniform Civil Code (UCC) in Article 44 of the Constitution.[14] In *Sheela Barse v State of Maharashtra*,[15] the Supreme Court stepped in and laid down guidelines for ensuring the protection of women prisoners from maltreatment in the light of UDHR, 1948, and observed that, "female suspects should not be kept in police lockup in which male suspects are detained. Interrogation of females should be made in the presence of female police officials." This is the first case in India, where the Supreme Court discussed the rights of women prisoners in the light of international instrument.

In this period though the Court attempted to view the cases on women in the human right dimension, there is no evidence of harmonization of civil and political rights from the international instruments into the domestic law except in *Sheela Barse* v. *State of Maharashtra*.[16] This phase is etched in the minds of all human rights activists for yet another interesting reason. It saw the emergence of a highly activist justice, V.R. Krishna Iyer, former Judge, Supreme court of India. He emerged as the champion of human rights. In this case he observed that, "the women are continuing to suffer from womb to tomb. Still, women are subjected to sexual offences like rape, sexual slavery, enforced prostitution and forced pregnancy besides being subject to gender bias in almost every walk of life." This phase is also significant because the National Commission for Women was constituted by the Indian government in 1992 to periodically appraise it about the position of women and their needs.

This phase saw few cases on gender equality. Women found a champion of their cause in the Court.

Fourth Phase

India ratified the *Beijing Declaration* and unreservedly endorsed the *Platform for Action (1995)* and Outcome Document adopted by the UN General Assembly Session on Gender Equality, Development & Peace for the 21st Century. This document was titled "*Further actions and initiatives to implement the Beijing Declaration and the Platform for Action*". The Indian Parliament enacted the *Protection of Human Rights Act, 1993* to give effect to the international obligations.

Women in India are accorded right to equality and the constitution guarantees that there shall be no discrimination on the basis of sex. The secular dimension of the Constitution permits the continuation of personal laws which are dealt in Articles 25-28. Accordingly, in law relating to marriage, succession, adoption, maintenance and guardianship, the traditional discrimination of women continues with certain modifications. In this matter the Government of India openly accepted in its periodic report submitted before the *UN Committee on the Elimination of Discrimination Against Women* and stated that, "the personal laws of the major religious communities had traditionally governed marital and family relations, with the government maintaining a policy of non-interference in such laws in the absence of a demand for change from individual religious communities."[17] By viewing the report, CEDAW Committee noted that "steps have not been taken to reform the personal laws of different religious and ethnic groups, in consultation with them, so as to conform to the Convention," and cautioned that "the government's policy of non-intervention perpetuates sexual stereotypes, son preference and discrimination against women." Further, the Committee urged the government to withdraw its declaration to Article 16, paragraph 1 of the Convention and to work with and support women's groups as members of the community in reviewing and reforming these personal laws and expected the government to follow the directive principles in the Constitution and Supreme Court decisions and enact a Uniform Civil Code (UCC) that different ethnic and religious groups may adopt.[18]

The Human Rights Committee (HRC) of the *International Covenant on Civil and Political Rights, 1966* at its meeting held on 30th

July 1997, after considering the third periodic report of India observed that "women in India have not been freed from discrimination and expressed serious concern that they 'are subjected to personal laws which are based on religious norms and which do not accord equality in respect of marriage, divorce and inheritance rights.' and stressed that the enforcement of personal laws based on religion violates the rights of women to equality before the law and non-discrimination." Therefore, the Human Rights Committee did not favour such a violation of the human rights of women in India to continue and recommended to the government of India "to take effort and strengthened towards the enjoyment of their rights by women without discrimination and that personal laws be enacted which are fully compatible with the Covenant."[19] The only justification recently given by government of India before various international monitoring committees is that it does not want to interfere in the personal affairs of any community without being requested by the members to do so. India signed CEDAW in 1980 and ratified it in 1993. Now India is legally bound under the international law to implement CEDAW. Except for *Domestic Violence Act*, passed in 2005, it is observed that the legislature and executive are yet to frame effective laws at the domestic level to give effect to India's international obligations. This paves the way for harmonization of laws by the judiciary as an organ of the State to implement the international human rights instruments at the domestic level.

Initially the Supreme Court was hesitant to interfere in the personal laws. In *Gulam Abbas case*, the question of interference in the customary religious rights was raised before the Supreme Court. The Court observed that the State could not interfere with the established customary rights to perform the religious functions.[20] Such practices are treated as integral part of every religion. Otherwise the non-essential and non-secular aspects will be clothed with religious sanction and may claim to be treated as religious practices which may not be an essential and integral part of a religion.[21] Hence, the Court preferred to maintain a careful balance between the freedom of an individual or the group in connection with their religion.[22] In another case, the Court held that "the fundamental rights should not touch with the personal laws of the parties."[23] The Court further observed that religious rights are subject to health of the society. Religious freedom under Article 25(2)[24] is subject to laws made for social welfare and reform. In *Lily Thomas* v. *Union of*

India,[25] the Supreme Court further observed that, "Religious freedom guaranteed under Article 25 of the Constitution should not encroach upon a similar freedom of other persons."

For the first time in Indian legal history the Supreme Court referred the international instruments in personal laws. In *C. Masilamani* v. *Idol of Sri Swaminathaswamy*,[26] the Court referred the conflict of gender equality with the Hindu personal laws. In this case the provisions of *Universal Declaration of Human Rights* (UDHR), *Convention on the Elimination of All Forms of Discrimination against Women* (CEDAW) and *UN Declaration of Right to development* were invoked for the interpretation of testamentary disposition of any property in accordance with the Section 30 of the *Hindu Succession Act*.[27]

In this connection, the Court observed that, "The State should take all appropriate measures including legislation to modify or abolish gender discrimination in the existing laws, regulations, customs and practices which constitute discrimination against women...facilities and opportunities not only are to be provided for, but also all forms of gender -based discrimination should be eliminated. It is a mandate to the State to do these acts. Property is one of the important endowments or natural assets to accord opportunity, source to develop personality, to be independent, right to equal status and dignity of person. Therefore, the State should create conditions and facilities conducive for women to realize the right to economic development including social and cultural rights."[28] The Court invoked the international human rights instrument and expanded the rights of women.

Again in *Valasamma Paul* v. *Cochin University and Others*[29], a Syrian Catholic lady belonging to forward community married to a Latin Catholic, a backward community, was appointed as a lecturer under reserved category provided for Latin Catholic. It was challenged before the Supreme Court. It was contended that giving benefit of reservation to such person will amount to playing fraud on Constitution and frustrate benign Constitutional policy under Articles 15(4) and 16(4). The appellant contended that due to her marriage she herself was subjected to all the environmental disabilities to which her husband was subjected and to which all members of the backward class in the region are subjected to. So she cannot therefore be discriminated once again by denying equality given by Article 16(4). She further contended that birth itself is not a determinative factor for claiming protective discrimination given to backward class people. Environmental and social disabilities are also relevant factors.

Taking into consideration the question of harmonization of personal laws and the Constitutional goals, the Court observed that "Human rights are derived from the dignity and worth inherent in the human person. Human rights and fundamental freedoms have been reiterated in the Universal Declaration of Human Rights. Democracy, development and respect for human rights and fundamental freedoms are inter-dependant and have mutual reinforcement. The human rights for women, including girl child are, therefore, inalienable, integral and an indivisible part of Universal Human Rights. The full development of personality and fundamental freedoms and equal participation by women in political, social, economic and cultural life are concomitants for national development, social and family stability and growth cultural, social and economical. All forms of discrimination on grounds of gender is violative of fundamental freedoms and human rights. Convention for Elimination of all forms of Discrimination against women was ratified by the UNO on December 18, 1979 and the Government of India ratified as an active participant on June 19, 1993 acceded to CEDAW and reiterated that discrimination against women violates the principles of equality of rights and respect for human dignity and it is an obstacle to the participation on equal terms with men in the political, social, economic and cultural life of their country; it hampers the growth of the personality from society and family, making more difficult for the full development of potentialities of women in the service of the respective countries and of humanity."[30] The court also felt that the establishment of New International Economic Order (NIEO) will contribute significantly towards the promotion of equality between men and women.[31]

In this case the Court pointed out the definition of Section 2(d) of the *Protection of Human Rights Act, 1993* and held that the principles embodied in CEDAW and the concomitant 'right to development' have became an integral part of the Constitution and the Human Rights Act and so enforceable. It is interesting to note that irrespective of reservation in Articles 5(e), 16(1), 16(2) and 29 of CEDAW, the Court viewed this in the light of Articles 15(1), (3), 21 of the Constitution. The observation of the Court remained as *obiter dicta* and was not reflected in the decision. The Supreme Court quashed her appointment on the ground that she was not entitled to the benefit of reservation under Article 16(4). It is found that the Court merely referred the international human rights instruments in this case.

In *Madhu Kishwar* v. *State of Bihar*,[32] the Supreme Court invoked CEDAW and harmonized into the Hindu personal laws and ensured the equal share of women in the ancestral property, even against the existing statutory provisions. The Court drew inspiration of gender justice from CEDAW by ignoring India's reservation on Articles 5(a) and 16(1) of the Convention.[33] By referring the instrument, the Court stated that the same should be the integral scheme of the Fundamental Rights and the Directive Principles of the Indian Constitution. It harmonized Article 2(e) of CEDAW which enjoins the State parties to breathe life into the dry bones of the Constitution,[34] and interpreted Section 2(f) of the *Protection of Human Rights Act, 1993*[35] with Articles 3, 14 and 15 of CEDAW,[36] which embodies concomitant right to development as an integral scheme of the Indian Constitution and the *Protection of Human Rights Act, 1993*. So in this case the Supreme Court harmonizes the international human rights instrument with existing statutory legislation by equating gender justice with 'right to life'.

But the majority found these arguments as of limited persuasion in view of India's reservation to CEDAW in the matter of personal law. It could prevail only to the extent of recognizing right to maintenance. The adverse impact of discrimination is made good by falling back upon right to life in the light of international legal norms." Like in the previous case, it is also found that the Supreme Court only referred the international human rights instruments into the domestic law though it was not taken for reaching the decision.

Again the nature of Hindu Personal Laws was examined by the Supreme Court in *Gita Hariharan and Another* v. *Reserve Bank of India.*[37] In this case the Court had to construe Section 6(a) of *Hindu Minority and Guardianship Act, 1956*[38] and Section 19(b) of the *Guardian and Wards Act, 1890.*[39] This Section was challenged as violative of equality clause of the Constitution, in as much as the mother of the minor is relegated to an inferior position on the ground of sex alone since her right, as a natural guardian of the minor, is made cognizable only 'after' the father. The Court relied upon the CEDAW and the *Beijing Declaration*, which directs all State parties to appropriate measures to prevent discrimination of all forms against women. It was held by the Court that the domestic Courts are under an obligation to give due regard to international conventions and norms for construing domestic law when there is no inconsistency between them.

In this case, C. Banerjee J., observed that: "though nobility and self-denial coupled with tolerance mark the greatest feature of Indian womanhood in the past and the cry for equality and equal status being at a very low ebb, but with the passage of time and change of social structure the same is however no longer dormant but presently quite loud. This cry is not restrictive to any particular country, but world over with variation in degree only. Article 2 of the UDHR[40] provided that everybody is entitled to all rights and freedom without distinction of any kind whatsoever such as race, sex or religion and the ratification of the convention for CEDAW by the UNO in 1979 and subsequent acceptance and ratification by India in June 1993 also demonstrate the same."

Further Chief Justice Anand while delivering the judgment on behalf of M. Srinivasan, and C. Banerjee. J.J. held that "both parents are duty bound to take care of person and property of their minor. Minor was in exclusive care and custody of mother where father for any other reason unable to take care of minor, because of his physical and mental incapacity mother can act as natural guardian of minor. All action of mother would be valid even during life time of father who is deemed to be absent for the purpose of Section 6(a) of the *Hindu Minority and Guardianship Act, 1956* and Section 19(b) of the *Guardian and Wards Act, 1980*". In this, the Court interprets the provisions of the domestic law in the light of the international instruments and expands the rights of women by liberal interpretation.

It was the first time in India, the Supreme Court comprehensively dealt with the right of working women against sexual harassment in *Vishaka* v. *State of Rajasthan*.[41] In this case, for the effective enforcement of basic human rights of gender equality and to protect working women from sexual harassment and abuse, the Court issued guidelines for the employer in working places as well as other responsible persons and institutions to observe the guidelines. Despite the absence of domestic law on sexual harassment of working women, the Court referred Articles 11 and 24 of CEDAW[42] and states that "In the absence of domestic law occupying the field, to formulate effective measures to check the evil of sexual harassment of working women at all work places, the contents of international conventions and norms are taken for the purpose of interpretation of the guarantee of gender equality and right to work with human dignity." Further the Court observed that "any international convention not inconsistent with the fundamental rights and in harmony with its spirit must be read into these provisions of the Constitution and enlarge the meaning and content thereof, to promote the object of the constitutional guarantee." On the basis of the international instruments, the Court issued guidelines obliging employers in work places as well as other responsible persons and institutions to observe the recommendations of CEDAW. Further the Court supported the decision on the basis of 'doctrine of legitimate expectation' and by referring to the objectives of the judiciary mentioned in the Beijing Statement of 1995.[43]

In *Apparel Export Promotion Council* v. *A.K.Chopra*[44], the Supreme Court once again examined the sexual harassment of women in working place. In this case, a manager attempted to assault his subordinate. Though the employer did not make any physical contact with her, he was removed from his service as a private secretary to the Chairman of the Apparel Export Promotion Council. But the High Court directed the reinstatement of the employer in a different branch of the office, at least for a period of two years. This order of the High Court was challenged before the Supreme Court. The question before the Court was whether the physical contact with the female employee is an essential ingredient of the charge. Did the allegation that the superior 'tried to molest' a female employee at the place of work, constitute an act unbecoming of good conduct and behaviour expected from a superior? What should be the nature of the approach on the part of the law courts in cases involving sexual harassment more generally? The Court referred to CEDAW and ICESCR, holding that the "Courts are under an obligation to give due regard to the international conventions and norms for construing domestic laws more so when there is no inconsistency between them and there is a void in domestic law".[45] The Court overturned the order of the High Court and held that "any lenient action in such a case is bound to have demoralizing effect on working women. Sympathy in such cases is uncalled for and mercy is misplaced."[46]

The pushing of young girls of fallen women into prostitution is another human rights issue discussed during this phase. In *Gaurav Jain case*,[47] the main question before the court was: What are the rights of children of prostitutes? What are the methods to segregate them from their mother and others so as to give them protection? What kind of care and rehabilitation can be given to bring them into the mainstream? What scheme should be evolved to eradicate prostitution? What sustenance can be provided to the victims of flesh trade? These were the questions raised before the Supreme Court in order to consider the rights of children of fallen women and to evolve a scheme to eradicate prostitution. In this regard the Court referred extensively to the *UN Declaration on the Rights of Child,* the *UN Standard Minimum Rules for the Administration of Juvenile Justice,* along with the UDHR and CEDAW in support of its decision. It issued several directions for creating juvenile homes for the rehabilitation of child prostitutes and neglected children, this bringing harmonization and expanding the human rights available to children of fallen women.

In another instance, the Supreme Court upheld the social justice principle by invoking international human right instruments. In *Municipal Corporation of Delhi* v. *Female Workers (Muster Roll) and another*[48] the question was whether having regard to the provision contained in *Maternity Benefit Act, 1961*, the women engaged either in casual basis or muster role basis on daily wages and not in regular employment were eligible for maternity leave? While upholding the rights of the female workers to receive maternity leave benefit, the Court relied upon the doctrine of social justice as embodied in Article 23 of *Universal Declaration of Human Rights, 1948*[49] and Article 11 of the CEDAW[50] and held that the provisions of the same must be read into the 'service contracts' of Municipal Corporation. In this case the Court referred and recognized the international human right instruments.

'Rape' has been held to be a violation of a person's fundamental rights guaranteed under Article 21 of the Constitution. It is a crime not only against the person of a woman, it is a crime against the society as such. It destroys the entire psychology of a woman and pushes her into deep emotional crisis. Rape is therefore the most hated crime. It is a crime against human rights and is violative of the victim's most cherished right, namely, right to life which includes right to live with human dignity as contained in Article 21.[51] In *Chairman, Railway Board* v. *Chandrima Das*[52], a woman from Bangladesh was gang raped by the employees of railways in a room at 'Yatra Niwas' of Howrah station at Calcutta. In this case the question was raised whether fundamental rights can be expanded and extended to give relief to foreign nationals or not? The Court held that relief can be granted to the victim for two reasons, firstly, on ground of domestic jurisprudence based on Constitutional provisions and secondly, on the ground of human rights jurisprudence based on UDHR, which has the international recognition as the "*Moral Code of Conduct*" having been adopted by the General Assembly of the UN. The Court held that the word 'life' has been used in Article 21 of the Constitution and recognized basic human rights in the same sense as understood in the UDHR. Hence there is no reason why it should be given a narrow meaning. According to the tenor of the language used in Article 21, it will be available not only to every citizen of this country, but also to a 'person' who may not be a citizen of the country.

The Court considered the relevance of the provisions in UDHR and *UN Declaration on the Elimination of Violence against Women,* 1993 and observed that, "the International Covenants and declarations as adopted by the UN have to be respected by all signatory states and the meaning given to the above words in those declarations and covenants have to be such as would help in effective implementation of those rights. The applicability of the UDHR and the principles thereof may have to be read, if need be, into the domestic jurisprudence." The 1993 UN declaration defines violence in a comprehensive manner, and adopts a synthetic approach by stating that women are entitled to the equal enjoyment and protection of all human rights, which would include *inter alia* the right to life, equality, liberty and security of person. In the *Chandrima Das case*, harmonization occurred in two dimensions and expanding the rights available to citizens event to foreign nationals with reference to this particular issue.

'Gender Equality' in the employment opportunities was considered by the Supreme Court in several cases in the light of international instruments like UDHR, ICCPR, ILO, CEDAW, etc. In a recent case, *Anuj Garg & Ors* v. *Hotel Association of India & Ors.*[53] the Constitutional validity of Section 30 of the Punjab Excise Act, 1914, which prohibits employment of a man under the age of 25 or any woman in any part of such premises in which liquor or intoxicating drug is consumed by the public was raised before the Court. It was a classical counter of the Individual rights *v.* Community orientation of rights. In this instant case the provisions of UDHR, 1948 was invoked before the Supreme Court for 'Gender Equality' and to throw the doors open for women also. Justice Sinha holding the legislation to be unconstitutional, supported the rationale of his decision by referring to provisions in the preamble of the International Labour Organization, the Universal Declaration of Human Rights, International covenant on Civil and Political Rights, the Convention on Elimination of All forms of Discrimination against Women.

In the first two phases from 1950 to 1966 and 1966 to 1979, it is found that, there is no assimilation or harmonization of civil and political rights from international human rights instruments. But in the third phase the Supreme Court median attempt to promote the international human rights principles against gender inequality and gender discrimination. Especially in *Shella Barse case* the Supreme Court laid down guidelines in consonance with the UDHR, 1948. But mere mentioning of the international human rights instrument in these cases did not play any role in arriving at the decision. Later in the third phase from 1979 to 1993 and in the Fourth and last phase from 1993 to 2011, it is found that the Supreme Court not only referred, but recognized and consolidated the international human rights in the domestic legal set-up.

From the foregoing analysis, harmonization process undertaken by the Supreme Court is clearly evident. This process made deep inroads into even the personal laws, which have sanctions under the fundamental rights of Freedom of Religion (Articles 25-28). By doing so, the personal law which brings in discrimination, has been shaken up.

CONCLUSION

There are substantial constitutional and statutory provisions related to the rights of women. There are 11 cases in this category that has undergone the process of harmonization during the study period. Out of this, in 3 cases there was reference, 2 of the 3 cases related to labour and related to reservation. In the remaining 8 cases there was expansion and 5 out of the 8 expansion cases, related to crimes against women.

In *Sheela Barse,* the Supreme Court laid down guidelines for protecting women prisoner's human rights in prison. In *Visaka*, the court laid down detailed guidelines preventing sexual harassment of women in working place—It was further expanded in *Apparel Export* case. In *Gaurau Jain's* case, certain directions were issued in protecting the interest of the children of prostitutes in order to rehabilitate them. All the human rights available to women was extended to a foreign women in the *Chandrima Das* case. This case related to crime against women. Another interesting finding is that by widely invoking international instruments, the Supreme Court tried to render gender justice. There are 3 cases that resulted in expansion and all 3 are related to Hindu women. 2 of these cases related to women's equal right to inheritance and in 1 case women's equal right to guardianship.

The Supreme Court directed the State in *Masilamani* case, to take all appropriate measures including legislation to modify or abolish gender discrimination in the existing laws, regulations, customs and practices which constitute discrimination against women. It held that the State should create conditions and facilities conducive for women to realize the right to development. In *Madhu Kishwar* case, the Court interfered in the personal laws of Hindus by harmonizing CEDAW principles and thus supporting equal share for women in the ancestral property rights. This move was against the existing statutory provisions.

In *Gita Hariharan* case, the Hindu women's right of guardianship over the minor child was accorded even during the life time of the father. Here too there was expansion. Thus, it is obvious that harmonization was made by the Supreme Court in the rights of women whenever they are deprived of their rights on grounds of gender. This was especially true in the case of Hindu women.

Notes and References

1. Irving Kristol, On the Democratic idea in America, New York : Harper, 1972.
2. Article 2 of the ICCPR provides:
   1. Each State party to the present Covenant undertakes to respect and to ensure to all individuals within its territory and subject to its jurisdiction the rights recognized in the present Covenant, without distinction of any kind, such as race, colour, sex, language, religion, political or other opinion, national or social origin, property, birth or other status.
   2. Where not already provided for by existing legislative or other measures, each State Party to the present Covenant undertakes to take the necessary steps, in accordance with its constitutional processes and with the provision of the present Covenant, to adopt such legislative or other measures as may be necessary to give effect to the rights recognized in the present Covenant.
   3. Each State Party to the present Covenant undertakes.
   4. To ensure that any person whose rights or freedoms as herein recognized are violated shall have an effective remedy, not withstanding that the violation has been committed by persons acting in an official capacity.

5. To ensure that any person claiming such a remedy shall have his right thereto determined by competent judicial, administrative or legislative authorities or by any other competent authority provided for by the legal system of the State, and to develop the possibilities of judicial remedy.
6. To ensure that the competent authorities shall enforce such remedies when granted.

Article 3 of the ICCPR: "The State Parties to the present Covenant undertake to ensure the equal right of men and women to the enjoyment of all civil and political rights set forth in the present Covenant."

3. V. Vijayabalan, "New Dimension of Human Rights", *Cochin University Law Review*, Vol. XXIV, Number 1&2.
4. Article 2(1) of the ICESCR, 1966 provides that the state party undertake to respect and to ensure to all individuals within its territory and subject to its jurisdiction the rights recognize in the covenant without any discrimination.
5. Upendra Baxi, From Human Rights to the Right to be a Woman (ed.), Amitha Dhanda & Archana Parashar, "Engendering Laws,"(1999), p. 13.
6. Article 14 of the Constitution says that 'the State shall not deny to any person equality before the law or the equal protection of the laws within the territory of India.'
7. Article 15(4) states that 'Nothing in this article or in clause (2) of Article 29 shall prevent the State from making any special provision for the advancement of any socially and educationally backward classes of citizens or for the Scheduled Castes and the Scheduled Tribes.'
8. Article 23 states that:
   1. Traffic in human beings and beggar and other similar forms of forced labour are prohibited and any contravention of this provision shall be an offensive punishable in accordance with law.
   2. Nothing in this article prevent the State from imposing compulsory service for public purposes, and in imposing such service for public purposes, and in imposing such service theState shall not make any discrimination on grounds only of religion, race, caste, or class or any of them.

   Article 24 states that: No Child below the age of fourteen years shall be employed to work in any factory or mine or engaged in any other hazardous employment.
9. Article 243(D)(3) states that: "Not less than one-third (including the number of seats reserved for women belonging to the Scheduled Castes and Scheduled Tribes) of the total number of seats to be filled by direct election in every Panchayat shall be reserved for women and such seats may be allotted by rotation of different constituencies in a panchayat."
   Article 243(T)(3) states that: "Not less than 1/3rd (including the number of seats reserved for women belonging to the Scheduled Castes and the Scheduled Tribes) of the total number of seats to be filled by direct election in every Municipality shall be reserved for women and such seats may be allotted by rotation to different constituencies in a Municipality."

10. Dowry Prohibition Act, 1961, Immoral Traffic (Prevention) Act, 1986, Indecent Representation of Women (Prohibition) Act, 1986, Commission of Sati (Prevention) Act, 1987, Child Marriage Restrain Act, 1929 as amended in 1956, National Commission for Women Act, 1990, Prenatal Diagnostic Techniques (Regulation and Prevention of Misuse) Act, 1994, Maternity Benefit Act, 1961, Protection of Women from Domestic Violence Act, 2005, Equal Remuneration Act, 1976, the Hindu Marriage Act, 1955 amended Act in 1976, The Marriage Amendment Act, 2001, the Immoral Traffic (Prevention) Act, 1956 as amended and renamed in 1986, Dowry Prohibition Act, 1961 and amended Act, 1984, Child Marriage Restrain Act, 1976, Medical Termination Pregnancy Act, 1971, the Indecent Representation of Women (Prohibition) Act, 1986, Commission of Sati (Prevention) Act, 1987, the Protection of Women from Domestic Violence Act, 2005.
11. According to Oxford Dictionary, Doctrinaire Research means adhering rigidly to the theories or principles often regardless of its practicality or appropriateness.
12. Yusuf Abdul Aziz *v.* State of Maharashtra, AIR 1954 SC 321.
13. Mohammed Ahmed Khan *v.* Shah Bano Begum, AIR 1985 SC 945; Also See Mrs. Mary Roy *v.* State of Kerala, AIR 1986 SC 1011.
14. Article 44 of the Constitution states that the State shall endeavour to secure for the citizens a uniform civil code throughout the territory of India.
15. Sheela Barse *v.* State of Maharashtra, AIR 1983 SC 378.
16. ibid
17. United Nations, Report of the Committee on the Elimination of Discrimination Against Women, Supp. No. 38, A/55/38, 22nd Session 17th January-4th February, 2000 and 23rd Session 12-30th June 2000, General Assembly Official Records, New York, 2000 at p. 8.
18. India's declaration to CEDAW. With regard to Articles 5(a) and 16(1) of the CEDAW, "the government of the republic of india declares that it shall abide by and ensure these provisions in conformity with its policy of non-interference in the personal affairs of any Community without the initiative and consent."
19. Concluding Observations of the Human Rights Committee, India, U.N. Doc. CCPR/c/79/Add.81 (1997)at http://www.umn.edu/humanrts/hrcommittee/india1997.html.(visited on 15/12/2010).
20. Gulam Abbas *v.* State of U.P, AIR 1981 SC 2198.
21. Tilakayat Shri Govindalalji Maharaj *v.* State of Rajasthan, AIR 1963 SC 1638.
22. A.S. Narayana *v.* State of A.P, AIR 1996 SC 1765.
23. Krishna Singh *v.* Mathura Ahir, AIR 1980 SC 707.
24. Article 25(2) of the Constitution stated that: "Nothing in this article shall affect the operation of any existing law or prevent the State from making any law:
    a) Regulating or restricting any economic, financial, political or other secular activity which may be associated with religious practice.
    b) Providing for social welfare and reform or the throwing open of

Hindus religious institutions of a public character to all classes and sections of Hindus.

Explanation I – the wearing and carrying of kirpans shall be deemed to be included in the profession of the Sikh religion.

Explanation II – In sub-clause (b) of the Clause (2), the reference of Hindus shall be construed asincluding a reference to persons professing the Sikh, Jains or Buddhist, religion and the reference to Hindu religious institutions shall be construed accordingly."

25. AIR 2000 SC 1650.
26. C. Masilamani *v.* idol of Sri Swaminathaswamy, AIR 1996 SC 1697.
27. Section 30 of the Hindu Succession Act stated that: Testamentary succession: Any Hindu may dispose of by will or other testamentary disposition any property, which is capable of being so disposed of by him, in accordance with the provisions of the Indian Succession Act, 1925 or any other law for the time being in force and applicable to Hinndus.
Explanation—The interest of a male Hindu in a Mitakshara coparcenary property or the interest of a member of a tarwad, tavazhi, illom, kutimba or kavaru in the property of the tarwad, tavazhi, illom, kutumba or kavaru in the property of the tarwad, tavazhi, illom, kutubu or kavaru chall, notwithstanding anything contained in this Act or in any other law for the time being in force, be deemed to be property capable of being disposed by him or by her within the meaning of this section.
28. AIR 1996 SC 1697; (1996)8 SCC 525).
29. AIR 1996 SC 1011.
30. Valasamma Paul *v.* Cochin University and others, AIR 1996 SC 1011, para. 25.
31. Article 1 of NIEO defined that "discrimination against women" to mean "any distinction, exclusion or restriction made on the basis of sex which has the effect or purpose of impairing or nullifying the recognized enjoyment or exercise by women, irrespective of their marital status on the basis of equality of men and women, all human rights and fundamental freedoms in the political, economic, social, cultural, civil or any other field."
Article 2(b) enjoins upon the State parties, while condemning discrimination against women in all its forms, to pursue, by appropriate means, without delay, elimination of discrimination against women by adopting "appropriate legislative and other measures including sanctions where appropriate prohibiting all discrimination against women; to take all appropriate measures including legislation, to modify or abolish existing laws, regulations, customs and practices which constitute discrimination against women.
Article 2(c) enjoins upon the State to ensure legal protection of the rights of women on equal basis with men, through constituted national tribunals and other public institutions against any act of discrimination to provide effective protection to women.
Article 3 enjoins upon the State parties that it shall take, in all fields, in particular, in the political, social, economic and cultural fields, all appropriate measures including legislation to ensure full development and advancement of women for the purpose of guaranteeing them the exercise

and enjoyment of human rights and fundamental freedoms on the basis of equality with men.

Article 13 states that "the State parties shall take all appropriate measures to eliminate discrimination against women in other areas of economic and social life in order to ensure, on a basis of equality of men and women".

32. (1996) 5 SCC 125.
33. The most obvious uses of CEDAW are in the area of gender equality. CEDAW has played an important role in the drafting, reform and judicial interpretation of the gender equality provisions in domestic constitutions in many countries. (Ruth Rubio-Martha I. Morgan, **Constitutional Domestication of International Gender Norms, in Gender and Human Rights** (Karen Knop, ed. Oxford University Press, 2004).
34. Article 2(e) of CEDAW states that 'to take all appropriate measures to eliminate discrimination against women by any person, organization or enterprise.'
35. Article 2(f) of the Protection of Human Rights Act, 1993 states that: 'International Covenant' means International Covenant on Civil and Political Rights, 1966, International Covenant on Economic, Social and Cultural Rights, 1966 adopted by the General Assembly of the United Nations on the 16th December 1966 (and such other covenant on Convention adopted by the General Assembly of the United Nations as the Central Government may by notification and specify.)
36. Article 3—States parties shall take in all fields, in particular in the political, social, economic and cultural fields, all appropriate measures, including, to ensure the full development and advancement of women, for the purpose of guaranteeing them the exercise and enjoyment of human rights and fundamental freedoms on a basis of equality with men.

Article 14—(1) States parties shall take into account the particular problems faced by rural women and the significant roles which rural women play in the economic survival of their families, including their work in the non-organized sectors of the economy, and shall take all appropriate measures to ensure the application of the provisions of the present Convention to women in rural areas.

(2) State parties shall take all appropriate measures to eliminate discrimination against women in rural areas in order to ensure, on a basis of equality of men and women, that they participate in and benefit from rural development and, in particular, shall ensure to such women the right.

Article 15—(1) State parties shall accord to women equality with men before the law,

(2) States parties shall accord to women, in civil matters, a legal capacity identical to that of men and the same opportunities to exercise the capacity. In particular, they shall give women equal rights to conclude contracts and to administer property and shall treat them equally in all stages of procedure in courts and tribunals.

(3) States parties agree that all contracts and all other private instruments

of any kind with a legal effect, which is directed at restricting the legal capacity of women, shall be deemed null and void.
(4) States parties shall accord to men and women the same rights with regard to the law relating to the movement of persons and the freedom to choose their residence and domicile.

37. Gita Hariharan *v.* Reserve Bank of India, AIR 1999 SC 1149.
38. Section 6(a) of Hindu Minority and Guardianship Act, 1956, stated that the natural guardian of a Hindu minor's person as well as in respect of the minor's property (excluding his or her undivided interest in joint family property) are in the case of a boy or unmarried girl—the father, and after him, the mother provided that the custody of a minor who has not completed the age of five years shall ordinarily be with the mother.
39. Section 19(b) of the Guardianship and Wards Act, 1890, describes that 'Nothing in this Chapter shall authorize the Court to appoint or declare a guardian of the property of a minor whose father is living and is not in the opinion of the Court, unfit to be guardian of the person of a minor whose father is living and is not, in the opinion of the Court, unfit to be guardian of the person of the minor.
40. As adopted and proclaimed by the UN General Assembly in its resolution No. 217 (III).
41. MANU/SC/0786/1997.
42. Article 11 of CEDAW states that:
    1. State parties shall take all appropriate measures to eliminate discrimination against women in the field of employment in order to ensure, on a basis of equality of men and women.
    2. In order to prevent discrimination against women on the grounds of marriage or maternity and to ensure their effective right to work, States parties shall take appropriate measures.
    3. Protective legislation relating to matters covered in this article shall be reviewed periodically in the light of scientific and technology knowledge and shall be revised, repealed or extended as necessary.
    Article 24 states that 'State parties undertake to adopt all necessary measures at the national level aimed at achieving the full realization of the rights recognized in the present Convention.
42. According to the Court, the objectives of the judiciary mentioned in the Beijing Statement are:
    a. To ensure that all persons are able to live securely under the Rule of Law;
    b. To promote, within the proper limits of the judicial function, the observance and the attainment of human rights; and
    c. To administer the law impartially among persons and between persons and the State.
43. According to the Court, the objectives of the judiciary mentioned in the Beijing Statement are:
    a. To ensure that all persons are able to live securely under the Rule of Law;
    b. To promote, within the proper limits of the judicial function, the observance and the attainment of human rights; and

c. To administer the law impartially among persons and between persons and the State.

44. 1999(1) SCALE 57 at 68; MANU/SC/0014/1999.
45. *Ibid.*, Para 28.
46. *Ibid.*, Para 30.
47. Gaurav Jain *v.* Union of India, MANU/SC/0789/1997.
48. (2000) I LLJ 846 SC.
49. Article 23 of UDHR declares that:
    1. Everyone has the right to work, to free choice of employment, to just and favourable conditions of work and to protect against unemployment.
    2. Everyone without any discrimination, has the right to equal pay for equal work.
    3. Everyone who works has the right to just and favourable remuneration ensuring for himself and his family an existence worthly of human dignity and supplemented, if necessary, by other means of social protection.
    4. Everyone has the right to form and to join trade union for the protection of his interests.
50. *Supra* 59.
51. Bodhisattwa Gautam *v.* Subhra Chakraborthy, AIR 1996 SC 922.
52. (2002)2 SCC 465; AIR 2000 SC 988.
53. AIR 2008 SC 663.

15

Socio-Legal Issues of Women in Mining Industry in India

N.B. Chandrakala

INTRODUCTION

Women are affected by mining as individuals, as workers and as community and family members. The health hazards and degeneration of health conditions of women and children is one of the most serious impacts of mining. Here women's health has to be understood from a larger perspective of direct and indirect impacts; the exposure of women and children to mine disasters and mine pollution as well as to the reduction in quality of life due to denial of access to food security, natural resources and livelyhoods. In India, this poses a much more dangerous situation as impacts of mining have been diverse depending on the nature of the minerals extracted and the extent of exploitation. Despite people suffering from several forms of ill-health, physical and mental deformities, constant exposure to toxic wastes and chronic diseases as a result of mining, there is a tragic gap in the availability of scientific studies and data on the health hazards of mining in India and more so, on the women in mining. The necessity for economic development has provided an ideal opportunity for mining industries to walk away from any responsibility towards the health of communities and workers they affect.[1]

The apathy, lack of understanding and political will, gross corruption of the government enhances the scope of the industry to continuity with impunity. As health issues are considered technical and scientific, the complaints and evidences from communities and workers, of the relations between mining operations and their ill-health are brushed under the carpet by the law implementing monitoring and judicial authorities, on the pretext of improper and inadequate scientific corroboration. Pitted against these forces are the women in the mining regions, whose health issues in general also, marginally addressed in the country.[2] Our development policy especially in the context of economic activities like mining, do not take into account women's health as important indices for human growth and development. Hence, mining is one of the largest sustainable industries. How true is this in the context of Indian women rural, tribal and urban poor who cannot articulate the victimization of their bodies for the extraction of minerals?

HEALTH IMPACTS OF MINING ON WOMEN

Women are employed in secondary activities such as cutting, sorting, quarrying and loading and unloading. Constant contact with dust and pollution and indirectly through contamination of water, air etc., cause severe health hazards to the women mineworkers. As majority of the women workers are contract laborers, and paid on a daily wage basis[3]. There is no economic security or compensation paid due to loss of workdays on account of health problems. Meager or no compensation is given during pregnancy period that puts a strain on incomes and health.

Even during pregnancy women have to work in hazardous conditions amidst noise, air pollution that have adverse effects on their off-springs. The work conditions, work timings, leave facilities, etc., and have significant impact on women's health. Children are also unsafe and indirectly affected right from conception and birth as women are forced to take their children to the mining areas and expose them to high levels of dust, pollution, mine explosives and accidents[4].

The women suffer from several occupational illnesses such as respiratory problems, silicosis, TB, arthritis etc., apart from terminal illness a more concurrent band chronic problem of women working in mines is the development of muscular and back pains, wearing out of joints spondilocys, etc. diseases of general physical incapacity in many unorganised firms the mine owners take very young people for work. In some places though the women were being given iron and mineral supplements they often suffer from these occupational hazards.[5]

Majority of health problems in mining regions are caused due to unchecked pollution and high levels of toxicity, mine tailings and mine disasters. the lands water bodies air and environment are polluted due to constant release of chemical wastes the dust generated by blasting and excavation and the dumping of mine wastes and over burden lands and neighbours.

ENVIRONMENTAL HAZARDS IN MINING PROJECTS

Mining from time immemorial as remain a major environmental concern . the mining of mineral resources weather by open cast or underground methods has adverse environment impact. The magnitude and significant impact varies depending up on the method of mining and beneficiation. The general environmental problems associated with most mining projects is depletion and degradation of existing surface water and aquifers, tailings leakage leaching from dumps , land degradation and large scale deforestation[6]. Despite laws and regulations constituted for the environmental protection of the mining areas, there are serious health hazards due to wastes generated from mines.

Hazardous mineral like asbestos whose extraction and processing have been banned in other countries are still being operated in India and the toxic implications on the environment and on their health as a result of this exposure.[7]

BLASTING AND MINE ACCIDENTS

Communities living around the mine sites are constantly vulnerable to mining accidents. Mining companies use explosives for blasting which result in houses cracking and accidents during working hours in the fields. Similarly mine pits around houses and agricultural fields may gradually get filled with contaminated water and debris and result in accidents. Companies often have not shouldered such responsibility for such accidents and neither pay compensation nor give medical treatment to the affected workers.

SEXUAL EXPLOITATION

As in many other areas discrimination is need towards employing women especially unmarried women and girls. They are the easy prays to the contractors, mining officials and other mine workers. Women working in mines rarely report sexual exploitation due to fear of loss of employment. Serious health problems such as aids and other communicable[8] diseases which are uncommon among tribal communities are becoming rampant in mining towns. Women living in the mining regions are highly susceptible for sexual assault.

Atrocities on women mostly by migrant workers contractors and mine owners and even higher level management staff are common in mining towns. For instance , in a remote tribal area of Vizag district in AP where Indian Rayons and industries was laying a road for a calcite mining project women complained of sexual assaults and gang rapes by the company staff members. In spite of several representations to the local authorities there was total apathy towards the situation.

LEGISLATIVE PROTECTION FOR WOMEN MINERS

In India the legislature has provided adequate safeguards for protection of women workers in mines[9]. The Mines Act, 1952 has laid down guidelines for the protection of workers employed in mines and regulates the working conditions and amenities for them. To ensure its implementation Mines Rules, 1955, Metali Ferrous Mines Regulation, 1961 and the Maternity Benefit (Mines) Rules, 1963 has been framed. The Mines Act was amended in 1983 to extend its scope. The 1993 National Mineral Policy addresses the issue of adverse effects of mining on the environment and recycling of metallic scrap and mineral wastes. Legal provisions related to abandonment and restorations of mines have been laid down by the Constitutional Mineral Conservation and Development Rules 1988 specify the need for providing a plan for dealing with in environment.

The Air (Prevention and Control of Pollution) Act[10] and Environment (Protection)[11] Act, provides safeguards for prevention of air pollution and emissions-related activities shall be controlled and kept in permissible limits.

CONCLUSION

Women working in Mines are detrimental to gender equality,

health and socio-economic conditions. The problems inherent in mining are the work conditions, work timings, leave facilities etc have significant impact on women's health. Despite of various legislative safe guards the environmental safety of mine workers especially women's situation neither has little improvement nor has been any benefits provided to them during their work or during accidents or disasters. Implementations of these laws are inadequate. Government has to set-up monitoring mechanisms to ensure better health and safety of women workers.

Notes and References

1. Bhanumathi, K., Status of women affected by mining in India: Mines, Minerals and People, India, www.samataindia.org.
2. S.M. Chaturvedi, 'Labour and Industrial Laws', 12th edition, 2001.
3. Rabi N. Misra, Sonali, Environment and Forest Resources Management, Edited by, 2008, viii, p.104.
4. Prof. S.N. Misra, Labour and Industrial Laws, 27th edition, 2013.
5. Dr. Meenu Paul, Labour and Industrial Law, 2001.
6. Prof. S.N. Misra, Labour and Industrial Law, 27th edition, 2013.
7. Rabi N. Misra, Sonali, Environment and Forest Resources Management, Edited by, 2008.
8. www.legalserviceindia.com.
9. The Mines Act, 1952.
10. The Air (Prevention and Control of Pollution) Act, 1981.
11. Environment (Protection) Act, 1986.

16

Right to Information in Women Empowerment

Y. PADMAJA RANI AND S. PADMAJA

"Yatra Naryanthu Pujithe Ramanthe thatra devatha".

"It is from women, the condemned one, that we are conceived and it is from her that we are born. It is to women that we are engaged, and married. It is she who keeps our race going. It is women through whom we establish our socialities. Then why denounce her from whom even the kings and the great men are born".

—Saint Guru Nanak

"You can tell the condition of a nation by looking at the status of its Women".

—Mr. Jawaharlal Nehru

INTRODUCTION

Ancient Period

Scholars believe that in India, the women enjoyed equal status with men in all fields of life. Works by ancient Indian grammarians such as Patanjali and Katyayana suggest that women were educated in the early Vedic period Rigvedic *versus* suggest that the women married at a mature age and were probably free to select their husband. Scriptures such as Rigveda and Upanishads mention several women sagas and seers, notably Gargi and Maitreyi. However, later (approximately 500 B.C.), the status of Women began to decline with the Smritis (Manusmriti) and the Islamic invasion of Babar and the Mughul empire and later Christianity curtails women's freedom and rights.

Medieval Period

The Indian Women's position in the society further deteriorated during the medieval period when Sati, Child marriages and a ban on widow remarriages because part of social life in India. The Muslim conquest in the Indian sub-continent brought the Purdah practice in the Indian Society. Among the Rajputs of Rajasthan, the Jauhar was practiced. In some parts of India, the Devadasis of the temple women were sexually exploited.

Inspite of these conditions, some women excelled in the fields of politics, literature, education and religion. Razia Sultana became the only woman monarch to have ever ruled Delhi. The Gond Queen Durgavathi ruled for fifteen years. Jahangir's wife Nur Jehan effectively wielded imperial power and was recognized as the real force behind the Mughal throne. Mughal princesses Jahanara and Zebunnisa were well known poets. In South India, many women administered villages, towns, divisions and added social and religion institutions.

British Rule Period: European scholars observed in the 19th Century that Hindu women are "naturally Chaste" and 'more virtuous' than other women. During the British Raj, many reformers such as Raja Ram Mohan Roy, Ishwar Chandra Vidyasagar, Jyothirao Phule etc., fought for the uplift of women all that efforts led to the abolition of Sati practice, child marriages, etc[1].

Independent India: Women in India now participate in all activities such as education, politics, media art and culture, service sectors, Science and Technology etc. Indira Gandhi who served as Prime Minister of India for an aggregate period of 15 years is the World's longest serving woman P.M. The status of any woman is determined by her rights, duties and liabilities *vis-à-vis* the society and family members. Any change in the Social pattern of society has it's impact on women. In our country where the main cultural trait is 'Mathru devo Bhava'—Mother is God, where everyone is supposed to hold woman in high esteem, statistics do speak in a different way. There is molestation every 26 minutes, cruelty every 33 minutes, kidnapping every 43 minutes, eve teasing every 51 minutes, rape every 54 minutes and dowry death every 102 minutes.

Women who sincere ancient ages were respected and worshipped as in carnation of Shakthi and today[2] victimized by Crimes not only from birth, but from 'Womb to tomb' for centuries past, women all over the world have not only been denied full justice, social, economic and political but as a weaker sex they have been denied full justice, social-economic and political but as a weaker sex they have been used, abused, exploited and discarded them to their fate and times. Women constitute about one half of the global positions due to gender difference and times immemorial.

ROLE OF RTI ACT IN WOMEN EMPOWERMENT

In many societies around the world, women never belong wholly to themselves; they are the property of others throughout their lives. Their physical well-being—health, security and bodily integrity—is often beyond their own control. Where women have no control over money, they cannot choose to get health care for themselves or their children. According to the United Nations Population Fund, around the globe, home and community are not safe havens for a billion girls and women: At least one in three females on earth has been physically or sexually abused, often repeatedly and often by a relative or acquaintance. By the World Bank's estimate, violence rivals cancer as a cause of morbidity and mortality for women of childbearing age. Even within marriage, women may not be able to negotiate when and what type of sex to have, nor to protest their husbands' multiple sex partners. Poverty and exclusion push some girls and women to engage in sex work, almost always the desperate, last choice of people without other choices.

Further, the U.S. Department of State indicates that up to 800,000 people are trafficked across international borders annually: 80 percent of these are women and girls, and the majority are forced into the sex trade. And in the midst of conflict and natural disaster in countries around the world, women's risk of violence skyrockets. Systematic rape as a weapon of war has left millions of girls and women traumatized, forcibly impregnated, and/or HIV positive.

These factors combined explain why today more women than men around the world are HIV positive.

Vulnerable sections of our society as they battle social and economic norms which are derogatory on humanitarian grounds. This is particularly true for women issues. Though we have crossed the first decade of the 21st century traditional patriarchal norms continue to relegate women to secondary status within the household and workplace. Even now women are married young in most parts of India, quickly become mothers, and are then burdened by stringent domestic and financial responsibilities. Consequently this drastically affects women's health, financial status, education, and political involvement. They are frequently malnourished since women typically are the last member of a household to eat and the last to receive medical attention. Additionally, only 54 percent of Indian women are literate as Compared to 76 percent of men. Women receive little schooling and also suffer from unfair and biased inheritance and divorce laws. These laws prevent women from accumulating substantial financial assets, making it difficult for women to establish their own security and autonomy. On the work front women are still abysmally paid compared to their counterpart and sexual harassment is commonplace. While eve teasing is rampant on Indian roads of late rape and molestations have increased making it imperative for women to be aware of self defense measures. In that context the RTI can be a real savior. This paper looks at RTI case studies and tries to find out how it has worked for women. Women have been at the centre of this movement as sixty percent of the members of Mazdoor-kisan Shakti Anghathan (MKSS) are women. It is these women and men who provide the breadth of vision that characterises MKSS. For them, the RTI is not just a campaign for the right to information. It is a campaign that links together all the natural rights of citizenship—to food, to wages, to work, to dignity, and to a life free of violence.

Right to information entitles the citizens of a country to have the right of access to official information held or in the custody of the government thus promoting transparency and accountability. Once citizens know what their government is doing on their behalf they are in a better position to monitor and where necessary hold those in public offices accountable for their decisions, actions or non-action.

However[1], if we specially talk about role of right to information in women's empowerment, then yes this Act has the potential in its own way in creating conditions for the woman to take recourse to a better well-informed decision-making process, even in her day-to-day life. Right to Information Act facilitates women self dependency while continuing of access to information and technology affects people in general and in most cases women are most affected and the advancement of women has been affected by lack of access to vital information that relates to their rights, therefore the availability of an Act that guarantees free access to relevant and timely information is crucial for women's empowerment.

Moreover, with this Act in place, women can also access information on issues like domestic violence, harassment at workplaces, whether police is refusing to register an FIR in serious dowry related cases and deaths. Of late, Vinita Kamte wife of IPS Officer Ashok Kamte who died fighting attackers during 26/11 Mumbai attack in her Book To The Last Bullet brought to the light the various lapses on part of the Indian security system that lead to the killing of many including Ashok Kamte. The expose was based on the information gathered with the provision of Right to Information Act in place. In an interview to the news portal Vinita Kamte clearly stated that the post-mortem report of the deceased police officer was also obtained through a request made under Right to Information Act.

RTI not only strengthens women in difficult circumstances but also make things better for school and college girl dropouts, women with disabilities, women entrepreneurs, women SHG leaders, grassroots women leaders and women in general.

It is said[3] that when one is equipped with knowledge in various aspects a lot of mishaps can be prevented, hence, information is a boon to women's empowerment and Gender Equality. Lack of information leads to hindrance to lot of things such access to health, education, social and economic reforms, etc. Information Act certainly accelerates the empowerment process of women and since world now recognizes the fact that women are the accepted agents of development and the crucial role that women play in development process. Acknowledging the huge potential especially in the group dynamics of women Self Help Groups it becomes essential that these SHG make efforts to build intra and inter-social group alliances so as to build them as a formidable force and increase their bargaining power to push government to implement the rights that are available to women in definitive term in the forms of legal entitlements, case law judgments, government schemes and programmes and budgetary allocations. Beyond being a fundamental right in itself, Right to Information also crucially facilitates the exercise of other rights.

Therefore, it is necessary to explore how successful Right to Information Act is in the context of woman issues.

RTI FOR LEGITIMATE RIGHTS

Individual women have certainly received help as we see Khetramani Samantrai recovering her right to land because of RTI. She had been constantly visiting the district office for the last one and a half years for her original land deed but the clerk concerned did not hand over the documents to them. While this case may happen irrespective of gender, women have also been able to fight such distinctions through RTI.

RTI FOR GENDER INEQUALITY

In India gender inequality plagues the society. In many areas of life women are not deemed fit to carry out the responsibilities compared to men. The RTI can bring relief as in the case of the women of Ramgarh village in Chhattarpur district in Madhya Pradesh's drought-affected Bundelkhand. They have battled administrative apathy and non-cooperation by elected representatives to find a solution to the severe water problem they were facing. With the help of Mahila Samiti, the women used the right to information (RTI) to get relevant information to press for their demands. The long-drawn-out struggle began in February 2006 when women belonging to three self-help groups in Ramgarh, formed by Mahila Samiti, called a meeting to discuss the villager's water problem. At the meeting it was pointed that there was water in one of the village wells, but that the well had to be deepened and a parapet built around it to ensure that the water remained clean and that there were no accidents. The women decided to ask the men of the village to attend a meeting the following day, to discuss how the task could be undertaken. The next morning, the men joined the meeting and volunteered to help deepen the well. A sum of Rs. 200 was collected from each family and the digging began. However, work had to be discontinued in April when, after digging up to 20 feet, they struck solid rock. Paan Bai recalls: "This took us by surprise. We did not have the money to call for a machine. So we just gave up."

The women then made their way to the Mahila Samiti office in Chhattarpur, and it was decided to use the RTI Act to get information on the availability of funds from the district panchayat. One of the women, Benni Bai Ahirwar, says: "We got a right to information form and, with the help of some Mahila Samiti field workers, fighting Social Injustice, Getting justice in a rape case is an uphill task and evidence can play a crucial role. When Sabruddin's daughter's rapists due to legal nuances were not getting proper punishment he turned to the Right to Information Act in a bid to pin the accused down. Sabruddin filed an application at the district magistrate's office under the Act. He sought information on whether three of the accused, who were lodged in a juvenile jail, were actually minors. While surrendering in court, the trio had submitted documents which said they were minors. Sabruddin used RTI to find out whether the trio had armed licenses. If it was proved that they had such licenses then they would not be juvenile. His daughter had also said that the prime accused was not a juvenile. Through RTI he also sought to find out whether the three accused had driving licenses then he would be able to prove that they did not fit the juvenile description. The case demonstrates the power of RTI in supporting women victims of social injustice.

CONCLUSION

Yet the main failure of the Act has been that it has not been invoked. Even in the urban region people are not aware properly about the different circumstances under which the right to Information Act is applicable. Due to illiteracy and also lack of proper knowledge most of the time women are not aware of their rights. For this actually the participation from women activist group or self help group is needed. The Act is there, provisions are there to implement it but participation is missing as they don't know how to participate, an awareness level of men is 26% while for women it is only 12%. RTI properly implemented can be a boon to the women. But that women need to come forward to claim their right. The Mahila Samitis also need to play a crucial role in educating the advantages of utilizing the RTI. Though the act has certainly elevated the position of the women lot more can be done. As Aruna Roy, the protagonist of RTI points out that the presence of women is essential for, according to Ms. Roy, women instinctively understand what it is to be marginalized, and, over time, men in the movement have begun to understand the importance of involving women. Women fear to complain about violence, for fear of security or loss of social image.

Delayed process in setting of cases . technicalities of law coming in the way of justice system. Lack of adequate social support with in and outside the home. Effective legal measures should be taken for implementation of laws.

Regrettable, due to the lack of awareness about the essential link between Right to Information and women's well-being that there is a limited participation of women in regards to it. Therefore, in this regard women's organization need to create, develop and invest is sustained training education and capacity building on Right to Information Act as a crucial element for all organizations working with woman's rights, special emphasis need to brought to bear on the linkages between women's rights, social justice, public participation, reform and the capacity of women to engage with these issues through information. The linkage between the participation and realization of almost all other rights cannot happen or envisaged without information itself.

Notes and References

1. Law relating to women by Dr. T. Padma, K.P.C. Rao.
2. The Law relating to Human Rights by Lohit, D. Naikar.
3. Miles to go effectiveness of RTI for Women by Madhuka Bakshi, Kolkat, did not receive the original documents in spite of producing the receipt of the deed. On 13th July 2006 she went to the RTI camp held in Bhubaneswar, seeking guidance as to how she could redress her grievances using RTI. The case was discussed with the Public Information Officer (PIO) of the DSO. When the volunteers insisted in registering the complain through RTI, the PIO intervened and asked the officials to look into the case and produce the land deed papers immediately. The head clerk then produced the document in 15 minutes and officially handed it over to Khetramani who finally got justice after resorting to the RTI tool.

17

Legal Aid to Women

I. RAMA SUNDARI AND N.B. CHANDRAKALA

INTRODUCTION

In India, women represent half of the population, but status of women is not remarkable in the society. In a society where glaring social injustice and exploitation, inequality of status and opportunity inequality of income exist, there is no room for equality. In the early vedic period women enjoyed a position on par with men. They were considered as "two wheels of the same chariot". In Rig Veda period women were even exalted to the position of goddesses. We have masculine names like Laxminarayana, Sita Rama, Ramasatyanarayana, etc. Most of the female names of rivers are Ganga, Yamuna, Saraswati, etc. The status of women was deteriorated in Muslim period, several restrictions were imposed on her rights. During the British reign, in the later half of the 20th century, Legislations were framed to protect the women rights but their implementation is not effective. Women were denied of rights. They were subjected to Gender discrimination, harassment, violence and exploitation of labor. The constitution aimed at giving women equal status as men by laying Fundamental Right of Equality.

The constitution guarantees rights of equality,[1] life, liberty to women. Women due to poverty and ignorance of rights are unable to fights against violation of rights and to seek remedy in a court of law. Women suffered from inequality on economic and social plane for centuries and now it is high time it needs to be removed by the constitutional process and perhaps the implementation of Directive Principles enshrined in Part IV of the Constitution would be right step in this direction. The Core issue of 'equal justice to all' and the attention of the Bar, Bench and Law Reformers during the post-independence era and all efforts are being made to protect the rights of women. Access to the court depends upon the payment of court fees and fee of lawyer. In so far as the woman is unable to obtain access to courts of law due to poverty and ignorance, for protection of rights, justice has become unequal, laws which are meant for her protection have no meaning and to that extent fail in their purpose. Hence, the concept of Legal Aid has adopted to provide equal access to justice. Legal aid is the only way to provide equal opportunity to obtain justice.

LEGAL AID

Legal aid, as a significant welfare right, is not the exclusive product of political right to seek defense in a court of law. But it is an outcome of the twentieth century struggle against poverty to ensure just human living to the people at large. In the traditional sense, legal aid included appointment of a lawyer at the expense of state, exemption of court fee, process fee other payable fee. In its wider sense, legal aid also includes public interest litigation, Lok Adalats, Legal Literacy; which are important limbs of legal aid.

The new encyclopedia Britannica defines legal aid as the professional legal assistance given, either free or for a nominal sum, to indigent persons in need of such help.[2] Lord Denning[3] has aptly, observed that "Since the second world war, the greatest revolution in the law has been the mechanism and evolution of the system of legal aid and it is a fundamental human right.

Dr. N.R Madhava Menon,[4] academician and legal aid activist defines "Legal Aid means not only a representation through lawyer at state expense in court proceedings but will include legal advice, legal awareness, legal mobilization, public interest litigation, law reform and a variety of strategic and preventive services which instead of assisting such individuals on a case-by-cases will help them as a class to avoid helplessness arising from poverty and promote equal access to justice."

Justice Krishna Iyer and Justice Bhagawati are the pioneers of Legal Aid Movement.

According to Iyer, An effective legal service programme covers three distinct services: (1) Legal Aid; (2) Legal Advice; and (3) Preventive Service. While the first item of legal service, namely, Legal Aid is purely litigation-oriented, the second item, Legal Advice, refers to advice on legal problems which may arise in the life of an individual and it may include drafting of documents and negotiations with a view to settling a dispute so that it does not require to be taken before a Court or Tribunal. The third item of Legal Service is preventive Service, which a legal service organization can render to the poor as a class. Its sole purpose is to prevent, on a mass scale, through education, instructional changes, organization of the poor etc., the innumerable injustices which the poor as a class suffer and from which it is apprehended, there is no escape for them except by revolution.[5]

INTERNATIONAL PARAMETERS OF LEGAL AID

At the International Plane, Legal Aid as Human Right is implicit in the covenants, conventions, obliges the state responsibility to provide legal aid which ratify them. Legal services were provided in countries like USA, UK, Canada, Spain, Denmark, obliging the state to provide legal service, at state cost to be represented by professional lawyers and public defenders.

Universal Declaration of Human Rights 1948, recognised indirectly the provision relating to legal aid. The declaration of Human Rights[6] was adopted by the General Assembly on December 10, 1948.

The group of Articles dealing with Legal Aid is Art.7, 8, 10. The Right to Legal Aid under this Article is based on the principle of equality that no one should be denied the opportunity of fair trial because of his/her indigence. These equality rights can be effective only when individuals are given opportunity to obtain legal aid and assistance when required so that they may have access to the Courts for a fair and impartial trial. Article 8 provides that everyone has the right to an effective remedy by the competent national tribunals for acts violating fundamental rights granted to him by the Constitution or by other laws. Article 10 provides that everyone is entitled in full equality to a fair and public hearing by an independent and impartial tribunal, in the determination of his rights and obligations and of any criminal charge against him. Here, guarantee has been given that equality will be maintained to a fair hearing in civil as well as in criminal cases.

The European Convention on Human Rights, 1953: Right to Legal Aid, Remedy & Equality. Article 6(3)(c) of the conventions deals with Legal Aid in Criminal cases. Article 6(3)(c) provides that "Every one charged with a criminal offence has to defend himself in person or through legal assistance of his own choosing, or, if he has no sufficient means to pay for Legal Assistance, to be given it free when the interests of justice so require". The Convention provides Legal aid, to a person charged with a criminal offence, to defend himself. The rights under this convention are the right to life and a general right of non-Discrimination. Article 13 of the convention provides that everyone, rights and freedoms as set forth in this Convention are violated shall have an effective remedy before a national authority notwithstanding that the violation has been committed by persons acting in an official capacity. Article 14 of the Convention provides that "the enjoyment of rights and freedoms set forth in this convention shall be secured without Discrimination on any ground such as sex, race, colour, language, religion, political or other opinions, national or Social Origin, associated with a national minority, property, birth or other status.

INTERNATIONAL COVENANT OF CIVIL AND POLITICAL RIGHTS, 1966

The Declaration of Human Rights was also followed by two significant instruments, which transformed the principles enunciated in the Declaration into treaty provisions and established legal obligation on the part of each ratifying country. These instruments were: International Covenant on Civil and Political Rights and its optional protocol, and The International Covenant on Education, Social and Cultural Rights. Civil and political rights are sometimes called the 'first generation' of human rights[7].

Article 26: All persons are equal before the law and are entitled without any discrimination to the equal protection of the law. In this respect, the law shall prohibit any discrimination and *guarantee* to all persons equal and effective protection against discrimination on any ground such as race, colour, sex, language, religion, political or other opinion, national or social origin, property, birth or other status.

The American Convention on Human Rights: Legal Aid is implicitly mentioned in Convention under Articles 7, 8, and 24. The right to free legal services is an essential ingredient of fair trial for a person accused of offence and it is implicit in the guarantee of Art.8. The detenue right to consult legal counsel is provided to protect the liberty of person.

CONSTITUTIONAL FRAMEWORK OF LEGAL AID

The coin word in the preamble is" we the people of India". It connotes that constitution was adopted and enacted by the people of India. The preamble speaks of justice, social, economic, political and equality of status and opportunity. The constitution inscribes justice at the first promise of the Republic, specifying the constitutional goal is to protect the interest of the weaker sections of the society and poor. Article 14[8]. Mandates Equality before law and Equal Protection of Laws to all. Indian Constitution not only proclaims equal justice in the preamble but also guarantees equal justice to all under Art.14. The principle of equality imbedded in Art. 14 provides Legal Aid without any discrimination to equal access to law and justice. Article 21[9] protects the life or personal liberty of every person. It guarantee against the deprivation of personal liberty. Person cannot be deprived of his life or liberty except according to the procedure established by law. The procedure to deprive person liberty is fair, just and reasonable. The Right to Free Legal Service is an essential ingredient of reasonable, fair and just procedure for an accused person and is implicit in Art. 21. Every arrested person has right to consult and to be defended by legal practitioner of his choice. The right to representation by counsel is essential to fair-trial.

Directive Principles of State Policy and Legal Aid

Part-IV deals with Directive Principles which are fundamental in the Governance of State. Art 38[10] mandates the state to laydown policies to promote the welfare of the people and to secure social order. (State to promote a just social order and socio-economic justice). On the recommendation of Mr. Swaran Singh Committee, a new Article 39-A was inserted by the constitutional (42) Amendment Act, 1976. Legal Aid has become a constitutional directive under 39-A, to ensure equal justice as promised in preamble and equality. In pursuance of 39-A, the Legal Service Authority Act, 1987 was enacted to provide legal assistance.

Legal aid and the criminal procedure code: Section 304 of the Cr.P.C. 1974 confers the accused the right of legal aid at the expense of the government in cases triable by court of session and (appeals).

Order XXXIII of civil procedure code (Amendment Act, 1976) deals with indigent person's right to have Legal Aid.

Judicial Recognition of Right to Legal Aid as Fundmental Right

The Supreme Court recognised Right to Legal Aid is a fundamental right under Art. 21 and it has reinforced by 39-A.[11] The Supreme Court[12] held that free legal aid to the indigent and poor accused is implicit under Art. 21 of the constitution. The court observed "Right to Speedy Trial" as a Fundamental Right is implicit in the guarantee of life and personal liberty as enshrined in Art. 21 of the constitution.

In *Hoskot case*[13], Supreme Court held that the right of appeal is implicit in Art. 21. The court issued guidelines to the Prison Authorities to furnish copy of judgment to convicted persons at free of cost so that the service of lawyer can be made available to him and if he is poor or indigent, the state shall pay remuneration for the lawyer. The Supreme Court in decided cases held that right to counsel implies Right to have an effective and experienced Lawyers.[14] The court observed that it is a mandatory duty on the magistrate to inform the poor accused persons the right to have legal assistance. The court vitiated the trial on the ground that state has not provided legal representation to accused. The judicial precedents reveal that state irrespective of financial ability, duty is cast to provide legal assistance to poor at state cost. Legal aid is not charity, it is constitutional imperative.

LEGAL SERVICES AUTHORITIES ACT, 1987[15]

Under the spirit of 39-A of the constitution the Parliament enacted The Legal Services Authority Act, 1987. The object of the Act is three-fold, to Constitute Legal Services Authorities, to provide free and competent legal services to the weaker sections of the society to ensure that opportunities for securing justice are not denied to any citizen by reason of economic or other disabilities and to organize Lok-Adalats to secure that the operations of the legal system promotes justice on a basis of equal opportunity. The Act came into force from 1995. It was amended by the Legal Service Authorities (Amendment) Act 1994, (59 of 1994), 1996 (1 of 1996), and 2002, (37 of 2002).

The Act Defines Legal Services Under Section 2(c) including the rendering of any service in conduct of any case or other legal proceeding before any court or other authority or tribunal and the giving of advise on any Legal matters. The Act empowered the State to establish a Four Tier System of providing speedy and informal justice at the National, State, District and Taluk Levels. Accordingly, Legal Services Authorities have been constituted at the National Level, State Level and District Level wherein the services of the bench, the bar and other persons in the allied fields like legal education and social services are being utilized.

Sections 3 to 5 of the Legal Services Authority Act deals with the National Legal Services Authority, to supervise and regulate legal services throughout the country. The power to constitute this authority vests with the Central Government. The National Legal Services Authority is a statutory body which has been set-up on 5th December, 1995 for implementing and monitoring legal aid programmes in the country. The Legal Aid is not a matter of charity but it can be claimed as a matter of right. For a long period, legal aid has been a subject of governmental policy and the National Legal Aid Programme has been organized through various rules and schemes sponsored by the State Governments.

NATIONAL LEGAL SERVICES AUTHORITIES SCHEMES

- Establishing Permanent and Continuous Lok Adalats in all the Districts in the country for disposal of pending matters as well as disputes at pre-litigative stages.
- Establishing separate Permanent and Continuous Lok Adalats for Government.
- Accreditation of NGOs for legal Literacy and Legal Awareness campaign.
- Appointment of "Legal Aid Counsel" in all the Courts of Magistrates in the country.
- Publicity to Legal Aid Scheme and programmes to make people aware about legal aid facilities.
- Emphasis on competent and quality legal services to the aided persons.
- Legal aid[16] facilities in jails.
- Setting up of Counseling and Conciliation Centers in all the Districts in the Country.
- Sensitisation of judicial Officers in regard to Legal Services Schemes and Programmes.
- Publication of "Nyaya Deep", the official newsletter of NALSA.

The National Legal Literacy Mission (NLLM) was constituted by National Legal Service Authorities: Its main object is to empower the poor and disadvantaged persons, particularly woman and children through legal literacy by making them aware of their rights; to lead them to live their life with dignity and to enjoy equality before law, to ensure justice and further facilitating them in this respect through free legal service programmer available under the Legal Service Authorities Act, 1987.

Address of Supreme Court Legal Services Committee[17]

Central Public Information Officer for Supreme Court Legal Services Committee, 108, Lawyers Chambers, Supreme Court Compound, New Delhi, Ph : 011-23388313.

Appellate Authority

Shri P.K. Bajaj, Deputy Registrar, Supreme Court of India and Secretary, Supreme Court Legal Services Committee, 108, Lawyers Chambers, Supreme Court Compound, New Delhi, Ph : 011-23073970

Andhra Pradesh State Legal Services Authority

The A.P. State Legal Service Authority with an intention to facilitate access to justice for all formulated a positive plan of Action for efficient and effective dispension of Legal Services, it includes. Constitution of High Court Legal Service Committee, 23, DLSA and 108, Mandal L.S. committees. The scheme of APSLSA are:

- Establishment of Permanent Lok Adalats u/s. 22B of L.S. Act.
- Expansion of Lok Adalat net and organization of Mega Lok Adalat.
- Appointment of Full Time Secretaries for DLSA.
- Celebrating Nation Legal Service Day on 9th Nov.
- Delivery of Legal Services by phone, post, legal counseling.

MODES OF DELIVERY OF LEGAL SERVICES[18]

1. *By Phone*: On 8th November, 2005. A Toll Free Telephone Number 1800-425-2999 was installed in the office of the A.P. State Legal Services Authorities and Services are available to the public for receiving Legal Services and Legal advice free of cost.

2. *By Post* : The Authorities attends to the representation received by Post from the public, renders legal aid and advice.
3. *Legal Counseling*: The Authority organized counseling centers at every district, and also organizing special counseling centers such as jail counseling, juvenile counseling, family counseling, etc. to make the people understand about relevant enactments and the bring them to amicable settlement in all the compoundable and petty cases.
4. *Para Legal Volunteers*: To identified and trained para-legal Volunteers to act as effective co-ordinators between the L.S.A. and the needy and deserving citizens.

A SCHEME FOR THE PROJECT OF PARA-LEGAL VOLUNTEERS (Under the Plan of Action for the year 2009-2010)[19]

The Project of Para-Legal Volunteers is aimed at imparting legal awareness to volunteers selected from certain target groups who in turn act as harbingers of legal awareness and legal aid to all sections of people. The Volunteers are expected to act as intermediaries between the common people and Legal Services institutions and thereby removing barriers of access to justice. Initially, the volunteers are identified from the NSS units in Colleges, creditworthy NGOs and credible social organizations and Women Self Help Groups.

THE NATIONAL LEGAL SERVICES AUTHORITY (LEGAL AID CLINICS) SCHEME, 2010

The Legal Aid Clinics, set-up under this scheme are of two types. Clinic Constituted by Legal Service Institutions and permanent legal aid clinic in law colleges in University. The aim of the Scheme is to provide an inexpensive local machinery for rendering legal services of basic nature like legal advice, other services like preparing applications for job card under the MGNREGA Scheme, liaison with the government offices and public authorities and helping the common people who come to the clinic for solving their problems with the officials, authorities and other institutions also shall form part of the legal services in the legal aid clinic.

- Organization of workshops and seminars

- Providing Legal Services to victims of trafficking and HIV and preparing plans for implementation of "Naya Sankalp Project.
- Rendering Legal Service to Prisoners. Maintaining, Keeping Grievance boxes in the prison, establishing legal aid cells in prison. Appointment Legal Aid Counsel.
- To give training to Legal Aid Workers in Alternative Dispute Resolution.
- To spread Legal awareness and legal literacy through organizing camps.
- Tendering proper legal advice offices.
- Appointment of Legal Aid Counsel and Duty Counsel.
- Evolution of uniform policy for implementation of Sec. 89 of the code of Civil Procedure.
- Rending Legal Service to the Mentally challenged people.

The Address of A.P. High Court Legal Services Committee[20]

Nyaya Seva Sadan, City Civil Court Complex, Puranihaveli, Hyderabad Tele Fax Nos. 040-23446704 Website apslsa.ap.nic.in Secretary:040-23446704, (Districts & Sessions Judge) 9440621436.

DISTRICT LEGAL SERVICES AUTHORITIES

The Honorable High Court of A.P. and the A.P.S.L.S.C. have posted judicial officers of the rank of senior civil judge as full time secretaries for the DLSA. The Secretaries conduct their offices at District Head Quarters at Nyaya Seva Sadan situated in District Court premises performs their duties and functions to achieve the objectives of the Act. Under the direct supervision and control of Chairman DLSA and the Secretary shall also act as Nodal Officer in the district for implementation of Legal Service Activities. In order to promote legal service activities, Secretary convenes meetings; organize seminars and workshops and also interactive sessions for legal awareness with different cross-sections of the society

APPOINTMENT OF LEGAL AID COUNSEL AND DUTY COUNSEL

Legal Aid Counsel: The Secretaries of DLSA with the approval of the Chairman appoints legal aid counsel on the basis of merit and seniority to provide legal aid to all needy citizens, particularly to prisoners, to provide legal aid to under-trial prisoners, in remand hour and other eligible categories (S. 12 women). They shall submit monthly report to the DLSA, giving particulars of remand. The duty of secretaries is to regulate monitor the performance of services of Legal Aid Counsel and report to the A.P. State Legal Services Authority once in every quarter.

Duty Counsel: Authorities prepares the panel of Advocates, willing to take up legal aid cases. They will assign the brief of the legal Aid beneficiaries to the duty counsel. Secretaries interact with legal aid beneficiaries periodically and enquire about the progress of the case and difficulties facing in conducting the cases.

Address: Secretary District Legal Services Authority, Visakhapatnam, Ph.9440901061.

Secretary District Legal Services Authority, Vizianagaram, Ph. 9440901062.

The Vital Part of this Act, is Chapter XII Secs.12 and 13 provisions provide free legal services to those enlisted under Sec. 12[21] Every person who has to file or defend a case shall be entitled to legal services under this Act if that person is-Sec.12(c) a woman[22]

Legal Service Authorities: Alternative Dispute Resolution Techniques

As a part of the Preventive Strategic Legal Aid Programme the Legal Services Authorities are adopting various techniques of ADR to prevent litigation at an initial stage such as Mediation, Conciliation, Negotiation and Counseling. It is noteworthy that Counseling Centers are established by the Government Departments, i.e. Women and Child Welfare Department, Commission to give advise to Women, to solve women problems, in cases where problems were not solved for those issues legal assistance to be provided.

SPECIAL PROGRAMMES FOR WOMEN

The Legal Service Authorities Organize special prorammes for women.

Mahila Lok Adalat: For settlement of pre-litigation disputes and pending cases of matrimonial and family nature a permanent Lok Adalat bench is constituted. The Authorities conduct seminars and workshop relating to women problems and measures to eradicate it and to protect the interest of women.

Welfare of Devadasis: A regional initiative is organized on 10th & 11th September, 2005 at Tirupathi Temple Town on challenges faced by the society in liberation of Devadasi from the Traditional bondage stigmas and the discrimination and significance of legal literacy and contribution of legal aid in empowerment of such vulnerable communities. Participation from the States of A.P., Tamil Nadu, Karnataka and Maharashtra has attended the Summit.

"Naya Sanklap" Project for Prevention of Trafficking and HIV/ AIDS.

The Authorities conducts special programmes for women:

1. National Legal Aid Week for Women—1st March to 8th March
2. National Legal Literacy Week for Women – 8th March to 15th March.
3. Benefit of Mother's Breast Feeding Children in the first week of August every year.
4. National Legal Services Day – 9th Nov.
   - I. May Day – 01st May
   - II. World Mental Health Day – 10th Oct – World Dental Health Week
   - III. Children's Day – 14th November
   - IV. Legal Aid Cell for Women.

The Authorities constitutes Legal Aid Cell for women for effective implementation of the protection of women from Domestic Violence providing legal aid to the victims and to provide assistance to the protection officers and service provider in implementation of the Act.

Legislation relating to Women: Legal literacy and legal aid.

NATIONAL COMMISSION FOR WOMEN ACT (1990)

The National Commission for Women was set-up as statutory body under the National Commission for Women Act, 1990 in January 1992. The commission has endeavored to uplift the status of women in the society and tackle the issues of speedy justice, child marriage, awareness of women, etc.

The Protection of Human Rights Act, 1993

The National Human Rights Commission and State Human Rights Commission has endeavored to give a positive meaning and content to the objectives set out in the Protection of Human Rights Act, 1993 for better protection of human rights. The function of the commission is to create awareness, sensitizing public authorities for promoting and protecting human rights in the country.

The Family Courts Act, 1984 is intended to "promote conciliation in, and secure speedy settlement of disputes relating to marriage and family affairs and for matters connected therewith". In all such cases, the primary objective is to preserve the institution of marriage and to promote the welfare of children through settlement of disputes by conciliation and counseling. For the first time, the law provides for judges to take the assistance of professionals, counselors, medical experts and NGOs.[23] In a radical departure, parties are not entitled to take, as of right, the assistance of lawyers. Section 13 provides for the appointment of the lawyer to be an exception and not the rule . The Bombay High Court as expressed the view that Section 13 does not bar the presence of the advocate and whenever necessary the court should freely make available the services of the advocate. The court functions with the assistance of services like family counseling and reconciliation service, legal aid service and enforcement service.

THE PROTECTION OF WOMEN FROM DOMESTIC VIOLENCE ACT, 2005

The phenomenon of domestic violence is deep-routed in our social and personal life. Among all types of violence against women domestic violence is the most serious one because it happens silently. Domestic violence is undoubtedly a human rights issue and serious deterrent to development. It is, therefore, proposed to enact a law keeping in view the rights guaranteed under Articles 14, 15 and 21 of the Constitution to provide for a remedy under the civil law which is intended to protect the women from being victims of domestic violence and to prevent the occurrence of domestic violence in the society. *The Protection of Women from Domestic Violence Act*, 2005 was enacted toProvide for more effective Protection of the rights of women guaranteed under the constitution who are victims of domestic violence[24] of any kind occurring within the family. The very nomenclature indicates that the Domestic Violence Act is not restricted to violence perpetrated against a woman by her husband or in-laws. It includes under its protective umbrella every woman living in a domestic relationship as member of a family with the person indulging in violence who in this case must invariably be of the male gender.

For the first time a great departure is made under this Act enabling women to fight out for her rights being in the house of her husband or the person with whom she has been residing. She can be of any relationship with the respondent of the nature of marriage or adoption. Therefore, for the first time civil relief is vested with Magistrate[25], doing criminal work. Even under section 125 of Cr.P.C. which governs the maintenance aspect, is primarily intended to provide expeditious monetary relief to prevent the wife, children of parents being driven to penury become destitute. In fact the aspect of maintenance is integral part of Hindu adoption and Maintenance Act and other related enactments. The Domestic Violence Act is a step further where under a woman can obtain protection order, primarily intended to keep the women under a same roof along with the respondent and she along with her children coming under the above category being provided with maintenance in the shape of monetary order and similar other orders. The Act has been designed to create certain civil rights, some declaratory (for example, the right to protection against domestic violencc) and some substantive (for example, the right to maintenance, right to compensation on account of the domestic violence, right to reside in a shared household, right to custody of children, right to medical expenses, etc.) It shall be the duty of the Protection Officer to assist the Magistrate in the discharge of his functions under this Act; to maintain a list of all service providers providing legal aid or counseling, shelter homes and medical facilities in a local area within the jurisdiction of the Magistrate. One of the most important features of the Act is the woman's right to secure housing. This right is secured by a residence order, which is passed by the Magistrate.

LEGAL AID AND GOVERNMENT DEPARMENT

Women Child Welfare Department

Project Director, Women & Child Welfare Development Acts as a Protection Officer discharge functions as define under Section 5 of the Domestic Violence Act. The complainant, will be given assistance, like counselling, police assistance, shelter home, medical facilities and legal Aid. The Department provides Advocate for Women Victim.

CONCLUSION

Gender Discrimination, still exist in modern society. Women were exploited and subject to violence like child marriage, dowry, domestic violence, etc. The principal beneficiary under Legal Services Authority Act being Woman, she can approach and avail free Legal

Services from the Legal Services Authorities. Legal literacy and Legal Awareness is the only road which lead the suffering majority, to the door of equality and access to Justice. Women to be conscious of their rights and obligations, then only through Legal process she can have remedy for her rights. Legal Aid functionaries should strive for effective implementation of policies to safeguard the interest of Women. It is a social obligation on the part of Legal Luminaries, Academicians, Advocates and Para Legal, Voluntaries to create Legal Awareness and to provide Legal protection to Women.

Notes and References

1. Article 15(1) of the constitution of India grants Equality to women. Article 15(3) empowers the state to make special provisions for the protection of Women and children. Article 16 (1) guarantees equality of opportunity to Women in Public Employment.
2. The New Encyclopedia Britannica, Vol. 1974 (ed.), p. 122.
3. Jitendra Bhatt, Not a closing chapter Lord Denning: A Don or Doyen? In the realm of law reforms and legal aid. N. Madras Law Journal 1999(2) pp. 2-6.
4. N.R. Madhav Menon, Legal Aid and Justice for the Poor (Article) in Upendera Baxi (ed.) Law and Poverty: Critcal Essays 1988, p. 366.
5. Report of the Legal Aid Committee (Government of Gujarat), (1971), p. 127.
6. Gen. Ass. Resolution 217-A (iii) of 10 December, 1948, Gen.Ass.Official Records, Third Session, Part I. Resolutions (U.N. DOC.A/810), pp. 71-77.

   Article 7. All are equal before the law and are entitled without any discrimination to equal protection of the law. All are entitled to equal protection against any discrimination in violation of this Declaration and against any incitement to such discrimination.
7. Civil rights cover rights to protect physical integrity, procedural due process rights, and non-discrimination rights.

   "Political rights' enable one to participate meaningfully in the political life of one's society, and include rights such as freedom of expression, assembly, and association, and the right to vote.
8. Art. 14 State shall not deny to any person equality before law and equal protection of law within the territory of India.
9. Art. 21: No person shall be deprived of life or liberty except according to the procedure established by law.
10. Art. 38: The state shall strive to promote the welfare of the people by securing and protecting as effectively as it may a social order in which justice, social, economic and political, shall inform all the institutions of national life.
11. 39A : Equal Justice and free legal aid, Hussainara Khatoon *v.* Home, Secretary, Bihar, AIR 1979 SC 1369, AIR 1978 SC 1548.

    Ins. by Constitution (42 Amendment) Act, 1976 Sec. 8 (w.e.f. 3-4-1977).

12. Hussanaria Khatoon *v.* Home Secretary, State of Bihar, AIR 1979 SC 1360.
13. M.H. Hoskot *v.* State of Maharastra, AIR 1978 3 SCC 544.
14. Kishore Chand *v.* State of Himachal Pradesh, 1990 Cr.L.J 2289.
15. http://hslsa.nic.in/HANDBOOK/1. LSAA, 1987.
16. *Ibid.*
17. http;//nalsa.com site visited on 5.5.2010.
18. Andhra Pradesh State Legal Services Authority (Activities up to July 2006), p. 12.
19. http//nalsa.com site visited on1.5.2010.
20. http//apslsa.ap.nic.in site visited on 1.5.2010.
21. Section 12 deals with the persons entitled to avail free legal services.
22. Definition of Woman; sec 10 of IPC. The word man denotes a male human being of any age; . the word woman denotes a female human being of any age. A girl of six years was held to be a woman respectively under this section.
23. (Section-6) Appointment of counsellors, officers, and other persons who may be required to render assistance to the family court. Section 13 of the Act favours dispensation of the service of the lawyer proviso to Section 13 provides that the family court may seek the assistance of legal expert as amicus curiae in the interest of the justice.
24. Section 3 of the Domestic Violence Act Defines "domestic violence" to include "any act, omission or commission or conduct" of the man in question in relation to the aggrieved woman in case it attracts any of the following four clauses: (a) harms or injuries or endangers the health, safety, life, limb or well-being, whether mental or physical, of the aggrieved person or tends to do so and includes causing *physicals* abuse, *sexual* abuse, *verbal* and *emotional* abuse and *economic abuse;* or (b) harasses, harms, injuries or endangers the aggrieved person with a view to coerce her or any other person related to her to meet any unlawful demand for any dowry or other property or valuable security, or (c) has the effect of threatening the aggrieved person or any person related to her by any conduct mentioned in clause (a) or clause (b); or (d) otherwise injures or causes harm, whether physical or mental, to the aggrieved person.
25. R.K. Gauba, Domestic Violence Law—A Recipefor disastor? Naya Deep, Vol. VIII, Issue 3, July 2007, pp. 20-59.

18

Right to Education

Specific Focus on Girl Child

ARUNA SRI LAKSHMI AND N.B. CHANDRAKALA

> *"Education of Girl Child is not a matter of Charity, it is an obligation".*

According the girl child her rightful share of human dignity and opportunity for development is not a concession to be given but an obligation to be fulfilled on the part of civil society. Such an obligation is not only ethical or moral but also legal as well so that the girl child can overcome the perils surrounding her. The girl-children are an essential social segment, which must be accorded recognition, provided of the opportunities, assured of the justice in case of atrocities and malpractices in implementing or extending the opportunities. The girl-children are considered to be essential social segment, because this segment speaks of the pre-womanhood and the protection of such segment always empowers the women.

The right of girls to education is one of the most crucial of all rights because education plays an important role in enabling girls to secure other rights. Education is the foundation for girl's development towards adult life. Education is important because it enables the girl child:

- to develop and realize her full potential as a human being;
- to develop the ability to think, question, and judge independently;
- to develop a sense of self-respect, dignity and self-confidence;
- to develop and internalize a sense of moral values and critical judgment;
- to love and respect fellow beings and nature;
- to develop civic sense, citizenship, and values of participatory democracy; and
- to enable decision-making.

Right to Education of every girl child is clearly a human right. It is an inalienable right. Education is a human right with immense power to transform. The cornerstones of freedom, democracy, and sustainable human development rest on its foundation.

INTERNATIONAL CONCERNS

The right to free and compulsory education, without discrimination with quality has been reaffirmed in all International Human Rights Conventions. The Right to Education has been a key element of all most every international declarations[1] on human rights since the U.N was established. Constitutions and laws in most countries recognize the Child's Right to Education.

NATIONAL COMMITMENTS

Education to girl children was recognized in the Constitution of India wherein it emphasized that the girl child had a right to free elementary education. "The State shall endeavour to provide within a period of 10 years from the commencement of the Constitution, free and compulsory education for all children until they attain the age of 14 years[2]"Articles 39(F), 46, 47 lend further support to this constitutional directive. However, it took decades to make free and compulsory education a reality. In due course in many of the cases like Francis Mullin case, Mohini Jain case and Unnikrishnan case, etc., which came before the Supreme Court, the Court observed and emphasized that right to life includes right to education under Article 21. Right to life under Article 21, includes right to live with dignity all that goes along with it i.e., including right to education.

All the landmark decisions given by the judiciary categorically recognized that education is the right of every child/person and that the State is under an obligation to provide. However, it took more than six decades to make free and compulsory education to all children a fundamental right. Later in the year 2002, a new Article 21A was inserted in the Constitution which made free and compulsory education a fundamental right to all children in the age group of 6-14 years which reads as follows:

> "The state shall provide free and compulsory education to all children of the age of six to fourteen years in such manner as the State may, by law, determine."

This Article clearly spells out the responsibility of the State to extend and provide free and compulsory education to all the children of the age six to fourteen years. It vests the discretion with the state to decide the manner and means of achieving the same. Pursuant to this amendment the Parliament enacted *The Right of Children to Free and Compulsary Education Act*, 2009. This Act is to provide to every child full time elementary education of satisfactory and equitable quality in a formal school.

The Salient features of The Right of Children to Free and Compulsory Education Act, 2009 are:

- Free and compulsory education is to be provided to all children of India in the 6-14 age groups.
- No child to be held back expelled or required to pass a board examination until completing elementary education.
- A child who completes elementary education (up to 8th class) shall be awarded a certificate.
- The Act calls for a fixed student- teacher ratio.
- 25 percent reservation for economically disadvantaged communities in admission to Class I in all private schools is to be made.

It mandates improvement in quality of education—

- School teachers will need adequate professional degree within 5 years or else will lose job.
- Financial burden will be shared between State and Central government.
- There would be partnership between government schools, government aided and unaided schools in providing elementary education to all children between 6-14 years of age.

CRITICAL APPRAISAL OF THE ACT

A review of the Right of Children to Free and Compulsory Education Act, 2009 indicate that there are undoubtedly remarkable features in the Act. Yet a critical examination of the Act indicates that it suffers from certain lacunae. One distinct feature of this Act is that under Section 4, if children above 6 years, who have either not been admitted to any school or admitted but could not complete elementary education have the right to be admitted to a class appropriate to his or her age for completing elementary education and also special training to enable such children to be at par with other children and also making the said children entitled for free education till the completion of their elementary education even after 14 years.

In the context of girls indeed, it is an appreciable step taken by the legislation wherein it aimed at achieving the goal of education for all and to reap the benefits of education. It enables the girl children, who do not join in the school or who discontinue their studies on account of poverty or on account of a pessimistic attitude in the family that a girl child does not need education and that their role is only recreation and procreation, to go to schools.

Under Section 5 of the Act the children are bestowed with another right, i.e. right of transfer to another school. Section 5 provides a child girl or boy the right to seek transfer from one school to another either within a state or outside and for immediate issue of transfer certificate to such child and also for liability for disciplinary action against the in charge of the schools delaying the issuance of transfer certificate. However delay in producing the T.C shall not be a ground for either delaying or denying admission in such other school.

Section 6 of the Right to Free and Compulsory Education Act 2009 reiterated that right to education places a burden not only on State, but also on parents or guardian of any child and on the child himself/herself and that the appropriate government and the local authority are require to establish a school within such area or limits of neighbourhood where a school is not established. Under Section 10 of the said Act provided that "It shall be the duty of every parent or guardian to admit or cause to be admitted his or her child or ward, as the case may be, to an elementary education in the neighbourhood school.

Importantly this provision is in consonance with the fundamental duty cast on the parents under Article 51-A(k) of the Constitution. Accordingly, the parents are duty bound to admit their children in the school. It is to be noticed that it is only a duty rather than an obligation. However, there is no any action that is taken against the parents who fail to admit their children. This lacuna has to be filled by the legislation by a suitable amendment. In a country like India where more than 30 million people are living below poverty line and where it is everyday struggle for existence, and their attitude that girls presence at home to take care of the siblings and cooking food would not encourage the parents to send girls to school. For them the RTE Act, 2009 remains a myth than a reality.

There is a provision under Section 14 that no proof of age of any child could not be a ground to deny her/him of admission into primary school. Similarly no child would be denied admission to a school even in the midst of an academic year under Section 15. Section 16 of the Act says that no child girl or boy will be held back in any class or expelled till he completes his elementary education. Thus, education has to be imparted without touching the child. Under the new system failing is not allowed. This provision may have been incorporated so as to improve the school dropout rate and the retention of children in the schools. On the other hand it must also be borne in mind that it hampers the development of child. A child who does not develop learning efficiency, value of performance in the schooling years, after 14 years of age, the child will find it harder to catch up in the senior classes. In turn she develops frustration in life, feel deprived and cannot deal with performance expectations in life and in life she/he cannot deal with failure or accept failure. Perhaps the Act intended that a child is allowed to acquire knowledge and develop with a free mind and an incentive for the children and parents to join them in the school whereby that they need only to study but need not pass any examination may have been the objectives. But unless performance evaluation is done through board examination it would only hinder the child's development.

Such a mechanism would only help the government to evaluate how successful the RTE Act, 2009 has been to achieve the goals of enrolment, retention, and not to drop out of the school and nothing more. The roaring sounds of attainable goals of the all round development of the child will be utterly defeated. Section 17 delineates that "no child shall be subject to physical or mental harassment thus no corporeal punishment can be imposed".

Prohibiting physical punishment is no doubt laudable but the word 'mental harassment' under Section 17 is not defined. This loophole empowers the students to complain against the teacher of 'any behaviour' as mental harassment. In turn it reduces the effectiveness of teachers to contribute to the development of the child. It is therefore necessary to rectify and define what constitutes mental harassment precisely.

A welcome feature of the Act is incorporation of Section 21 which provides for constitution of School Management Committee, consisting of the elected representatives of the local authority parents or guardians of children admitted in such schools and teachers. Any discrimination towards girl children can be questioned by those elected representatives who are parents or guardians. However, it is also provided that 50 per cent of the members of such committee shall be women.

Section 29 aims at integrated personality development of the children and clauses (a) to (h) are incorporated with the following objectives. The academic authority shall take into consideration the conformity with the constitutional values of all round development of the child, Building up of child's knowledge and potentiality, learning through activities, medium of instruction to be in the mother tongue. To make child express views with a free mind and continuous evaluation of child understands. Another remarkable feature of the Act is any violation of the RTE Act is subject to jurisdiction of the National Commission on Protection of the Children's Rights, 2005.

IMPLEMENTATION OF THE ACT—ABCs OF EDUCATION

To develop the above said lofty objectives in the child and the success of the RTE Act can be assessed only when the ABC's of education are implemented. The implementation of education, as a remedial measure to emancipate the girl children, must be explicitly be careful of the following factors called ABCs. Education must simply not be limited to impart the ABCs but, it must be careful about.

A—to speak of access to education, attendance to educational institutions and attainment of knowledge;

B—to speak of building one's own personality, becoming the most potential section of the society and nation; and

C—to speak of cherishing the values of character, conduct and cultural assimilation.

Without these ABCs, any education can not uplift a social group or emancipate a specific section like the girls. Education is not simply a scholastic medium, but it conducts any member of the mankind into life and living.

ACCESS TO EDUCATION

This is the primary step to provide education to the girls in particular and children in general. The absence of lack of infrastructural facilities like crèches in the agrarian zone as well as the industrial zone are not providing openings. However, the RTE Act, 2009 under section... provided for neighbourhood schools. It is to be waited to see whether neighbourhood schools serve the purpose.

ATTENDANCE TO EDUCATIONAL INSTITUTIONS

Once the children join the school, they must habituate themselves for attending to the school. In the villages two factors are hindering them. One is the gross rate of illiteracy prevailing in not creating a harmonious atmosphere to make the children to attend to the school. The girls tended to lose one due to burdens of household chores, inadequate nutrition as well as few chances of tuition in case they encountered in difficulties.

FACTORS AFFECTING GIRLS ACCESS TO EDUCATION

The pedagogic factors are another reason. The flexible structure with the learning role, the text book-based teaching by the middle class teachers are promoting absenteeism. The methods like learn while play and others are not effectively practiced, particularly in the rural scenario. Even though each and every one knows the significance of school and schooling, everyone is ignoring the same as per his/her convenience. In the same way the institutional factors like the existence or absence of:

(a) Girls schools, women teacher schools and single teacher schools;
(b) Incentives such as scholarship, mid-day meals, books, stationery and the like;
(c) Appropriate physical structures such as buildings, drinking water facilities, toilettes; etc.
(d) Child care facilities; and

(e) Private schools have a vital bearing on the girls' access to the schools.

Lesser attendance to the schools at the primary level can be remedied only if children are attracted through play method.

SOCIAL EMPOWERMENT OF GIRLS THROUGH EDUCATION

The social empowerment, practically, means the potential energy of the girls and women in carrying down the cultural heritage and social personality with a contemporary application. But the policy-makers approach of treating the reduction of the gender gap in basic education, which may, for them, serve as an effective tool for women empowerment. Can it promote the human dignity? Human dignity is nothing but human worth. Unless human dignity is promoted social empowerment cannot be realised.

Human dignity of girls can be promoted and can be achieved only through the implementation of human values in the regular school curriculum through EHV, i.e. Education in Human Values as advocated by the world spiritual leader Bhagavan Sri Satya Sai Baba is the only effective mechanism to realize the cherished goals of the Constitution. It is based on 'educare'. 'Educare' i.e., the method of bringing out and inculcating the inherent values of truth, righteousness, non-violence, peace and love and understanding in the human being. As Bhaghvan Sri Satya Sai Baba said "if human values take root in the educational system, the emerging individuals will have the following attributes. They will want Peace and Justice in a world that acknowledges the rule of law and in which no nation or individual need to live in fear: Freedom and Self-reliance to be available to all; the Dignity and work of every person to be recognized and safe-guarded, all people to be given an opportunity to achieve their best in life; and they will seek equality before the law and equality and opportunity for all."[3] They alone would mould the children into responsible citizens of the country. Education without 'educare' has no meaning and every child should be subjected to such method of education where in it realizes the source of life. The source i.e., the values should become the force of life. They should be able to realize that education is not merely information but it is transformation. The child should be trained towards 'We' rather than 'I'. 'We' in turn it reflects on 'We the people' as enshrined in the Constitution.

The cherished values of the Preamble i.e., Justice, liberty equality and fraternity as enshrined in the Constitution are automatically imbibed and mould them into future citizens of India, and the supreme asset of the Nation. Quality education with value additions like right conduct, truth, peace and love and non-violence would promote the integrated personality of the child. A girl with such education would be an asset to a family, Society and Nation.

THE GENDER GAP IN BASIC EDUCATION

The lack of equilibrium in the demand–supply ratio, in the primary education and also the secondary and higher educational levels, is very much aggravated by the gender gap. It is much a concern to identify, and adopt remedial measures to reduce, and if possible to eradicate the gender gap. The gender gap can be understood, in the context of India, only in the wider context of female disadvantage. Gender bias pervades all spheres of life and society and it influences political decision-making as well as intra-familial attitudes and values. Still the country is not in a position to root out the social emphasis on gender disparity and the in-built social inequality. In such a situation, is there a scope in near future to launch programmes for the universal empowerment of women in India? Experience across the country has demonstrated that, even among the most disadvantaged communities there is a keen desire to learn and to educate children. Given the right environment, the education of the girls has been up with gusto, with illiterate mothers' demanding schools for their daughters.

Cultural barriers, poverty, distance from schools, the lack of female teachers and inappropriate curricula are the major drawbacks that are working against the promotion of the basic education for the girls. Unless the gender bias or discrimination are totally annihilated, the women cannot have opened avenues to carve themselves out with full rate of empowerment.

EDUCATIONAL STATUS OF THE GIRLS

Unless and until the girls are educated, they cannot enjoy a status of being educated. It is found that among the girls there is no equal distribution of the educational services extended by the government. The gender disparity, which is already prevailing, has a say in the lack of equilibrium in this aspect. There are certain international standards set for the purpose of promoting educational status. In the urban areas is found some change. The movements like large scale industrialisation and openings through the media to observe the life styles of different social groups are creating a felt need for education. They are thinking that education is an essential tool for leading a successful life within the limited resource structure. This may be the case with some middle income groups and low income groups.

To sum up and observe, the poor are guided by the instantaneous results in material prosperity and as they are not in a position to invest their money and time, they are wont to diverse the sources of girls. It is reducing their educational status. More significant one is the presence of early marriages in such communities. The middle income groups and middle class are guided by market persuasions. The opulent sections are guided by personal reasons. To be specific these three do not have a set goal of achieving some status for woman and the girl is made a scapegoat in this process. It is clear that the nation is marching ahead to bring 100 per cent literacy. It is found that the children between 6 to 11 years consisting of 47,918 and children between 11 to 14 years was 79,175 who were not going to school and out of which some were drop-outs. Surprisingly the school drop-outs are more among boys than girls[4]. The passing of the RTE Act, 2009 is hope legally that girls will equally get educated along with the boys crossing all the impediments in their way as this is a progressive legislation.

The UNESCO report on Education stated the aim of education thus :

Learn to know
Learn to do
Learn to be

Learn to live together, which is appropriate in the context of girls' right to education because—

"If you educate a man, you educate an individual;
if you educate a woman, you educate a family"

Notes and References

1. The U.N. declaration of Human Rights, 1948, the 1959 Declaration of the Rights of the Child, the 1966 International Covenant on Economic, Social and Cultural Rights, 1989 Convention on the Rights of the Child, the World Declaration on Education for all 1990, the 1990 World Declaration on Survival, Protection and Development of Children, the

1995 Beijing Declaration and the 1996 Amman Affirmation, all express a commitment to Education as a right.
2. Article 45 of the Constitution of India.
3. www.sathyasaiehv.org.uk
4. Eenadu Daily News paper published on 13th May 2011.

19

Women and the Problems Related to Food Security in Rural Area

CH. VENKATESWARLU

"As long as women do not have the same rights in law as men, as long as the birth of a girl does not receive the same welcome as that of a boy, so long we should know that India is suffering from partial paralysis. Suppression of women is inconsistent with principles of ahimsa (non-violence)".

—Mahatma Gandhi, *Harijan*, August 18, 1940

INTRODUCTION

Women are responsible for half of the world's food production, and in most developing countries they produce between 60 and 80 percent of the food. Yet, women continue to be regarded as home producers or assistants on the farm, and not as farmers and economic agents on their own merit. Women receive a small fraction of assistance for agricultural investments; empowering women farmers is vital to lifting rural communities out of poverty, especially as many developing nations face economic crisis, food insecurity, HIV/AIDS, environmental degradation and increasing urbanization.

In developing countries, among the poor, rural women are the poorest and more vulnerable. Empirical evidences suggest that women in rural areas are more adversely affected by poverty than men. The incidence of poverty among rural women is on the rise in most of the developing countries. The issues of gender bias and equity point to the double burden women have to bear—that on being poor and being a woman. Further strategies and programmes for development had largely overlooked the question of gender equity. The present paper discuss the reduce poverty view the poor rural women as the recipient of benefits of development, instead of active participant and still poor rural women have the least access to basic needs such as food, health and education.

Women are important in our society. The role of women in society has been greatly overseen in the last few decades but now it is coming to a more positive perspective. Until the second half of the 20th century, women in most societies were denied some of the legal and political rights according to men. The man often made the final decision on all household matters, because he had the money. But women at presently enter the all type of employment, earn the money equal with men, so the position of women was changed compared with the past. Even today in the rural area women facing number of problems, there is no proper nutritional food due to the poverty, illiteracy and other cultural problems. The Governments made several attempts to eradicate poverty and provide food security to rural women.

HUNGER AND POVERTY

Hunger, which usually follows food shortages, is caused by a complex set of events and circumstances [social, economic and political factors] that differ depending on the place and time. Although hunger has been a part of human experience for centuries and a dominant feature of life in many low-income countries, the causes of hunger and starvation are not very well understood. Our understanding of the main causes of hunger and starvation has been hampered by myths and misconceptions about the interplay between hunger and population growth, land use, farm size, technology, trade, environment and other factors.

Poverty cannot be defined simply in terms of lacking access to sufficient food. It is also closely associated with a person's lack of access to productive assets, services and markets. Without access to these, it is unlikely that production and income earning capacities can be improved on a sustainable basis. Rural poverty is related to food insecurity, access to assets, services and markets; income-earning opportunities; and the organisational and institutional means for achieving those ends[1].

Throughout the history and in many societies, inequalities of women and men were part and parcel of an accepted male-dominated culture. It is a complex historical process, which requires detailed study before one can conceive of a viable strategy to improve and sustain the status of women in society. One of the basic factors causing unequal share of women in development relates to the division of labour between the sexes. This division of labour has been justified on the basis of the childbearing function of women and this is biologically important for survival. Consequently, distribution of tasks and responsibilities between men and women in a given society has mainly restricted women to the domestic sphere. Mass poverty and general backwardness has further aggravated the inequalities[2].

While the women's childbearing and child-rearing functions are respected in many countries, there has been very little recognition of women's actual or potential contribution to the economic, social and cultural states. The role of women within the family combined with high level of unemployment and under-employment of the population in general, has led to the unequal state of priority to men in matters of employment[3]. It is understandable that women cannot be expected to join the army, for instance, as foot soldiers but Israel's well-known and rightfully feared *sabrahs* or women commandos have shattered the myth of man's physical superiority and thus priority for most jobs.

DISCRIMINATION AND UNDERDEVELOPMENT

It is relevant to consider some aspects of the marginalisation of the status of women in the world by having a look at the figures which are based on the documents of the United Nations. Some of the findings are:

Unemployment Rate: Male unemployment rate decreased by 11% from 1984 to 1988 while that of women, unemployment rate increased by 0.5% during the same period;

Women in the Informal Sector: Without legal protection or security, women depend on informal trade for their survival. In Third World countries, a high percentage of food vendors were women: in Nigeria 94%, Thailand 80%, 63% in the Philippines;

Inequality in Pay: All over the world women earn only two-thirds of men's pay and earn less than three-quarters of the wages of men doing similar jobs. Women form a third of the world's official labour force, but are concentrated in the lowest-paid jobs and are more vulnerable to unemployment than men;

Domestic Work: Women do almost all the world's domestic work and coupled with their additional work in the productive spheres - this means most women work a double day. Unpaid domestic work is regarded as women's work. Though it is vital work, it is invisible work, unpaid, undervalued and unrecognised. Yet, the women's contribution to society in this regard is enormous;

Agriculture: Women grow about half of the world's food, but own hardly any land, have difficulty in obtaining credit and are overlooked by agricultural advisors and projects[4]. In Africa, three-quarters of the agricultural work is done by women while in Asia, Latin America and the Middle-East, women comprise half of the agricultural labour force;

Health: Women provide more health care than all health services combined and have been major beneficiaries of a new global shift in priorities towards prevention of disease and promotion of good health[5];

Education: Women continue to outnumber men among the world's illiterates by about 3:2 ratio, but school enrollment boom is closing the education gap between boys and girls;

Political Affairs: Due to poorer education, lack of confidence and greater workload, women are still under-represented in the decision-making bodies of their countries.

WOMEN AND FOOD SECURITY ISSUES

Not only do women produce and process agricultural products but they are also responsible for much of the trade in these and other goods in many parts of the third world. In many parts of the world, women continue to play an important role as rural information sources and providers of food to urban areas. This may involve food from the sea as well as from the land. Although women rarely work as fisher people, they are often involved in net-making and the preparation and sale of the catch.

Women's roles and status all over the world are generally determined by social institutions and norms, religious ideologies, eco-systems and by class positions. The Indian social systems exhibit such grave disparities. Indian women are not a homogeneous group. Their traditional roles are not identical in all strata of society. Norms and taboos governing their roles and behaviours within and outside the family, the structure of family organisations and social practices and the positions accorded to women in a community differ considerably across regions, cultures and levels of socio-economic development[6].

It is needless to emphasise on the significant contribution of women to agricultural production and household food security. In the process of production, handling and preparation of food, women play a multiple role throughout the sequence. They are said to be "feeding the world". Do women really feed the world? Let us consider the evidence. On a global scale, women produce more than half of all the food that is grown. In sub-Sahara Africa and the Caribbean, they produce up to 80% of basic foodstuffs. In Asia, they provide from 50 to 90% of the labour for rice cultivation[7]. And in Southeast Asia and the Pacific as well as Latin America, women's home gardens represent some of the most complex agricultural systems known[8]. In countries in transition, the percentage of rural women working in agriculture ranges from about a third in Bosnia and Herzegovina to more than half in Poland. Across much of the developing world, rural women provide most of the labour for farming, from soil preparation to harvest. After the harvest, they are almost entirely responsible for operations such as storage, handling, stocking, marketing and processing.

Women in rural areas generally bear primary responsibility for the nutrition of their children, from gestation through weaning and throughout the critical period of growth. In addition, they are the principal food producers and preparers for the rest of the family. Despite their contributions to food security, women tend to be invisible actors in development. All too often, their work is not recorded in statistics or mentioned in reports. As a result, their contribution is poorly understood and often underestimated[9]. There are many reasons for this. Work in the household is often considered to be part of a woman's duties as wife and mother, rather than an occupation to be accounted for in both the household and the national economy. Outside the household, a great deal of rural women labour — whether regular or seasonal — goes unpaid and is, therefore, rarely taken into account in official statistics. In most countries, women do not own the land they cultivate. Discriminatory laws and practices for inheritance of and access and ownership to land are still widespread. Land that women do own tends to consist of smaller, less valuable plots that are also frequently overlooked in statistics. Furthermore, women are usually responsible for the food crops destined for immediate consumption by the household, that is, for subsistence crops rather than cash crops. Also, when data is collected for national statistics, gender is often ignored or the data is biased in the sense that it is collected only from males, who are assumed to be the heads of households[10].

These handicaps have contributed to an increasing "faminisation" of poverty. Since the 1970s, the number of women living below the poverty line has increased by 50%, in comparison with 30% for their male counterparts. Women may feed the world today, but, given this formidable list of obstacles placed in their path, will they be able to produce the additional food needed for a world population expected to grow by three billion in 2030. These international agreements specified that the role of women in agriculture and food security must be emphasised, in order to create the enabling political, social and economic environment required for the eradication of hunger and poverty.

Under Commitment-I of the World Food Summit Plan of Action agenda, governments committed themselves to:

- Support and implement commitments made at the 4th World Conference on Women that a gender perspective is mainstreamed in all policies;
- Promote women's full and equal participation in the economy...including secure and equal access to and control over credit, land and water;
- Ensure that institutions provide equal access for women;
- Provide equal gender opportunities for education and training in food production, processing and marketing;
- Tailor extension and technical services to women producers and increase the number of women advisors and agents;
- Improve the collection, dissemination and use of gender-disaggregated data which distinguishes between males and females[11];
- Focus research efforts on the division of labour and on income access and control within the household; and
- Gather information on women's traditional knowledge and skills in agriculture, fisheries, forestry and natural resources management.

CONCLUSION

Rural women have a central role to play in achieving food security. Stronger legislation and effective programs are greatly needed at the national and regional level to invest in their potential. Good governance, ecologically efficient agriculture, land access, food security and social protection, and linking smallholders with efficient markets. It is essential that strategies for rural women's empowerment are understood in relation to the mix of factors that impact their lives.

This paper has provided a snapshot of what is and could be done to strengthen commitments for rural women. Much more can be presented, including a better overview of best practices and lessons learned in the field. The case studies submitted for the Forum highlight the potential of development cooperation to support women's entrepreneurial spirit and leadership and to even scale-up those initiatives that are working. They also capture some of women's coping and savings strategies as well as alternative farming methods. Practitioners can be learning about women's decisions through engagement and dialogue. There is a long way to go to ensure that the voice of women is being heard and that the needs of women farmers are seriously taking into account... Let us work together to create an enabling environment in which women can participate fully in decision and policy-making processes in the areas of agriculture and rural development.

Notes and References

1. Women in Rural Development—A Report Issued by the Afro-Asian Rural Reconstruction Organisation {AARRO}, New Delhi, India.
2. Food Security Issues, WTO and Agricultural Cooperatives by Daman Prakash, International Cooperative Alliance Regional Office for Asia-Pacific, New Delhi.
3. Cooperatives and Poverty Reduction—Enhancing Social and Economic Imperatives by Daman Prakash, ICA ROAP, New Delhi.
4. Paradigm Shift in the Management of Agricultural Cooperatives in Asia by Daman Prakash and G.C. Shrotriya. Published jointly by the ICA Regional Office, and IFFCO, New Delhi.
5. Women in Farming and Improving Quality of Life in Rural Areas. Published by the Asian Productivity Organisation—APO, Tokyo, Japan.
6. Women and Law from Impoverishment to Empowerment, Lalita Dhar Parihar, Eastern Book Company, Lucknow, 2001.
7. Women in Agriculture and Rural Development by Maithili Vishwanathan. Published by Rupa Books Private Limited, New Delhi.

8. Cooperative Leadership Training for Women – Report of the Regional Seminar held in Malaysia in December 1997. Issued by the ICA Regional Office for Asia and the Pacific, New Delhi.
9. Women's Health and Human Rights. Published by the World Health Organisation, Geneva.
10. The Contribution of Cooperatives to Social Development – The Cooperatives as Social Actor by Daman Prakash, ICA ROAP, New Delhi.
11. Gender Dimensions of Agriculture and Rural Employment: Pathway out of Poverty. FAO, IFAD, ILO, 2010.

20

Cyber Crimes Against Women

Indian Perspective

K. SAMATHA

INTRODUCTION

In India, cyber crime against women is relatively a new concept. Although we have Information Technology Act, 2000 , but it turned out to be a half baked law as the operating area of the law stretched beyond electronic commerce to cover cyber attacks of non-commercial nature on individuals as well. It mostly covered commercial crimes and economic crimes, it miserably failed to prevent the growth of cyber crime against individuals, including women[1], The term 'cyber crime against women' in India is mostly used to cover sexual crimes and sexual abuses in the internet, such as morphing the picture and using it for purposes of pornography, harassing women with sexually blackmailing/harassing mails or messages, etc. or cyber stalking. The majority of the cases reported to the police are of the nature of sexual crimes and most of them are booked under the Section 67 (which was meant to cover pornography and obscenity in the internet) of the Information Technology Act, 2000.[2] Most of the women who are falling prey to cyber crimes are illiterate women. Another disturbing factor is the alarming rate of divorce in the country, which is also fuelled by some of the cyber crimes committed on women. Many chat-based friends or Face book-hooked buddies today enjoy teasing their lady friends by using words such as "awesome body", "sexy", and "attractive", etc., which are actually the beginning of obscenity. They slowly take their female friends into confidence and start discussing about their own problems like a true friend. The emotionally oppressed or family-wise depressed Indian woman is a soft target. These guys then turn their successful Net-based friendship into a strong bond and gradually proceed to send obscene or derogatory talks[3]. In India 966 cyber crime cases were registered under IT Act during the year 2010 and 356 cases were registered under IPC Sections during the year 2010.

The cyber crimes specially targeting women are Cyber stalking is the use of the Internet or other electronic means to stalk or harass an individual, a group of individuals, or an organization. It may include the making of false accusations or statements of fact as in defamation, monitoring, making threats, identity theft, damage to data or equipment, the solicitation of minors for sex, or gathering information that may be used to harass.[4] This stalking is not new, it has been exist from time immoral, like domestic violence, stalking is a crime of power and control. And it can be carried out in person or via electronic mechanisms[5] Statistics show, and law enforcers confirm, that the majority of cyber crimes are related to obscenity. Mumbai tops the list in these crimes, followed by Delhi. It is believed that about 75% of all cyber crimes are targeted at women, adolescents, and children[6]. A study conducted on 72 women by Megha Desai and K. Jaishankar states that 12.5% of the respondents had intimate relationship with their cyber stalker before the stalking started. According to the research, 62.5% cases of harassment started through emails and online chats[7]. There was a famous case Manish Kathuria who was recently arrested by the New Delhi Police. The offender, Manish Kathuria was stalking the victim, Ritu Kohli by illegally chatting on the website 'MIRC' using her name and exploiting her personal details. He gave out her residence phone number and invited people to chat with her. This resulted in Ritu receiving obscene phone calls, she contacted the Delhi Police. An arrest was made under section 509 of the Indian Penal Code for outraging the modesty of Ritu Kohli[8].

CYBER PORNOGRAPHY

In India those who involve and see immoral acts are not

regarded as right thinking persons. Obscenity is one of those immoral acts which is directly relates to the people notion of morality, it potentially disturb public order and harm the peace and tranquility in the society. These obscene acts called in the name of cyber pornography in cyber space strike against the morality, public order and peace tranquility of a society and therefore it has tendency to destroy the very roots of social values[9] Pornography on the net may take various forms. This would include pornographic websites, pornographic magazines produced using computers to publish and print the material and the Internet to download and transmit pornographic pictures, photos, writings etc. Internet has provided a medium for the facilitation of this crime. Cyber porn as it is popularly widespread. Almost 50% of the web sites exhibit pornographic material on the Internet today. Pornographic materials can be reproduced more quickly and cheaply on new media like hard disks, floppy discs and CD-ROMs. The new technology is not merely an extension of the existing forms like text, photographs and images. Apart from still pictures and images, full motion video clips and complete movies are also available. As It is very bad for society to ruins lives and corrupts the adolescents and adults minds so the pornography should be blocked or banned not only in developing countries like India but also all other countries where there is no restriction.

CYBER DEFAMATION

According to Wikipedia, Cyber defamation is a crime conducted in Cyber Space, usually through the Internet, with the intention of defaming others. Sending defamatory email, writing derogatory comments on facebook, orkut or other social networking sites also constitute cyber defamation[10]. Unfortunately cyber defamation is not defined by the IT Act, 2000 and it is treated by the criminal justice system under the same provisions of cyber pornography or publication of obscene materials in the internet (Section 67 of the IT Act 2000: whoever publishes or transmits or causes to be published in the electronic form any material which is lascivious or appeals to the prurient interest or if its effect is such as to tend to degrade and to corrupt persons who are likely, having regard to all relevant circumstances, to read see or hear the matter contained or embodied in it shall be punished on the first conviction with imprisonment of either description for a term which may extend to five years and with fine which may extend to one lakh rupees and in the event of a second or subsequent conviction with imprisonment of either description for a term which may extend to ten years and also with a fine which may extend to rupees two lakh. The offence is well explained in the IPC under Section 500 which mentions punishment with simple imprisonment which may extend to two years or with fine or with both; and under Section 501 which states that "whoever prints or engraves any matter, knowing or having good reason to believe that such matter is defamatory of any person, shall be punished as per Section 500".[11]

Email Spoofing

E-mail spoofing is a term used to describe fraudulent email activity in which the sender address and other parts of the email header are altered to appear as though the email originated from a different source. By changing certain properties of the email, such as the From, Return-Path and Reply-To fields, ill intentioned users can make the email appear to be from someone other than the actual sender. One of the best examples of Cyber spoofing is Gujrat Ambuja's Executive Cases, in this case the perpetrator pretended to be a girl for cheating and blackmailing the Abu Dhabi based NRI. [12].

Morphing: Morphing is editing the original picture by unauthorized user or fake identity. It was identified that female's pictures are downloaded by fake users and again re-posted/uploaded on different websites by creating fake profiles after editing it. This amounts to violation of I.T. Act, 2000 and attracts sec. 43 and 66 of the said Act. The violator can also be booked under IPC also[13]. The Times of India reported that in October, a Delhi-based beautician told the police that her photograph was flashed on a porno portal along with her mobile number.

Cyber Flirting

Generally cyber flirting may be considered very minimal petty offence that starts when perpetrator force the victim to hear obscene songs, messages and it may consequently result in cyber sexual defamation and breach of thrust. Again this can be treated as the flip side of IT Act that except Section 72 which deals with the breach of confidentiality and privacy there is no other support that can be offered by the Act to the victim[14].

Cyber bullying is the use of the Internet and related technologies to harm other people, in a deliberate, repeated, and hostile manner[15]. The main aim and objective behind such crime may be to defame the target out of anger, hatred or frustration or secondly when the perpetrator wants to make simple fun of his friends, classmates, juniors or unknown net friends. In *United States* v. *Lori Drew* (2006) is one of the examples of cyber bullying. In this case on October 17th, 2006, thirteen-year-old Megan Meier received a message from a boy named Josh Evans saying, "The world would be better-off without you". She took his words to heart and she was found dead twenty minutes later in her bedroom closet. She had hung herself. What makes this story even more tragic is that Josh Evans did not exist. He was the creation of Lori Drew; Drew was arrested in 2008 for violations of the Computer Fraud and Abuse Act but was acquitted in 2009[16].

Provisions of the IT Act, 2000 relating to cyber crimes and the loopholes of the IT Act, 2000.

- The object of the IT Act is crystal clear from its preamble which shows that it was created mainly for enhancing ecommerce hence it covers commercial or financial crimes i.e. hacking, fraud, and breach of confidentiality, etc. but the drafters were unaware about the safety of net users[17]. Even though Chapter XI of the IT Act deals with the offences such as Tampering with computer source documents (S. 65), Hacking with computer system (S. 66), publishing of information which is obscene in electronic form (S. 67) Access to protected system (S. 70), Breach of confidentiality and privacy (S. 72), Publication for fraudulent purpose (S. 74) IT Act 2000 still needs to be modified. It does not mention any crime specifically as against women and children. Whereas IPC, Criminal Procedure Code and Indian Constitution give special protection to women.
- Most of the cyber crimes remain unreported due to the hesitation and shyness of the victim and her fear of defamation of family's name. Many times she believes that she herself is responsible for the crime done to her. The women are more susceptible to the danger of cyber crime as the perpetrator's identity remains anonymous and he may constantly threaten and blackmail the victim with different names and identities. Although the women net suffers are very less in number in India, women still do not go to the police to complain against sexual harassment,

whether it is in the real world or the virtual world they prefer to ignore the matter as they feel that it may disturb their family life[18].

- Absence of female cyber cops and cyber cells is another big factor prohibiting the women victims from opening up. When such crimes happens against women she feels too embarrassed to speak to the male officers. Hence, either she does not complain of it or if she does, she tells to her friends and immediate family. But the complaint never reaches the police so it very important to have female cops to deal with such matters as women victims openly speaks up.
- Need for female counselors is the biggest need of the day for cyber crime relating to women in India. A woman victim feels traumatized after a horrifying experience in the internet. But unlike other crimes, these virtual crimes can not be seen or felt by others other than the victim herself. The trauma may lead her to total withdrawal from the society or even to suicide which only an expert female counselor can prevent by thorough counseling and moral support. In such extreme cases the family as a whole must be called in to give emotional strength to the victim. It is essential that such counselor must have some knowledge of cyber law .It could be quite similar to that of free legal aid and counseling offered by every court to women in general or even like the counseling sessions for matrimonial cases in the family courts.
- The female "judge": Last but not the least, there must be a compulsory post of woman adjudicator and woman chairperson in the Cyber Regulatory Appellate Tribunal who should hear the cases relating to cyber crimes against women. It is true that till now there is rarely any case of such nature which has reached the Cyber Regulatory Appellate Tribunal, but the time when such Still after amendment the IT Act of India is a law for E-commerce and not for general cyber crimes and this is the biggest problem with our Indian cyber law. It is not the women alone who suffer the most in the internet, but there are millions of men and children as well who are victimized every day in this "vicious web". Due to the absence of proper law on cyber crimes neither the victims, specially

women in this context can understand how they are being victimized, nor they feel to go for legal help as they think the problem is purely "trust-oriented", "breach of trust" or even "an accident" which could be further prevented by a simple strong warning to the wrong doer. This would no way help to solve the problem and on the other hand aggravate the situation more. The best solution for crimes against women in the internet would be to report the case to the police station or to the cyber cell with assistance of your trust parents.. The more the cases are reported, the more the scope of analyzing the various natures of cyber crime enhances and this will finally help the victims as the law and justice machinery to protect and prevent cyber crime; especially crimes against women[19].

CONCLUSION

Cyber violence against women is on the rise and there is a need to review the Information Technology Act, 2000, The Information Technology (Amendment) Act, 2008 and include cyber-harassment and cyber-exploitation in it. A stricter punishment should be interpreted so the perpetrators have fear in their mind to do such acts as new cyber crimes of cyber-violence against women, including cyber stalking, e-mail harassment and using internet to publish obscene information to exploit or embarrass women is taking alarming proportions. The police, judiciary and the investigative agencies need to stay abreast with the latest developments in web-based applications so that they can quickly identify the actual perpetrator. It is the job of the legal system and regulatory agencies to keep pace with the Technological developments and ensure that newer technologies do not become tools of exploitation and harassment. Governments can take legislative measures that ensure human rights; especially women's rights are protected online just as they are physical spaces. Legislation should not just protect users; however, it should also educate and inform all groups on how to exercise their communication rights. At the same time, Individuals must become savvy both online and offline; know how to take precautionary measures in cyberspace and how to seek remedy if their rights are violated.

Notes and References

1. Cyber Victimization of Women and Cyber Laws in India, http://www.igi-global.com/viewtitlesample.aspx?id=55537.
2. *Ibid.*
3. Adv. Prashant Mali, Cyber Crime against Women, http://www.csi-india.org/c/document_library/get_file?uuid=70d4bc4a-8548-4375-adb6-15654dc9d068&groupId=10157
4. http://en.wikipedia.org/wiki/Cyberstalking.
5. http://www.nij.gov/topics/crime/stalking/
6. Adv. Prashant Mali .,Cyber Crime against Women, http://www.csi-india.org
7. Desai, M. and Jaishankar, K., Cyber Stalking—Victimization of Girl Students: An Empirical Study, 2007.
8. *The Hindu,* Thursday, June 18, 2009.
9. Dr. J.P. Mishra, An Introduction to Cyber Laws, Central Law Publications, first Ed., Allahabad, India.
10. http://wizardlegal.in/blog/cyber-defamation/
11. Shobhna Jeet, Cyber crimes against women in India: Information Technology Act, 2000, http://www.elixirpublishers.com/articles/1351168842_47%20(2012)%208891-8895.pdf
12. *Ibid.*
13. R. Nagalakshmi, Cyber Crime Against Women, http://tnfwl.com/pdf/news_letter/CYBER_CRIME_AGAINST_WOMEN.pdf
14. Bhupinder Jit Kaur, Cyber Crimes against Women in India: Information Technology Act, 2000, *International Indexed & Refereed Research Journal,* ISSN 0974-2832, E-ISSN- 2320-5474, July, 2013, Vol. V, Issue-54.
15. http://en.wikipedia.org/wiki/Cyberbullying.
16. http://blog.koldcast.tv/2011/koldcast-news/8-infamous-cases-of-cyber-bullying/
17. Abhimanyu Behera, "Cyber Crimes and Law In India", XXXI, IJCC 19 (2010).
18. Bhupinder Jit Kaur, Cyber Crimes against Women in India: Information Technology Act, 2000, *International Indexed & Refereed Research Journal,* ISSN 0974-2832, E-ISSN- 2320-5474, July, 2013, Vol. V, Issue 54.
19. Cyber Law for the women, of the women, by the women: http://www.cyberlawtimes.com/articles/111.html

21

Role of Judiciary

V. SASI KALA

An impartial Judiciary is *sine-quo-non* for the smooth functioning of a judicial system. It is the third organ of the government and is charged with the deliverance of Justice to the aggrieved party. The Judiciary does not have a substitute in the present society. While the power of the Parliament to legislate is supreme, at the same time the Judiciary has been made the watch dog of Indian Democracy. As per the working of the Constitution for the past more than sixty years, a new role for the Judiciary has emerged.

Certain fundamental rights contain specific and positive provisions to protect the right of women. Article 15(3) which permits special provisions for women and children, has been widely resorted to, by the State and the Courts have always upheld the validity of the special measures in legislations or executive orders favoring women.

The Supreme Court has upheld the constitutional validity of proviso to Sec. 31(1) (a) of the Andhra Pradesh Co-operative Societies Act, 1964 and of the rules 22(c) and 22A(3)(a) framed there under relying upon the mandate of Art. 15(3). The proviso read with the said rules provided for nomination of two women members by the Registrar to the managing committee of the Co-operative Societies with a right to vote and to take part in the meeting of the Committee. The Court upheld the validity of these provisions on the ground that Art. 15(3) of the Constitution permitted the making of special provisions for women. The reservations made for women in educational Institutions and public employments are protected by Art. 15(3).

Some cases for protective discrimination in favor of women: A single Judge of Andhra Pradesh High Court has held that a beauty contest in decently represents any woman by depicting the figure of a woman, form, or any part thereof in such a way so as to have the effect of being indecent or denigrading women or injure the public morality would be violative of the provisions of the indecent representation of women (prohibition) Act, 1986 and also unconstitutional as it violates Article 14, 21, and 51-A of the constitution. In Yousuf Abdul Aziz *vs.* St. of Bombay.[1] In this case when the petitioner contended that even though the women may be equally guilty as an abettor, but only the men were punished, which violates the right to equality on the ground of sex. The Supreme Court upheld the validity of the provision on the ground that the classification was not based on the ground of sex alone. The Court obviously relied upon the mandate of Art. 15(3) to uphold this provision.

The Constitution and the Criminal Procedure Code have given certain basic rights to protect a person including the women in the administration of Criminal Justice system in India. The founding fathers did not visualize the changing circumstances and attitude and perceptions of the male dominated society in its approach towards women. The Supreme Court formulates the justified move as it reversed the Delhi High Court's decision consenting Air India's move of grounding Air Hostesses for being overweight. It not only quashed the termination also stayed all future termination of Air Hostesses on account of their being overweight. It is rightly mentioned by the Hon'ble Justice Bhagawati of Supreme Court of India in *Air India* v. *Nargeesh Meerza's*[2] case. The Supreme Court struck down the Air India and Indian Air Lines Regulations relating to retirement and pregnancy bar on the services of Air Hostesses as unconstitutional on the ground that the conditions laid down therein were entirely unreasonable and arbitrary.

Also in the case of *C.B. Muthamma* v. *Union of India*[3], the Supreme Court repealed the provisions of Indian Foreign Service (Conduct and Discipline) Rules, 1961 requiring a female employee to obtain permission from the government prior to marriage and was suppose to resign if the government decides that her marital commitments hamper her work. When our constitution guarantees Right to Work and the discrimination on basis gender by means of Directive Principles and Fundamental Rights wide Articles 41,15 and 16 such instances of gender discrimination should not be welcomed.

Articles 20, 21 of the constitution of India in general and Sec. 160, 163, 164 of Cr.P.C. specifically conferred the basic right of Women in the administration of Criminal Justice. Through the activist intervention of the judiciary, women at large have been enabled to get justice in matters relating to employment, protection against police atrocities, manhandling, inhuman conditions in prisons; slow approach of the judiciary etc., Indian Supreme Court is very pro-women which is excellent. In the last so many centuries, the Indian societal customs have taken away from movement more than they have given her so this quiet but a definite movement for empowering the women is very positive. These decisions which become precedents and *defacto* law have been accumulating over many years.

There are multiple precedents by judiciary for empowering women employees by protecting their rights. Despite being in the midst of globalization and increasing talk of Women Empowerment, discriminatory grounds still exist. Judiciary is continuously working to curb discrimination but time and again like epidemics, it resurfaces. The need is to put in efforts to work out a permanent solution to the issue.

The Hindu Succession Act of 1956 was the first time that by law in modern times, a woman was given the right to inherit the property. Before that for the absolute right to be inherited to a lady, the Will should have mentioned it in clear and unambiguous terms. After the Hindu Succession Act 1956, however, a daughter and wife was treated the same way as the male heirs. A spate of judgments were administered by Supreme Court thereafter where the injustice that was prevalent before the HSA 1956 was reversed by saying that any will that did not explicitly give absolute rights to a lady but recognized a 'relationship' with the owner that could inherit property, then property rights—however restricted—to such a relationship with blossom as absolute right automatically. This means that if a wife was not explicitly given absolute right in the will but rights to live and function in that property (or has any vestige of right to property) then automatically she gets absolute rights to that property. However, the courts have taken a traditional and strictly, literal view of provisions of Muslim women (Protection of Rights or Divorce) Act, 1986 according to which a Muslim divorce women can claim maintenance u/s 125 Cr.P.C.

Indian Judiciary has applied the principle of equality of status, opportunities and justices while interpreting statutes, relating to women's development and empowerment. For example, the Orissa High Court in *Gayatri Devi Panjari* v. *State of Orissa*[4] upheld the policy of Government to give preference to women while allotting shops on merit in addition to 30% observation for women in that regards. The Court opinioned that reserved for any category cannot be taken as a ceiling and the Government could prefer women over men ever if was reservation for women since the policy of reservations aims at ensuring the minimum while the policy of preference aims at facilitating the empowerment of the disadvantages sections of the people.

In another case, the Court extended the benefits of Maternity Benefits Act, 1961 to all women whether employed on regular, casual, daily wages or on muster role basis. The Court observed that: "A just social order can be achieved only when inequalities or obliterated and everyone is provided what is legally done, women, who contribute almost half of the segment of our society, have to be honored and treated with dignity at place where they work to earn their livelihood. Whatever be the nature of their duties, their avocation and the place where they work, they must be provided all the facilities to which they are entitled".

Upliftment and development of women has been at the centre of constitutional mechanism as well as the politicians, media, the civil society institutions and the judiciary, various provisions of a constitutions like right to equality contained in the Articles 14, 15, 15 (3), 42, 45, 46 and the provision relating to 33.3% reservation for women in the offices and the membership of the rural and urban local bodies aim at achieving the goals of empowerment , welfare and development on equal footing of women. General rural and urban development schemes and programmes enacted and implemented through various development plans and women and child specific programmes in particular since independence were indicative of the political commitment to bring about change in the social and economic status of women. The critical social change through social equality between man and woman was also attempted through social reform laws so as to remove social disabilities suffered by Hindu women in matters like marriage, divorce, succession, adoption and guardianship. The judiciary compensated for the inadequacies of these laws.

The constitution of India guarantees equality to women and various laws have been enacted to protect and empower women. But the pathetic situation of women prisoners languishing in jails is a serious problem. The concept of Human Rights is totally alien to such women. The press has frequently exposed the violence and sexual exploitation of women and youth in the jails. Though there are elaborate rules in the jail manuals to protect women, very few women know about them. As "women have a special claim to compassion, defense of dignity, human rights, protection of her sensitive needs and personal integrity". Majority of the women prisoners are from rural background, illiterate, shy and do not have courage to communicate their needs and grievances to the prison staff in the jails.

In *Sheela Barse* v. *State of Maharashtra*, the Court ruled that legal assistance to a poor or indigent accused arrested and put in jeopardy of her life or personal liberty is a constitutional imperative under Art. 39 A, 14 and 21. When it is not provided, injustice is likely to result. The Court directed the State of Maharashtra to provide separate lockups for females and guarded by female constables, interrogation by female police officers. Further, the Magistrate before when a woman prisoner is produced should inquire whether she had any complaint or maltreatment in police custody. Legal assistance is provided to prisoners and a lady judge make periodical visits to police lockups in the city of Bombay to hear to grievances of women prisoners.

Judicial activism of the Supreme Court gave a new dimension to the word 'personnel liberty' where prisoners rights were debated, observed. Justice Iyer acknowledged the prisoner's right to privacy also. Justice V.R. Krishna observed that Part III of the Constitution does not part company with the prisoner at the gates, and judicial over sight protects the prisoner's shrunken Fundamental Rights. Judiciary's role in issuing several directions to Central and State Governments to prevent violations of Human Rights of the women prisoners is laudable. Indian judiciary has been very emphatic on the issue of enforcing Art. 44 of Indian Constitution that enjoys a duty on the state to enact uniform civil code. Judiciary is convinced that uniform civil code is the charter of equality and dignity to women in India, specially belonging to the oppressed and suppressed Sections of the women in the country. Former Supreme Court Judge Justice P.

Sathasivam said the judiciary was performing the role of a social reformer by upholding the rights of women especially the victims of subordination and suppression. The judiciary's contribution is to improve the status of women their protection, access to Fundamental Rights and dignity could be discerned from a number of its interpretation of laws and the constitution. Speaking on the occasion Supreme Court Judge Justice Ranjana Prakash Desai referred to destruction of millions of female fetuses every year, rape, bride harassing, sexual harassment at work place, physical and mental cruelty, domestic violence and denial of property rights.

In the context of gender justice and equality the judiciary played a vital role of social reformer by upholding the rights of women and especially of the victims of subordination, suppression and subjugation. Judiciary has played this role both as a court of judicial restraint and as a progressive, dynamic, creative and proactive institution for social, economic and cultural transformation. The contribution made by the judiciary to the improvement of status of women, protection of and access to Fundamental Rights of women and provision of conditions of dignity of life can be discerned from a number of decisions delivered while interpreting laws and the constitution.

CONCLUSION

It is submitted that the women rights in India has undergone remarkable changes in the recent years with the activist intervention of the judiciary in protecting the Fundamental Rights of women in India (especially in cases like maintenance). This has led to be amendments in the existing laws framed by the founding fathers of constitution of India. Through such activist intervention of the Judiciary, women were getting justice in matters relating to employment, protection against police atrocities, manhandling inhuman conditions in prisoners, slow approach of the judiciary, etc.,

Therefore, I would like to conclude that the attitude of the people towards women in general and also the officials involved in the above matters has been in the optimistic track.

Notes and References

1. AIR 1954 SC 321.
2. AIR 1981 SC 1829.
3. 1979 SCC 260.
4. AIR 2000 SC 1531.

22

Women's Rights and Human Rights

S. FAIZUNNISA

INTRODUCTION

Women constitute half the world population, perform nearly two thirds of works hours, receive one-tenth of the world's income and own less than one-hundredth percent of world's property.[1] The problem of family violence, especially violence against women, is not a new one and evidence of such violations can found throughout in historical records of any culture. However, awareness about the extent and nature of these issues came to the forefront during 1970 in USA as a result of the national family violence survey. In India, it was only during the early 1980s, in the wake of dowry and related problems, that crimes against women came to be recognized as an important social problem. Late Smt. Indira Gandhi, former Prime Minister of India once told "our women have more rights than women of other countries, but there are large areas wherein women are suffering, where may be, they are not conscious of their rights." [2]

Human rights and fundamental freedoms are birthrights of all human beings and their protection and their protection and promotion is the first responsibility of State. Women constitute half of world population. However, devaluation of women, which is both physical and psychological, begins even before life begins. The patriarchal relationships and processes, which operate through gender, class, race, ethnicity and sexual orientation, are directly responsible for oppression and subordination of women and violation of their basic human rights.

VARIOUS PROVISIONS RELATING TO WOMEN'S HUMAN RIGHTS

The world Conference on Human rights at Vienna adapted declaration which is hallmark in the efforts to gain recognition of women's human rights and integrated their rights in the mainstream of United Nations human rights dialogue. The basic and most crucial international Human Rights Charter and conventions such as Universal Declaration of Human Rights (UDHR), 1948, International Covenant on Civil and Political Rights (ICCPR), 1966 and International Covenant on Social and Cultural Rights (ICESCR), 1966.

Convention on elimination of all forms of discrimination against women: On June 25, 1993, the World Conference on Human Rights at Vienna adopted the Vienna Declaration, which is a rights and integrated their rights in the mainstream of the United Nations human rights dialogue. The Declaration recognized human rights of women as an inalienable, integral and indivisible part of universal human rights and demanded that the equal status of women and the human rights of women be integrated into the mainstream of the United Nations system wide activity. It pressed for the eradication of all forms of discrimination against women, both hidden and overt. But the most important of all, the Vienna Conference, for the first time recognized the gender based violence against women in public and private life as a human rights concern. The Declaration specifically condemned gender based violence and all forms of sexual harassment and exploitation and called upon the General Assembly to adopt the draft declaration on violence against women. It welcomed the decision of the Commission on Human Rights to consider the appointment of a special rapporteur on the violence against women. This indeed is a big achievement. It has brought the issue of violence against women to the centre stage of all discussions.

Article 11(1)(f) of universal declaration provides that state parties shall take appropriate measures to eliminate discrimination against women in the enjoinment of right to protection of health and safety in working conditions including safeguarding the reproduction. With regard to the women, the Constitution of India contains many negative and positive provisions which go a long way in securing gender justice. While incorporating these provisions, the framers of the Constitution were well conscious of the unequal treatment meted out to the fairer sex, from the time immemorial. The history of suppression of women in India is very long and the same has been responsible for including certain general as well as specific provisions for the upliftment of the status of women. The rights guaranteed to the women are on par with the rights of men and in some cases the women have been allowed to enjoy the benefit of certain special provisions.

The Indian constitution reading Article 21[3] with Articles 39, 41, 42, 47, casts high priority burden on the state to bestow dynamic concern for ensuring the health of all its citizens, especially women and children and weaker sections. Supreme Court construed right to life as inclusive of right to livelihood. It covers freedom from decease deprives a person of his right to life, even liberty. The fundamental right of every person to equal protection of law under Article 14 of Indian constitution is a mandate to the Executive and Legislature to use their powers to protect to citizens equal rights[4].

The Directive Principles of State policy contained in Part IV of the Constitution incorporate many directives to the state to improve the status of women and for their protection. Article 39(a) directs the state to direct its policy towards securing that the citizen, men and women, equally have the right to an adequate means of livelihood. Article 39(d) directs the state to secure equal pay for equal work for both men and women. The state has enacted The Equal Remuneration Act, 1976 to give effect to this Directive Principle. Article 39(e) specifically directs the state not to abuse the health and strength of workers, men and women. Article 42 of the Constitution incorporates a very important provision for the benefit of women. It directs the state to make provisions for securing just and humane conditions of work and for maternity relief. The state tried to implement by enacting The Maternity Benefit Act, 1961. Article 44 directs the state to secure for the citizens a uniform civil code throughout the India. This particular goal is towards the achievement of gender justice.[5] The Supreme Court has highlighted the right of women in India to eliminate gender-based discrimination particularly in respect of property so as to attain economic empowerment[6]. The Court, while referring to the Vienna Declaration on the elimination of all forms of discrimination against women (CEDAW) which was ratified by the United Nations Organization on 18-12-1979 and by the Government of India on 8-8-1993 elaborately discussed the principles of equality of rights and respect of women dignity.

CONCLUSION AND SUGGESTIONS

A vast majority of women are ignorant of their protective rights or even their existence. The law has therefore remained an ineffective instrument of social change for equality of women. Through legal aid and literary services are available to women at all levels, women remain without intended protection. The need of the hour is to make the women to be aware of 'human rights' as 'women's rights'. In a world racked by violence women face rape, mutilation and death at the hands of not only common men but also of those in power including armed men. They are beaten by their husbands, they are stripped by upper caste men, they are subjected to rape and finally forced to die in a helpless society. Thus suffering contuses despite historic declaration by the international community that women's rights and human rights. Half of the Indian population too are women. Women have always been discriminated against and have suffered and are suffering discrimination in silence. Self -sacrifice and self denial are their nobility and fortitude and yet they have been subjected to all inequalities, indignities, inequality and discrimination.[7]

NOTES AND REFERENCES

1. A Report of the United Nations, 1980.
2. Article: Violence Against Women: A Human Right Violation, By Dr. Krushna Chandra Jena.
3. Right to freedom of life and personal liberty.
4. The dialectics and dynamics of Human Rights in India—V.R. Krishna Iyer.
5. Saralamudgal *v.* Union of India (1995) 3SCC 635.
6. C.M. Mudaliar *v.* Idol of Sri S. Swaminathaswami Thirukoil (1996) 8 SCC 525.
7. Justice K. Ramaswamy in Madhu Krishwar *v.* State of Bihar [(1996) 5 SCC 148].

23

Wife's Employment vis-a-vis Husband's Right to Restitution

An Unsettled Law

A. Aswini

INTRODUCTION

The home epitomizes the finer delicacies of the marital status. The bundle of indefinable rights and duties which bind the husband and the wife can perhaps be best understood only in the context of their living together in the marital home[1]. The essence of marriage is sharing of all happiness and sorrows, compromising with ups and downs and showing love and affection on each other, legally termed as *'Conjugal Society'*. *'Conjugal'* refers to anything pertaining to marriage or to husband and wife in their relations to each other[2]. *Society* means mutual consortium. Every marriage gives rise to bundle of rights to be enjoyed and duties to be performed for both the spouses. Right to have conjugal society or an obligation to provide conjugal society is one such straw in the bundle. Withdrawal from the matrimonial home by either spouse would inevitably involve a total or partial loss of consortium to either spouse which lies at the very root of the marital relationship.

Though the term *'Conjugal Right'* can't be fit into a straight jacket definition, we can give a comprehensive definition which includes right to mutual enjoyment of association, sharing of feelings of joy and sorrow, sympathy and confidence, dwelling together in the same habitation and sharing the intimacies of marital relations. When such is the sanctity of conjugal society in spousal relationship, sometimes due to various reasons and even without any reason, marital harmony lands up in crisis leading to various emotional setbacks.

Restitution of Conjugal Rights is one of the matrimonial reliefs available to either of the parties to the marriage in such a situation. It is available to all communities, irrespective of their religious affiliation. It is provided for Hindus u/s. 9 of Hindu Marriage Act, 1955; Christians u/s. 32 of Divorce Act, 1869; Muslims under general law; Parsis u/s. 36 of Parsi Marriage & Divorce Act, 1936 and for persons marrying in the civil form u/s. 22 of Special Marriage Act, 1954. The gist is that when either the husband or the wife has *'without reasonable excuse'*, *'withdrawn'* from the society of the other, the aggrieved party may apply, by petition to the family court for restitution of conjugal rights and the Court, on being satisfied of the truth of the statements made in such petition and there is no legal ground why the application should not be granted, may decree restitution of conjugal rights accordingly[3].

The granting or rejecting of the remedy depends on the successful proof of *'reasonable excuse'* clubbed with proof of *'withdrawal'* in the correct sense of the term. There is no hard and fast rule in determining what is *'reasonable excuse'* because it depends and differs from facts of each case. There are many cases wherein the judiciary recognized cruelty, desertion, bigamy, concubinage etc. as reasonable excuses. Similarly, temporary withdrawal of a spouse for petty quarrels without an intention to permanently forsake conjugal society does not come under this remedy. *'Withdrawal'* legally implies both the *'animus'* and *'factum'* to withdraw.

Does legislature intend *'employment'* as a reasonable excuse to withdraw from the conjugal society?

Whether employment of the wife in a place different from husbands place of employment can contribute a reasonable excuse to *withdrawal* from the matrimonial home thereby giving a right to restitution of conjugal rights to husband—is the main theme of this paper.

Post 1970's, women started taking up jobs either for economic necessity or for economic independence or for both. Luckier are those women who get an employment at the place of husband's employment. But always it doesn't happen. They are compelled to leave the matrimonial home since their place of employment is far away from husband's employment place. For this, husband may or may not give consent. Whether such leaving without husband's consent can be termed as *'withdrawal'* according to legal parlance is also a question to be addressed; because the term *'reasonable excuse'* has not been defined under the Codes and left out for judicial interpretations.

JUDICIAL INTERPRETATIONS

The Courts have been confronted with such situations in many cases. Some decisions tilted in favour of the husband and a few decisions are rendered in favour of the wife. A brief analysis of some of these cases is indicative of divergence in judicial attitudes and trends. Wife's right to gainful employment *vis-a-vis* Husband's right to restitution of conjugal rights has become a topic of debate which has not been settled at rest by the Apex Court.

Decisions tilting against wife

In *Tirath Kaur* v. *Karthar Singh*[4] the Punjab & Haryana High Court relied on Mulla's Hindu Law and observed that *refusal of wife to resign the job situated at a different place amounts to withdrawal from his society*. The position was reiterated by various High Courts in *Pothuraju* v. *Radha*[5], *Gaya Pd.* v. *Bhagawati*[6], *Surinder Kaur* v. *Gurdeep Singh*[7] and *P.V.P. Sharma* v. *Sesha Lakshmi*[8]. Similarly in *Kailash Wati* v. *Ayodhia Prakash*[9] the court analysed that *where the husband marries a woman already in employment, he doesn't give up his right to claim a common matrimonial home with his wife. Rather the wife by necessary implication consents to marital duty of living with her husband as a necessary incident of marriage.*

Another issue raised in this case was whether husband has got superior right to establish matrimonial home? The Court held it affirmatively because under Hindu Law larger family obligations are imposed on man to maintain his wife, children, aged parents and other dependents of the family under Hindu Marriage Act, 1955, S.125 Cr.P.C. and S.18 of Hindu Adoption and Maintenance Act 1956. Hence, he must have a say over the place of matrimonial home so as to discharge his duties effectively through his earnings. The onerous legal obligations shall be correlated to the right to fix the matrimonial home. Even under Sastric Hindu Law, the obligation of the wife to live with her husband in his home and under his protection is clear and unequivocal. The court also observed that *though the decision tilted a little in favour of the husband it was inevitable because the decision was in the interest of the both to take as they can decide about their marriage which is otherwise irretrievably broken down.*

Decisions tilting in favour of wife

We find a set of High Courts viewing the situation in a different way. The Allahabad High Court took a liberal view. In a detailed judgment delivered by S.N. Katju J. in *Shanti Nigam* v. *R.C. Nigam*[10], the court observed: *women are now no longer confined within the walls of their houses. In view of the altered social and economic conditions both husband and wife may think it is necessary to work and contribute to the family chest. If she says that it is necessary for the upkeep of the family that she should also work and she would go to her husband whenever it is possible for her to do so and the husband could also come to her at his own convenience, it does not amount to 'withdrawal'.* Similarly in *Vibha Shrivastava* v. *Dinesh Kumar*[11] and *Prakash* v. *Snehalatha*[12], the Madhya Pradesh and Rajasthan High Courts respectively expressed *their recognition to the concept of equality of spouses in fixing the matrimonial home and husband's insistence and wife's refusal to resign her job were held not amounting to causing cruelty to husband* and husband's petition for divorce was dismissed.

In *Swaraj Garg* v. *K.M. Garg*[13], the Delhi High Court has taken a progressive view which held that *it is the high time that Mulla's Hindu Law is to be rewritten in the modern day context. The Sastric rules and the Dharma Sastras were apt for those conditions which speak about ideal situations and they are only recommendatory rules. In modern day when numerous women have taken up jobs to help their families and also to be useful member of the society sometimes wife may be more gainfully employed by the husband.* In such cases, it is wrong to say that wife doesn't have say in determining the place of matrimonial home. Any law which would give the exclusive right to the husband to determine the place of matrimonial home without considering the merits of the claim of the wife would be contrary to Art. 14 of the constitution which guarantees equality before law and equal protection of the laws to the husband and the wife. In this case, the court suggested that the choice of matrimonial home should be determined on the principle of common convenience, principle of consent, principle of comparative advantage and principle of balance of circumstances. However, the court lamented that such situations may bring about breakdown of marriage without anybody's fault. The principle of breakdown of marriage is only partially recognized as a ground for divorce under Indian laws whereas in England, it has been a separate ground for divorce. It suggested for amendment in Hindu Marriage Act to obtain divorce when the marriage is apparently broken down.

In *Jagdish Mangtani* v. *Geetha Jagdish Mangtani*[14], *wife insisted on not leaving the job to join her husband and husband prayed for decree of divorce on the ground of desertion.* The court came to the conclusion that *as the marriage had completely broken down, it had no other alternative but to pass divorce decree and no useful purpose would be served in asking them to maintain the spousal relationship.* A bird's eye view of various decisions rendered by different High Courts enable us to catagorise the decisions under five heads.

i) In some cases the wife's right to employment is given a back seat and husband's right to restitution of conjugal rights is honoured.
ii) In some cases, wife's right to employment is given priority and husband's right to restitution of conjugal rights is denied.
iii) In some cases, wife's right to employment is recognized and husband's right to restitution of conjugal rights was also granted as an inevitable alternative by deeming it to be a situation of breakdown of marriage if restitution of conjugal rights was to be denied.
iv) In few other cases, husband's claim for divorce is granted as it is deemed to be a case of breakdown of marriage.
v) Lastly, in some other situations, divorce is refused to the husband, honouring wife's right to employment. In such situations, the courts lamented upon their helplessness to give proper remedy to the deprived spouse because irretrievable breakdown of marriage is not provided under the matrimonial law as a separate ground for dissolution of marriage and also pointed out the necessity of incorporating the provision of irretrievable breakdown of marriage as a ground for divorce under sec. 13.

It is also clear that all these cases were decided by different High Courts and the point has not been set at rest by the Supreme Court.

Till then, the wife's right to gainful employment *vis-à-vis* husband's right to matrimonial relief either in the form of restitution of conjugal rights or in the form of divorce will be tilting in favour of either the wife or the husband. It is really a legal dilemma which awaits Apex Court decision. If restitution of conjugal rights is granted to the husband that means the wife's right to gainful employment is left unrecognized; on the other hand if the wife's right to gainful employment is recognized, the husband's right to restitution or divorce is to be given a back seat. Then it amounts to compelling the husband to lead a marital life without any substance in it. Hence, in many cases, the High Courts recognizing the wife's right to employment also granted relief to the husband only to free the parties from the clutches of non-functional marriages as no other alternative was found suitable. Reconciliation between both the rights in a harmonious way is a challenge to the judiciary.

LEGISLATIVE INADEQUACY

Here it is to be noted that the Law Commission of India in its 71st Report, 1978 highlighted the inadequacy of *'fault'* and *'consent'* theories of divorce to meet certain situations where in either no party is at fault or both the parties are at fault and one needs matrimonial relations to continue and the other doesn't. These are the situations wherein the marriage will have all the external appearances of marriage but in reality the substance of marriage is disappeared. In other words, marriage exists *dejure* but has ceased to exist *defacto* where by the very purpose of marriage gets frustrated. Law should not endeavour to preserve an unworkable marriage which would cause greater misery to both the parties. Hence the report recommended for incorporating irretrievable breakdown as separate ground for divorce under matrimonial law. Here it is to be noted that already there is S. 13(1-A) which provides for remedy in case of non-compliance with restitution of conjugal rights and non-resumption of cohabitation after judicial separation for a minimum of one year. These are termed as breakdown of marriage situation. But it is used in the restricted sense. It is a remedy only after a preliminary legal battle is fought by either of the parties. What we need under an amendment is a remedy for breakdown of marriage in a wider context, wherein no legal battle is fought previously. It is already existing in foreign countries where the Courts have discretion to dissolve a marriage if there was a separation of three or five years without any scope for reconciliation.

> *".... Public interest demands not only that matrimony should be maintained as far as and as long as possible but when a marriage has been wrecked beyond the scope of salvage, the same public interest demands such marriages to be put an end to... law can't turn a blind eye to such situations. When marriage becomes a fiction though supported by a legal tie, refusing to severe that tie not only doesn't serve the sanctity of marriage but also disregards the feelings and emotions of the parties"*[15].

Why the recommendation of Law Commission is not implemented till now?

There are arguments on both sides of the issue. It is apprehended that if irretrievable breakdown of marriage as a ground for dissolution of marriage is introduced, it would put human ingenuity at a premium and the doors of litigation will be thrown wide open. In most cases, husband may have it as a weapon at the cost of wife and children rather than wife taking it as a remedy. On the other hand, its need is emphasized by arguing that as human life has short span, situation causing misery can't be allowed to continue indefinitely. Hence the use and misuse of such a provision if introduced should be left to the discretion of the judges who are supposed to exercise it judiciously. Already an amendment was proposed in 1981 through a bill to provide for irretrievable breakdown of marriage under Sec. 13C and in that case it was proposed to have S. 13D as a safeguard for the wife whenever husband happens to be the petitioner in the light of incidental financial hardship to her. S. 13E was also proposed wherein divorce shall not be granted unless adequate provision is made for maintenance of the children. But it didn't come out as an amendment. Hence, out of apprehension that this remedy is having the potentiality of being misused by husband, some women's associations opposed passing of this amendment.

Observations

In view of the above discussion the situation is that :

- The judicial approach is oscillating and the point has not been set at rest by the Supreme Court leading to a judicial dilemma.
- The present matrimonial legislative provisions are inadequate to address the situation.
- The modern day concepts of women's right to

employment as fundamental right and priority to career at the cost of family are adding fuel to the uncertainty.

Suggestions

- *Pre-Marriage deliberation :* There is nothing wrong on the part of intending parties to the marriage to arrive at a consensus through deliberations regarding this issue before marriage itself. The parents should not hesitate to address this issue.
- *Clear vision :* Women should be very clear in their thinking and priorities. Certainty will be achieved by taking the decision either this way or that way before entering into matrimonial relationship.
- *Skill to balance :* Women should also acquire the skill of balancing their rights with their obligations and be smart wives, care taking mother and good working women.
- *Attitudinal change :* The Mindset of the husband as well as the family members also needs a rational outlook so as to extend their co-operation to the working women.
- *Role of Sociologist :* Sociologists have a greater role to play in this regard because any disturbance in the family, though a private affair, has the potential to disturb societal harmony because society is nothing but conglomeration of families and happy families make up a good society and broken up families reflect the social disharmony.
- *Pro-Women Government Policy:* Especially in case of married women employees, the Government should work out a conducive policy whereby a policy is to be formulated in service rules where in preference of work place to the women at or near the place of husband's employment should be given weight.
- *Legislative amendment :* It is high time, the legislature should bring about the amendment not only in Hindu Marriage Act but also in other matrimonial legislations so as to incorporate irretrievable breakdown of marriage as a specific ground for dissolution of marriage with necessary safeguards to protect the interests of wife and children.
- *Role of Family courts :* Apart from legal mechanism, marital dispute over wife's employment can be settled in a cordial manner in which both the parties would be the winners and to bring about this change the *onus* lies

heavily on the family courts which are special types of courts headed by judges well versed in family relations and conciliation skills.

CONCLUSION

To conclude, wife's right to employment and husband's right to conjugal society—both are equally important. The correct approach is not to give priority to one at the cost of another but to construe both the rights harmoniously. Women's employment contributes for the dignity and worth of women and boosts up her confidence. It adds economic value to the family, especially in the present day situation of ever escalating price index and ever growing needs of family consumption. However, a proper balance between family and career and between matrimonial rights and obligations will go a long way in preserving family harmony. Every one of the stakeholder has a significant role to play and the contribution of legislature through necessary amendment, executive through pro-women policies and judiciary through its judicious rendering of justice delivery system are of special significance. The motto is to minimize the marital friction and to maximise family union. Let neither wife's employment nor husband's ego come in the way of family union in the interest of their own children. Non-recognition of this truth will eventually lead to breakdown of marriage and ruin of family happiness.

Notes and References

1. Kailashwati *v.* Ayodhia Prakash, 1997 (79) PLR 216.
2. WHARTON's concise Law Dictionary (Universal Law Publishing Co. Pvt., Ltd., Delhi, 2010).
3. Section 9 of Hindu Marriage Act, 1955.
4. AIR 1964 Punj 28.
5. AIR 1965 Andhra Pradesh 407.
6. AIR 1966 MP 212.
7. AIR 1973 P&H 134.
8. AIR 1975 Andhra Pradesh 239.
9. *Supra* note 1.
10. (1971) All LJ 67, p. 7.
11. AIR 1991 MP 346.
12. AIR 2001 Raj 269.
13. AIR 1978 Del 249.
14. XLIV (1) 2008, Guj LR 309.
15. Naveen Kohli *v.* Neelu Kohli (2006) 4 SCC 558.

24

Women's Human Rights

Need for Health Care Services of HIV/Aids

RANI MANDA AND PADMA RAGAM K.

INTRODUCTION

AIDS has affected millions of women worldwide. This epidemic unfortunately remains an epidemic of women. (Michel Sidibé, Executive Director of UNAIDS). At the end of 2010 it was estimated that out of the 34 million adults worldwide living with HIV and AIDS, half are women. The AIDS epidemic has had a unique impact on women, which has been exacerbated by their role within society and their biological vulnerability to HIV infection. Generally, women are at a greater risk of heterosexual transmission of HIV. Biologically women are twice more likely to become infected with HIV through unprotected heterosexual intercourse than men. In many countries women are less likely to be able to negotiate condom use and are more likely to be subjected to non-consensual sex.

Additionally, millions of women have been indirectly affected by the HIV and AIDS epidemic. Women's childbearing role means that they have to contend with issues such as mother-to-child transmission of HIV. The responsibility of caring for AIDS patients and orphans is also an issue that has a greater effect on women. There are a number of things that can be done in order to reduce the burden of the epidemic among women. These include promoting and protecting women's human rights, increasing education and awareness among women and encouraging the development of new preventative technologies such as post-exposure prophylaxis and microbicide.

Globally, HIV/AIDS is the leading cause of death among women of reproductive age. The percentage of women living with HIV and AIDS varies significantly between different regions of the world. In areas such as Western and Central Europe, Eastern Europe and Oceania, women account for a relatively low percentage of HIV infected people. However, in regions such as sub-Saharan Africa and the Caribbean, the percentage is significantly higher.

Asia: UNAIDS estimates that nearly 4.8 million adults are living with HIV in Asia, approximately 34 percent of whom are women. The number of women living with HIV and AIDS in Asia varies greatly between different countries, and in places largely affected by the epidemic, such as India, the numbers vary between different states. Although women are often perceived to be at low risk of HIV infection because it is not common to have more than one lifetime sexual partner, a great number of women are put at risk of HIV infection as a result of their husbands having unprotected sex outside of marriage or injecting drugs. It has been estimated that 90% of women living with HIV in Asia were infected by their husband or long-term partner. The number of adults living with HIV and AIDS in India is estimated to be 2.3 million, of which 38 percent are women. As HIV transmission in India is largely through heterosexual contact, the infection rate for women is increasing, and the low economic and social status of women continues to be a barrier to preventing new infections.

In countries such as Indonesia, Vietnam and Pakistan, HIV transmission is largely through injection drug use. Not only are female injecting drug users (IDUs) at a high risk of contracting HIV but also increasing numbers of women are becoming infected with HIV from male IDU partners.

RESPONSIBILITY AND CARE FOR HIV INFECTED

In areas with few palliative care facilities, when a person becomes ill from AIDS the care is usually a woman's responsibility. In Africa, for example, two-thirds of all caregivers for persons living with HIV and AIDS are women. This care giving is usually in addition to many other tasks that women perform within the household, such as cooking, cleaning, and caring for the children and the elderly. Caring for ill parents, children or husbands is unpaid and can increase a person's workload by up to a third. Women often struggle to bring in an income whilst providing care and therefore many families affected by AIDS suffer from increasing poverty. In some areas of sub-Saharan Africa where a family's livelihood relies on growing and maintaining crops, the death of farmers can lead to famine. The AIDS epidemic also affects young girls and elderly women. Often in households where both parents are ill from AIDS, the responsibility of main care is taken on by a daughter, even if it means that she has to miss school. If both parents die then it tends to be the grandmothers, aunts or cousins who then look after the orphans.

INEQUALITIES WITHIN THE FAMILY

Why women are difficult to protect themselves, because in some societies, women have few rights within sexual relationships and the family. Often men make the majority of decisions, such as whom they will marry and whether they will have more than one sexual partner. This power imbalance means that it can be more difficult for women to protect themselves from getting infected with HIV. For example, a woman may not be able to insist on the use of a condom if her husband is the one who makes the decisions. Marriage does not always protect a woman from becoming infected with HIV. Many new infections occur within marriage or long-term relationships as a result of unfaithful partners. In a number of societies, a man having more than one sexual partner is seen as the norm.

VIOLENCE AGAINST WOMEN

Women who are victims of sexual violence are at a higher risk of being exposed to HIV, and the lack of condom use and forced nature of rape means that women are immediately more vulnerable to HIV infection. A South African study concluded that women who were beaten or dominated by their partners were much more likely to become infected with HIV than women who were not. Another study of 20,425 couples in India found not only that HIV transmission was much greater in abusive relationships, but also that abusive husbands were more likely to be infected with HIV than non-abusive husbands. In countries where armed conflict is rife, there have been reports of rape being used as a 'tool of war'. Amnesty International reported that between 1999 and 2000 in every armed conflict that they investigated, the torture of women was reported. In some cases, women have been intentionally infected with HIV, with the aim of causing a 'slow death'.

WOMEN'S INHERITANCE AND PROPERTY RIGHTS

It is well fact that in many countries around the world, women do not have the same property rights as men. Especially in sub-Saharan Africa, property is typically owned by men and even when married, women still do not have as many property rights as their husbands. Inheritance rights are just as discriminatory, as when a husband dies, his property often goes to his side of the family and not to his wife. The denial of a woman's inheritance and property rights can increase her vulnerability to HIV. Not being able to own property means that women have limited economic stability. This can lead to an increased risk of sexual exploitation and violence, as women may have to endure abusive relationships or resort to informal sex work for economic survival.

FREEDOM FROM DISCRIMINATION

Discrimination against women is a fact of life in all regions of the world, to varying degrees, and manifested in varying ways. In many countries, women face difficulties finding and keeping paid work or earning a wage that is equivalent to men's. In some regions, they are not allowed to inherit or own property or are discouraged from doing so, meaning that a woman without male protection has very few ways to support herself or her children. Stigma and ridicule are still common in many courts and prevent women from bringing cases that could rectify some of the worst injustices.

The abuses of human rights that women deal with on a daily basis can become nearly insurmountable obstacles when HIV/AIDS is involved. One of the most serious economic effects of HIV for women has been the loss of property. A study in Uganda of HIV-positive widows revealed that 90 per cent of the women interviewed had difficulties with their in-laws over property and 88 per cent of those in rural areas were unable to meet their household needs. Also in Uganda, another study found that 37 per cent of widows compared to 17 per cent of widowers had migrated from their original homes because they were generally not entitled to inherit their husband's property and their families were likely to live elsewhere.

In many regions, the right to inherit land is linked to cultural practices like cleansing. Women have been thrown out of homes they helped pay for and lost all their property because they refused to have relations with a cleanser. Because of conditions like these, Human Rights Watch has called the problem of property rights in sub-Saharan Africa 'catastrophic', leading to women ending up "homeless or living in slums, begging for food and water, unable to afford health care or school fees for their children, and at grave risk of sexual abuse or exploitation." In most of South Asia, women also have difficulty inheriting or owning property, even in instances where they are legally allowed to do so.

PREVENTING HIV INFECTION

There are a number of issues that need to be addressed in order to prevent the spread of HIV infection. The following are relatively new preventative technologies that could directly benefit women.

- The female condom is the only female-initiated HIV prevention method presently available. These condoms can potentially help women to protect themselves from becoming infected with HIV if used correctly and consistently. However, although the female condom allows partners to share the responsibility of condom use, it still requires some degree of male cooperation.
- Post-exposure prophylaxis is an antiretroviral drug treatment that is thought to decrease the chances of HIV infection after exposure to HIV. This treatment could potentially benefit women who have been raped, if started within 72 hours of exposure. In many countries with high levels of sexual violence against women and high HIV prevalence, this treatment is not always freely available to women.
- Research is being carried out into the development of a microbicide—a gel or cream that could be applied to the vagina without a partner knowing and which would prevent HIV infection. Trials have been taking place for a number of years, but none have been successful and a microbicide for HIV prevention does not yet exist.

However, protecting women from HIV is not solely women's responsibility. Most women with HIV were infected by unprotected sex with an infected man. Preventing transmission is the responsibility of both partners, and men must play an equal role in this.

HIV/AIDS AND HUMAN RIGHTS

Human rights are fundamental to addressing the HIV and AIDS epidemic. On the one hand human rights violations fuel the epidemic by increasing people's vulnerability to infection. On the other, human rights violations often follow infection and people living with HIV and AIDS can be subjected to various forms of discrimination and ill-treatment, including harassment, arbitrary arrest and torture. Discriminatory policies and practices can also result in people being denied access to the information, support and services necessary to make informed decisions and to reduce their vulnerability and risk of infection. Everywhere in the world, HIV-positive people are still subject to serious forms of stigma and discrimination. They risk losing their jobs, being ostracized from their communities and being denied equal access to goods and services necessary to realize their human rights, and even the protection of the law. The vast majority of people living with HIV have inadequate access to care and treatment. All people, including people living with HIV, have a right to the highest attainable standard of health. Amnesty International believes that respecting, protecting and fulfilling the full range of human rights of all individuals is indispensable to reducing the rates of HIV infection, expanding access to care and treatment and mitigating the impact of the epidemic, including acts of discrimination and violence.

Human rights are inextricably linked with the spread and impact of HIV on individuals and communities around the world. A lack of respect for human rights fuels the spread and exacerbates the impact of the disease, while at the same time HIV undermines progress in the realization of human rights. This link is apparent in the disproportionate incidence and spread of the disease among certain groups which, depending on the nature of the epidemic and the prevailing social, legal and economic conditions, include women and children, and particularly those living in poverty. It is also apparent in the fact that the overwhelming burden of the epidemic today is borne by developing countries, where the disease threatens to reverse vital achievements in human development. AIDS and poverty are now mutually reinforcing negative forces in many developing countries.

The Relationship between HIV/AIDS and Human Rights in three Areas

Increased vulnerability: Certain groups are more vulnerable to contracting the HIV virus because they are unable to realize their civil, political, economic, social and cultural rights. For example, individuals who are denied the right to freedom of association and access to information may be precluded from discussing issues related to HIV, participating in AIDS service organizations and self-help groups, and taking other preventive measures to protect themselves from HIV infection. Women, and particularly young women, are more vulnerable to infection if they lack of access to information, education and services necessary to ensure sexual and reproductive health and prevention of infection. The unequal status of women in the community also means that their capacity to negotiate in the context of sexual activity is severely undermined. People living in poverty often are unable to access HIV care and treatment, including anti-retroviral and other medications for opportunistic infections.

Discrimination and stigma: The rights of people living with HIV often are violated because of their presumed or known HIV status, causing them to suffer both the burden of the disease and the consequential loss of other rights. Stigmatization and discrimination may obstruct their access to treatment and may affect their employment, housing and other rights. This, in turn, contributes to the vulnerability of others to infection, since HIV-related stigma and discrimination discourages individuals infected with and affected by HIV from contacting health and social services. The result is that those most needing information, education and counseling will not benefit even where such services are available.

Impedes an effective response: Strategies to address the epidemic are hampered in an environment where human rights are not respected. For example, discrimination against and stigmatization of vulnerable groups such as injecting drug users, sex workers, and men who have sex with men drives these communities underground. This inhibits the ability to reach these populations with prevention efforts, and thus increases their vulnerability to HIV. Likewise, the failure to provide access to education and information about HIV, or treatment, and care and support services further fuels the AIDS epidemic. These elements are essential components of an effective response to AIDS, which is hampered if these rights are not respected

PROMOTING AND PROTECTING WOMEN'S HUMAN RIGHTS

In many parts of the world there exist major inequalities between women and men in all aspects of living from employment opportunities and availability of education, to power inequalities within relationships. These gender roles can confine women to positions where they lack the power to protect themselves from HIV infection. As most of the inequalities that women face are denying them their basic human rights, it is thought that promoting these rights will enhance their status within society and help protect them against the risk of HIV infection. Protecting the human rights of women and girls also protects them from HIV/AIDS. More than any other disease in recent decades, HIV/AIDS has exposed the social inequities that make girls and women more likely to become infected, but women need more than rights in order to protect themselves. They need to know that they have such rights, that they can act in their own self-interest and that they will be supported by their communities and governments.

In many countries, women cannot take human rights for granted. They do not have access to the education and information that would help them learn how to avoid HIV infection. They are subject to violence, which robs them of control over their bodies and limits their ability to use methods to prevent HIV infection. This chapter looks at two aspects of human rights: instances where these rights appear to come into conflict with traditional practices such as early and forced marriage, female genital cutting (FGC) and 'widow cleansing' (a traditional practice in which widows are expected to have sexual relations, often with a relative of their late husband, in order to secure property within the family); and instances where women's ability to achieve economic independence is directly or indirectly affected by discrimination.

TRANSFORMING GENDER ROLES

Both men and women are affected by gender roles that define what it means to be a man or a woman. These gender-based expectations can increase vulnerability to HIV infection. For example, in many societies women are expected to be innocent and submissive when it comes to sex, preventing them from accessing sexual health information and services. For many men, masculinity is linked with taking risks and being tough, which can increase vulnerability to HIV infection and discourage men from seeking testing and treatment. Recognizing and challenging harmful gender roles is crucial to preventing the spread of HIV. Programmes that focus on men are equally important in protecting women from HIV, as they can transform men's attitudes and behaviour towards their partners, families and women in general.

INCREASING EDUCATION AND AWARENESS

Education is one of the most effective tools in preventing HIV infections. An estimate from the Global Campaign for Education suggests that if every child received a complete primary education, around 700,000 new HIV infections in young adults could be prevented every year. Education is particularly important for protecting girls against HIV infection. School can teach vital HIV prevention methods, such as condom use, having fewer sexual partners, and the importance of greater communication about HIV prevention between couples. Also, girls who frequently attend school are more likely to be able to make decisions about their sexual lives, are more independent, and are more likely to earn a higher income in the future. Increasing HIV and AIDS education can also help to reduce the stigma that people living with HIV and AIDS face. Eradicating stigma is important in the fight against HIV and AIDS because stigma can increase the vulnerability of a group that may already be at a higher risk of HIV infection. Sex workers, for example, are in many countries still both frowned on socially and criminalized. It is very difficult for these women to access the healthcare services they need in order to stay healthy if they risk arrest or punishment when their profession is known.

CONCLUSION

Women are physiologically more susceptible than men to HIV infection through unprotected vaginal intercourse, and the vast majority of women living with HIV are infected in this way. Women's physiological vulnerability to HIV infection is compounded by pervasive sexual and domestic violence and by women's entrenched social and economic inequality within their marriages and intimate relationships. HIV transmission between spouses is becoming more prevalent and there are indications that married women have a higher risk of infection than unmarried women. For example, adolescent brides in some African countries are being infected with HIV at a higher rate than their sexually active unmarried counterparts. Women have also suffered disproportionately from discrimination against people living with HIV/AIDS. The pandemic has led to increased gender-based violence as HIV-positive women are assaulted, prevented from having children, dismissed from employment, disowned, shunned by their families and communities, and sometimes even killed. Women are more likely than men to be held responsible for spreading the disease and to be labeled as promiscuous. Fearing violence, stigma, and ostracism, many women avoid taking HIV tests, thereby denying themselves crucial information about their health and excluding themselves from programs to prevent HIV transmission to their newborns.

References

Anju Bindra (2010): "HIV/AIDS Health Care and Human Rights", Manglam Publishers, Delhi.

Chenna Reddy, D. (2010): "Human Rights of Women", Manglam Publishers, Delhi.

Deshmukh, K.L. (2011): "Human Rights and International Law", Swastik Publishers, Delhi.

Jagannath Mohanty (2008): "Human Rights Education", Deep & Deep Publications Pvt. Ltd., New Delhi.

M.L. Janagambika (2010): "Social Work and Human Rights", Navyug Books International, Delhi.

Prasad. R.N. (2011): "Human Rights in India: An Analytical Perspectives", Kanishka Publications, New Delhi.

Raju, M.V. (2010): "Human Rights: Today and Tomorrow", Swastik Publishers, Delhi.

Reichert (2007): "Challenges in Human Rights: A Social Work Practice", Rawat Publications, New Delhi.

Singh, Schgal, B.P. (2008): "Human Rights in India: Problems and Perspectives", Deep & Deep Publishers Pvt. Ltd, New Delhi.

Wasiyoddin R. Mujawar (2009): "Social Justice and Human Rights", Manglam Publishers, Delhi.

25

Legislative Protection for Women in India

A Ladder For Women Empowerment

B. YUVAKUMAR REDDY AND S. DRAKSHAYANI

Human Rights are the natural rights, basic rights which should be enjoyed by all people in the society. Though at the global level and national level laws exist to protect the rights of human being man/woman in general but special consideration and concentration is required to recognize the rights of women. Gender jurisprudence is new ordering of society to emancipate and liberate women from the shackles of ancient law, traditions and customs whereby the new claims, interest and needs of the women are promoted and readjusted through law with men folk on a footing of equality, dignity and non-exploitation.

In a democracy, welfare state concept always prevails as important requirement. India, as the worlds, largest democracy, strictly adheres to the Socio-economic welfare of the people as the prime tasks of the makers of the state. Equality is the first principle of the constitution and in every governmental action, gender based-discrimination represents the very ugly face of the society. This issue is global with different degrees and very old in nature. It is a travesty of all cannons of social Justice and equity, the women who constitutes half of the world's population and work two-third of worlds working hours should earn just both of world's property and also should remain victim of inequality and injustice. Fay Welden, the British Novelist commented that "We are well enough attended to racism, seximalas, scarcely upsets us". The sex equality was paramount necessity for national development to eradicate discrimination and inequality and to provide enough opportunities for the exercise of women protection. Even god is regarded as half man, half woman popularly known as "Ardhanariswara" but the woman is neglected from womb to tomb or from ancient times to modern times that is as a girl she assists to their mother from six years onwards in fetching water from the pump, cleaning the yard and cleaning utenisils. The elder girls look after younger siblings. The sister stalls the babies' cries of hunger by singing songs or by distracting them. As a wife and mother woman is heavily loaded with multy responsibilities. All these activities are seems to be social in nature but behind it there will be 'force' which is the cause root for discrimination against women in general and girls in particular.

In India, there are various women policies, schemes, and legislatures for protecting women or eradicating discriminations but there are dearth in proviso's or with too many technicalities in the legislature. This impact may be on the organ of implementation and finally favours to the women are remains null. This paper is an attempt to study the protections available in India are really protects through legislative safeguards and the shortcomings that are coming for providing justice to women. The research paper is based on secondary data with the following objectives:

1. To enlight the schemes and policies available to protect women in India in general and girls in particular.
2. To describe the constitutional and legislative safeguards in India.
3. To study the role of organisations in Protection of Women Rights.
4. To identify the steps to be followed for protection of women rights.

CONVENTIONS, POLICIES AND SCHEMES IN INDIA

The life of Indian women had passed in different ways through different periods. If one looks at classical religio-juridical literature, the dharmasastras, the position of women in early India appears to be measurable and degrading. Manusmriti contains verses which are explicitly hostile towards women. The Post-modern treat equality as a social construct and since it is a product of patriarchy, feminist reconstruction new truth in place of old things within the frame work of democratic polity, our government has ratified various international conventions covenents, policies one among them is convention on elimination of all forms of Discrimination Against Women (CEDAW) in 1993. India is a party to the International Covenant on Civil and Political Rights and the International covenant on Economic, Social and Cultural rights adopted by general assembly of the United Nations on 16th December 1966 and to have the mechanism to deal with this rights enacted the protection of Human Rights Act, 1993 and the like.

The Government has also taken steps for incorporation of various schemes where a separate department is created to ensure development and welfare of women and children. The women welfare department was established in the erst while Madras State in 1952 with special programmes for women and children by converting the activities of women's civil cops started by the wives of the military officers to take care of the war widows and their children after II World War with the help of welfare activities.

The government has introduced women welfare department and this department initially was taken up the welfare approach to women's problems through community development workers. Formation of Mahila Mandals, District shelters and after Care Homes, etc. worked with rural women to stimulate the awareness. Later several schemes were taken place like direct investment on girl child, education to girl child, marriage after majority, and so on so forth. Since 1953 several steps were taken by the government for empowerment but the lack of practical implenmentation. Due to this several lacunae, draw backs were facing by the aggrieved women. This impact of the society has found by the commissions, academic conferences and legislature. The parliamentarians started introducing legislative safeguards for protecting women.

CONSTITUTIONAL MANDATE REGARDING PROTECTION OF WOMEN

The Constitution of India not only grants equality to women but also empowers the state to adopt measures of positive discrimination in favour of women for neutralizing the cumulative socio economic, educational, political disadvantages faced by them.

1. Article 14, Equality before law and equal protection of laws for women.
2. Article 15 states to make special protection for women.
3. Article 39(a) state to direct its policy towards securing for men and women equally the right to an adequate means of livelihood.
4. Article 39(d), equal pay for equal work for both men and women.
5. Article 42, maternity relief
6. Article 51(A)(e) to promote the spirit of brother hood amongst all the people of India and to renounce practices derogatory to the dignity of women.
7. Article 243, one-third of the seats to be filled by direct election and the same ratio for Chairpersons in the panchayats at each level and in Municipal Corporation as well.

LEGISLATIVE SAFEGUARDS FOR EMPOWERING WOMEN WITH THE HELP OF CONSTITUTION

The legislative measures has taken place to eradicate or to control violence against women The offences against women can be classified as crime against women in general law of crimes and special laws for protecting women in India.

General Law of Crimes: The general law of crime or law of crimes is Indian penal code. Outraging the modesty of women (Secs. 509 and 354), Rape and attempt to rape (Secs. 376 or 376r/w511), kidnapping or abduction of women or girls (Sec 363 to 373), Harassment of married women (Sec. 498-A), Consequential offences of harassment which are like Dowry Deaths, Homicide for dowry, abetment to commit suicide, or attempt to murder and the like. Harassment leads for filing of maintenance application and its consequences are matrimonial matters like Divorce, Judicial separation and Restitution of conjugal Rights.

SPECIAL LEGISLATIONS FOR PROTECTING WOMEN

The Legislative activism has taken place for protecting women in different dimentions initially the society was depending on only Indian penal code but some of the amendments were taken place in the year 1985 in IPC and also in Law of Evidence as well.

The Special statutory protections are :

1. Immoral Traffic (Prevention) Act, 1956
2. Dowry Prohibition Act, 1961
3. The Maternity Benefit Act, 1961
4. The Medical Termination of Pregnancy Act, 1971
5. Indecent Representation of women (Prohibition) Act, 1986
6. Commission of Sati (Prevention) Act, 1987
7. Prohibition of Child Marriage Act
8. Protection of Women Domestic Violence Act, 2005 and rules 2007.

India has a number of well-intended laws on protection of women, a few of them having been shown above. They have not achieved their objective owing to poor implementation, insufficient policing and lack of awareness and the year 2002 declared as women empowerment year. No doubt that the legislative trend from time to time depicts the honest attempt for betterment of women's status in the society as considerable inequalities, gender discriminations, harassment and violence but still the women are facing the unbearable drawbacks.

ROLE OF ORGANISATIONS IN PROTECTION OF WOMEN RIGHTS

Laws, particularly relating to women, cannot be successful without popular support and social change. NGOs and activists play an important role in creating awareness and informing citizens of their rights and options under law. An interesting example is that of the 'Bell Bajao' campaign against domestic violence. It was produced *pro bono* by advertising professionals in association with the Ministry of Women and Child Development and several human rights organizations. NGOs and public-spirited individuals can act as a bridge between State and victims, helping them escape situations of violence and also get justice through judicial channels.

CONCLUSION

The survey and review of legislative provisions particularly in criminal laws reveal that there are pitfalls in the wording or drafting of certain provisions in the legislations like Indian Penal Code, Dowry Prohibition Act, Criminal Procedure Code, Prevention of

Immoral Traffic Act and in Domestic Violence Act. In order to provide adequate safeguards to women empowerment the following steps may be taken:

- These too many legislations are creating confusion for proper action; all these legislations should be brought under one umbrella through making as one single statute as Law of Women and Girls protection act.
- Criminal laws has to be replaced from concurrent list of the constitution to union list so that uniformity can be maintained in the entire country
- In women offences technicalities should be dispensed and speedy disposal and Victim compensation should be given on the date of Judgement without following a separate enquiry as made in Sec. 357-A Crpc.
- Active role of voluntary organisations should be given in the statute for empowerment of women.
- Incorporation of saviour penal sanctions, positive implementation of statutes by active police.
- Legal services should be extended irrespective of social and financial status in women matters.

References

Hemalatha Devi V., 'Role of law in developing Asia', organised by Asian Law Institute, Faculty of law, National University of Singapore, 2004.

Subba Rao, T.V. and Hemalatha Devi, V., Women law and social change in women development perspectives from selected states of India, edited by Reddy, P.R. and Sumangala, p. 1998.

Viswanatha Reddy K., Cultural Ecology of Indian Tribes, Raj Publications, Delhi-2002.

Saxena D.R., Law, Justice and Social Change, Deep and Deep Publications, New Delhi, 1996.

Anil Trehan, Nyaya Deep, NLSA Volume XI, issue ivoct 2010, pp. 89 and 90.

Myneni S.R., Jurisprudence, 2001.

Pandey, J.N., Constitutional Law of India.

Women Development and Child Welfare Department Manual.

www.Parliament of India.nic.in

www.mosp.nic.in/mosp_upload/women-man P2010.

wwwlawyerscollective.org

26

Women's Health and Law

V. VIJAY LAKSHMI

Women share half of the population. Hence, it is very important to note that insufficient care or absence of health care of women is likely to cripple the other half of the society. A society with fifty percent unhealthy persons fails to achieve its goals. A sick girl child cannot become a healthy woman and an unhealthy woman cannot beget a healthy child. Children who are considered as future of the nation cannot lead the country towards light if they suffer from health complications. With fifty percent of population not maintaining good health hundred percent performances cannot be expected. Countries that do not capitalize on the full potential of one half of their societies are misallocating their human resources and undermining their competitive potential.[1] The overall progress of society, state or the world is dependent upon the health of a woman. Empowerment of a woman[2] thrives to achieve the health factor of a woman too. Among various dimensions of woman's empowerment like social, political, economic, health is also a major component. A holistic approach to women's health which includes nutrition, health services, access to comprehensive, affordable and quality health care is required, better employment conditions at work place, special attention from the family and society is required. Hence, attempts are made both at international and national level to achieve this objective. An attempt is made in this brief paper to discuss various aspects of women's health, the related legal perspectives, national policies and the concerned measures on women's health.

Protection of health of its subjects is one of the primary duties of any State. This duty becomes more significant when it is the question of protecting the health of women. Health care for women may be discussed under two broad methods. One is by enacting specific provisions on women related issues and entitling the women with certain rights and the other is by undertaking certain measures that would ultimately facilitate to achieve the required goal Health includes total well-being. It includes both physical and mental health.[3] it was first articulated in the 1946 Constitution of the World Health Organization (WHO), whose preamble defines health has "a state of complete physical, mental and social well-being and not merely the absence of disease or infirmity". The preamble further states that "the enjoyment of the highest attainable standard of health is one of the fundamental rights of every human being without distinction of race, religion, political belief, economic or social condition."

The 1948 Universal Declaration of Human Rights also mentioned health has part of the right to an adequate standard of living (art. 25). The right to health was again recognized as a human right in the 1966 International Covenant on Economic, Social and Cultural Rights. Right to health is a constitutional rights. "Right to health is not included directly in as a fundamental right in the Indian Constitution. The Constitution maker imposed this duty on State to ensure social and economic justice. Article 38 of Indian Constitution imposes liability on State that states will secure a social order for the promotion of welfare of the people but without public health we cannot achieve it. It means without public health welfare of people is impossible. Article 39(e) related with workers to protect their health. Article 41 imposed duty on State to public assistance basically for those who are sick and disable. Article 42 makes provision to protect the health of infant and mother by maternity benefit. The Directive Principles of State Policy are only the directives to the State. These are non-justifiable. No person çan claim for non-fulfilling these directives.

· *Judicial interpretations*: The Supreme Court has brought the right to health under the preview of Article 21. The scope of this provision is very wide. It prescribes for the right of life and personal liberty. The concept of personal liberty comprehended many rights, related to indirectly to life or liberty of a person. And now a person can claim his right of health.[4] In 1995, the Supreme Court held[5] that right to health and medical care is a fundamental right covered by Article 21 since health is essential for making the life of workmen meaningful and purposeful and compatible with personal dignity. The Supreme Court, while examining the issue of the constitutional right to health care under Arts 21, 41 and 47 of the Constitution of India in *State of Punjab* v. *Ram Lubhaya Bagga*,[6] observed that the right of one person correlates to a duty upon another, individual, employer, government or authority. Hence, the right of a citizen to live under Art. 21 casts and obligation on the state. This obligation is further reinforced under Art. 47; it is for the state to secure health to its citizens as its primary duty. No doubt the government is rendering this obligation by opening government hospitals and health centers, but to be meaningful, they must be within the reach of its people, and of sufficient liquid quality. Since it is one of the most sacrosanct and valuable rights of a citizen, and an equally sacrosanct and sacred obligation of the state, every citizen of this welfare state looks towards the state to perform this obligation with top priority, including by way of allocation of sufficient funds. This in turn will not only secure the rights of its citizens to their satisfaction, but will benefit the state in achieving its social, political and economic goals.

Thus, Article 21 which guarantees every citizen a fundamental right to life in its ambit and life implies a healthy life. Every person is equal before law and the right to equality and right against discrimination is enshrined under Articles 14 and 15 of the Constitution. Yet it is been realised that women do not in practice enjoy same status as do men. Their biological constitution and social implications make them comparatively weaker. Women are affected by as many of the same health conditions as men, but women experience them differently. The prevalence of poverty and economic dependence among women, their experience of violence, gender bias in the health system and society at large, discrimination on the grounds of race or other factors, the limited power many women have over their sexual and reproductive lives and their lack of influence in decision-making are social realities which have an adverse impact on their health.[7] Due to this they are been pushed to the back seat of development. Hence, unless they are been brought to the mainstream the overall progress of the society cannot be achieved.

State is empowered to make special provisions for women and children. Various factors influence the wellbeing of a woman. It cannot be assumed that various factors affect the health of men and women equally as both are biologically different. Some of the determinants that influence the women's health include: (i) Genetic factors, (ii) Environmental factors, (iii) Nutritional factors, (iv) Working conditions, (v) Practices in family, (vi) Economic factors, (vii) Education and (viii) Insufficient sanitation, housing, etc.

Genetic/health Factors: Genetic/health factors that affect a woman can be classified in three groups. One, that is common like deformity at the time of birth whether physical or mental, second is the defects that are more common to women and under third category factors that are exclusive to women can be grouped. Like the health problems related to cancer like cervical and breast cancers are more specific to women.[8]

Education is one such factor that makes lot of difference from a person not educated. An educated woman better understands the health perspectives of her personal health and the health aspects of family. It may be presumed that educated woman would be more capable in selecting quality of good, content of consumable goods including that of drugs, medicines and approaching for better medical care. Education is one of the important tools of health care. If individuals can be educated to have the essential information, skill and value to take care of their own health the incidence of illness is considerably reduced and management of illness when it does occur is made simpler and more economic.[9] Education, which plays a significant and remedial role in balancing the socio-economic framework of the country. Improvements in education are not only expected to enhance the efficiency but also augment the overall quality of life. Education is an instrument of social change and eliminates gender disparities and ensures equal opportunities. Social Empowerment and Education domain aims at converging and linking various schemes of Government of India focusing on women with special reference to the flagship programs of Ministry of Human Resource Development (MoHRD).[10] Utilization of postnatal care by women's education reveals that effect of education is quite significant towards promotion of utilization of postnatal care from public health institutions.[11] Earlier, education of a girl upto fourteen years was made free but now realising the importance of education, it is made a statutory right of every child to have free and compulsory right under the Right to Education Act.

Family factors: Among the family factors marriage, child-bearing, domestic environment in a matrimonial home is responsible for maintaining good health especially the mental health of a woman. It should not be thought that care is not required before marriage. Proper education, nutrition is required for a healthy growth of a gird child. Abolition of child marriage and solemnising a marriage of girl before the completion of eighteen years is void.[12] Health issues are also involved with respect to conception, pregnancy and child birth.[13] Medical Termination of Pregnancy Act, 1971 entitles women *inter-alia*, to terminate pregnancy by registered medical practitioner where its continuance would involve a risk to life of the pregnant woman or grave injury to the physical and mental health or where there is substantial risk that if the child were born, it would suffer from such physical or mental abnormalities as to be seriously handicapped if there is a danger to the health of the woman or there is danger for the new born. Violence against the woman whether it is physical or mental is made actionable under Indian Penal Code.[14] Dowry-related issues and domestic violence are strictly dealt under Dowry Prohibition Act, 1961 and Domestic Violence Act, 2005. Domestic violence is found to be associated with a range of symptoms and diagnoses such as respiratory conditions that includes allergies, breathing difficulties and various chronic lung conditions and cardiovascular diseases, bowel problems, pain and fatigue.[15] In addition to this in case of dissolution of marriage, for whatever reason, a woman is entitled to claim maintenance or alimony.[16] Psychological state of childless woman cannot be expressed. Hindu Adoption and Maintenance Act, provides an opportunity even to an unmarried woman to adopt a child.

Economic and financial issues: Economic and financial solvency brings lot of confidence and earns self-respect for woman. A woman can attend health issues personally and can take better care for her dependants. Share in ancestral property is a step in this direction. This is taken care by amending the Hindu Marriage and Right to Property Act, 1937 and the Hindu Succession Act, 1925. Recently, the Supreme Court has highlighted the right of the women in India to eliminate gender-based discrimination particularly in respect of property so as to attain economic empowerment.[17] The Court while referring to CEDAW[18] elaborately discussed the principles of equality of rights and respect of women's dignity.

Employment: One of the fastest growing trends in the world over the past two decades has been the increase in the number of women. Women have been joining the workforce with increasing numbers in sectors such as agriculture, industry and services making up 42 percent of the estimated global working population.[19] Working women have multiple roles to play. National Commission of Women on 'Self-employed Women and Women in Informal Sector', 1988,[20] stated that in order to understand the occupational health aspects, it is necessary in terms of physical and mental health to analyse in terms of physical stress, postural position and their effects, and occupational health-related problems.[21] Employment opportunities for women by following the 'reservation system' are another milestone that is achieved under Article 15(3) of the Constitution. State is required to secure equal pay for equal work for both men and women.[22] In *CESE Ltd.* v. *Subhash Chandra Bose,*[23] the court held that, the health and strength of a worker is an integral facet of the right to life. The aim of fundamental rights is to create an egalitarian society to free all citizens from coercion or restrictions by society and to make liberty available for all. The court, while reiterating its stand for providing health facilities in *Vincent* v. *Union of India*[24], held that a healthy body is the very foundation for all human activities. In a welfare state, therefore, it is the obligation of the state to ensure the creation and the sustaining of conditions congenial to good health.

Health, hygiene, insufficient sanitation and housing: Health problems related to employment is another area where the government is taking constant measures to protect the interest of women employees. National Institute of Public Co-operation and Child Development factors affecting the poor health status of women as unsafe drinking water, inadequate sanitation facilities, poor hygiene and housing conditions, disproportionate workload, physical and mental violence, etc.[25] Article 42 requires the State to make provision for securing just and humane conditions of work and for maternity relief. Article 39 (e)specifically directs the State not to abuse the health and strength of workmen and women. Factories Act prohibits employment of women in hazardous occupation. The 1987 amendment to Indian Factories Act, 1948 is made to deal with the occupational health and safety matters keeping in concern the physical and mental well being of the women. Maternity Benefit Act, 1961 specially enacted with an objective to secure just and humane conditions of work and for maternity relief. It regulates employment of women in certain establishment for certain periods before and after child birth and to provide for maternity and other benefits. The National Health Policy (2002) pointed out "social, cultural and economic factors continue to inhibit women from gaining adequate access even to the existing public health facilities. It highlighted women along with other under-privileged groups, as one who are significantly handicapped due to a disproportionately low access to health care.[26]

Proper sanitation and a safe house are *sine qua non* for a healthy house. In the absence of sanitation a person with all other resources may not lead a healthy life. Unhygienic surroundings cause him/her to suffer from various kinds of diseases. NFHS-3 survey has also revealed that every third woman in India is undernourished (33.0 per cent have low Body Mass Index) and every second woman is anemic (56.2 per cent women are anemic in the age-group of 15-49).[27] The cell would endeavour to achieve empowerment of women by convergence of different schemes/programmes, encourage health-seeking behaviour and fuel demand through awareness generation for appropriate services to meet women's health and nutritional needs from infancy to old age and would encourage women to make informed decisions about their health. Maternal mortality and foetal losses could be reduced considerably if women undergo delivery underhygienic conditions under the supervision of trained health professionals.

Studying environmental factors, specifically in the context of women's health, is important because it cannot be assumed that the environment will affect women and men in the same way. First, systematic differences in the way men and women live and work can result in significant differences in environmental exposures. Second, women's lives involve hormonal and metabolic changes that create opportunities for differential effects of similar environmental exposures as compared to men. Many of these biologic events influence the uptake, distribution, and storage of chemicals.[28]

Exploitation of women at workplace is another serious concern that causes deterioration of woman's health. The judicial pronouncements by the Supreme Court in Visakha case[29] where the guidelines laid down to remedy the legislative shortfalls are commendable. A Bill in this regard is pending before the parliament. It is observed in a study that with decreased employment opportunities, women/men are taking up self- employment but even in such cases also women faces violence and harassment from state machinery (police, administrative bodies), customers, male counterparts, from other agencies involved in trade like transporters, general public, etc[30].

Nutritional conditions: Life is not mere existence. The person should have a healthy body. It is the healthy food that keeps our body healthy. Lack of good food or insufficient food makes us weak and unhealthy. In the absence of balance diet the possibility of getting sick is more. Food needs are different for both men and women. Proper nutrition is a key determinant of health, both in childhood and beyond. The nutritional status of girls is particularly important due to their future potential reproductive role.

Environmental aspects: In *Virender Gaur* v. *State of Haryana*, the Supreme Court held that environmental, ecological, air and water pollution, etc., should be regarded as amounting to violation of right to health guaranteed by Article 21 of the Constitution. It is right to state that hygienic environment is an integral facet of the right to healthy life and it would not be possible to live with human dignity without a humane and healthy environment.[31] In *Subhash Kumar* v. *State of Bihar*,[32] the Supreme Court held that right to pollution-free water and air is an enforceable fundamental right guaranteed under Article 21. Further, the Supreme Court imposed a positive obligation upon the State to take steps for ensuring to the individual a better enjoyment of life and dignity and for elimination of water and air pollution.

Violence[33] against women is continuously in rise. Crimes against a woman especially that of serious nature like rape, cruelty, trafficking in women, bigamy, cause irreparable loss to the victim and also brings national shame.[34] The perilous impact on the health of women due to such barbarous acts is unquantified. As such criminal sanctions are imposed on the guilty.[35] The recent gang rape case of Delhi and in many other places and the strong protest from all sections of the society in the country, demanding capital punishment for such crimes appears to be appropriate. Protection of Women's Health by the State under Directive Principles and through Policy Measures:

Various schemes evolved by the Government from time to time either under its own research or investigation or from the reports of International Organisation or under the obligations of International Treaties and Conventions may be called as steps that are taken by the State to attend the health issues of women. Article 46 requires the State to promote with special care the education and economic interests of the weaker sections of the citizens. Obviously it directs towards a gender just society. The various special programmes and policies that have been formulated by the State since independence have had this objective.

In addition to the rights and policy issues of government there exist fundamental duties under the constitution. Article 51A(e) requires that the citizens of India renounce practices derogatory to the dignity of woman. In the India the Directive Principle of State Policy under the Article 47 considers it the primary duty of the state to improve public health, securing of justice, human condition of works, extension of sickness, old age, disablement and maternity benefits and also contemplated. Further, State's duty includes prohibition of consumption of intoxicating drinking and drugs are injurious to health. Article, 48-A ensures that State shall Endeavour to protect and impose the pollution-free environment for good health.

It may be expected that the proper implementation these schemes would definitely improve the health perspectives of the women. The National Commission of Women, a statutory body, is working in various fields of women and making recommendations to the government in this regard for necessary action. In addition to this it is to be remembered that enacting gender just laws is not enough to end the exploitation of women. The mental set-up in the society needs a change. Above all it is to be understood that it is the human right of every women that she should be treated first as an 'individual' than as mother, wife or daughter.

CONCLUSION

Constitution-makers included public health as Directive Principle of State Polivy because they were well-known about it that only inclusion of right to health as Fundamental Rights (F.R.) will hive only right but it will not ensure medical facilities. If right to health included as a F.R. then what happened it is clear that State can protect himself to say that who is going to take away your right for example if any person effected by T.B. defended for his right to health as a F.R., then State can protect to say that go and be healthy. T.B. is not caused to you by State. Thus right to health as F.R. cannot be give remedy for ill person. For treatment of T.B. there are so many component are requirement, i.e. Hospital, doctor, medicine. So constitution-makers included it in DPSP for to impose duty to State so that State will protect and improve public health. Due to this duty states are taking steps in this regard and hospitals are running in control of State to give free health service to public at large. There is no need of right to health for a person to be healthy. A person should have health entitlements, medical aid, medical assistance which provided by States.

Knowledge is power and its power comes through education so it is only education with the help of which woman can become independent, think freely and become capable of taking right decision bring forward their ideas, participate in all activities of life , light for their rights, work for their own development and finally development of welfare of society.[36] In addition to education proper working conditions, safe environment, hygiene, proper nutrition, is required. It is the duty of all of us to see that violence against women is not only condemned but we should shun away from such acts. It should not be forgotten that improving women's health matters to women, to their families, communities and societies at large. Therefore,improve women's health—improve the world.

NOTES AND REFERENCES

1. 'Women's Empowerment: Measuring the Global Gender Gap', an overview prepared by WORLD ECONOMIC FORUM, 2005. p. 1.
2. "...no tool for development is more effective than the empowerment of women. No other policy is as likely to raise economic productivity, or to reduce infant and maternal mortality. No other policy is as sure to improve nutrition and promote health—including the prevention of HIV/AIDS. No other policy is as powerful in increasing the chances of education for the next generation", Kofi Annan, Commission on the Status of Women marking Beijing +10, 28 February 2005 http://www.unohrlls.org/UserFiles/File/Publications/Genderperspectives.pdf [visited on 28-09-2010].
3. Mental health is recognized globally as being of enormous social and public health importance. World over, more women than men, suffer from common mental disorders (2) Several mental health issues arise from social, psychological and physiological differences on account of gender and need specific attention (3) Gender-based violence has far-reaching mental implications (4) Mental ill-health and its profound stigmatization carry with it a burden of human suffering that at times is not only incalculable, but incomprehensible to the non-afflicted onlookers. The situation can be much worse if the affected person is a woman. Kanchan Kumari, 'Women and children: mental health dimensions' Mental Health Care and Human Rights, NHRC PUBLICATION, 2008, edited by D. Nagaraja Pratima Murthy, ISBN- 978-81-9044117-5.
4. Sheeraj Latif Ahmad Khan, "right to health". (1995) 2 SCJ 29-34, at 30.
5. Consumer Education and Research Center *v.* UOI, AIR 1995 SC 636; See also Parmanand Katra *v.* Union of India, AIR 1989 SC 2039; Paschim Banga Khet Mazdoor Samity & Ors *v.* State of West Bengal & Ors, (1996) 4 SCC 37; Kirloskar Brothers Ltd. *v.* Employees' State Insurance Corporation, (1996) 2 SCC 682, AIR 1996 SC 3261, Vincent

Panikurlangara *v.* Union of India, AIR 1987 SC 990, (1987) 2 SCC 165; Unnikrishnan, J.P. *v.* State of A.P., AIR 1993 SC 2178 , (1993) 1 SCC 645.

6. 1998) 4 SCC 177: AIR 1998 SC 1703.
7. The Right to HealthFact Sheet No. 31 World Health Organization, p. 16 http://www.ohchr.org/Documents/Publications/Factsheet31.pdf[2-12-12]
8. National Health Profile 2008 reveals that 37.4 per cent of the cancer incidences are in cervix (19.1%) and breast (17.3%) which are women-specific.
9. R. Ramurthy, "Health for All", Social Justice in Health edited by S.C. Bhatia, 1988, p. 62 and p. 64.
10. http://nmew.gov.in/index1.php?lang=1&level=0&linkid=58&lid=166&ltypeid=2&domid=9[23-12-12]
11. http://planningcommission.nic.in/reports/peoreport/peoevalu/peo_2807.pdf. p. 82.
12. Hindu Marriage Act, 1955, Section 5.
13. According to the World Health Organization, 585,000 women die every year, over 1,600 every day, from causes related to pregnancy and childbirth. World Health Organization/UNICEF, 1996.
14. See Section 304-B [dealing with 'dowry deaths'. The punishment for such offences is imprisonment of seven years but may be extended to life imprisonment]; Section 313 [dealing with 'miscarriage' without the consent of women]; Section 354 [outraging the modesty of women]
15. Deborah Loxton *et.al.* 'History of Domestic Violence and Physical Health in Mid-life', Violence Against Women: *An International and Interdisciplinary Journal*, Vol. 12, Aug. 2006, Sage Publication, p. 715 at p. 727.
16. See Section 18(1) of the Hindu Adoption and Maintenance Act, 1956, Section 125 of Cr.P.C. Indian Divorce Act 1869, Parsi Marriage and Divorce Act, 1936 and Special Marriage Act, 1954.
17. C.M. Mudaliar *v.* Sri S. Swaminathaswami Thirukoil (1996) 8 SCC 525.
18. CEDAW refers to Convention on Elimination of all forms of Discrimination against Women, held at Vienna. India ratified this Convention in 1993.
19. H.L. Kalia, 'Women, Work and Family, 2005,Ravat Publication, p. 256.
20. The Commission's Task Force on Health (1998) found that each year, work -related injuries and diseases kill as estimated 1.1 million people world over.
21. Sareen *et. al.*, 'Women and Occupational Health', *Indian Journal of Industrial Medicine*, 43 (2), June 1997.
22. See Article 39 (d) of the Constitution and Equal Remuneration Act, 1976.
23. AIR 1992 SC 573: 1991 (2) SCALE 996.
24. AIR 1987 SC 990.
25. Statistics of Women in India, 2007, a study on Health and Nutrition by Ministry of Women and Child Development (India).
26. Mainstreaming Gender Perspective in the National Health Programmes: The Challenges Ahead L.K. Piang, Poonam Khattar and Deoki Nandan,

Journal of Population Research, Volume 33 Number 1 January-March, 2010, p. 34 at p. 35.

27. http://nmew.gov.in/index1.php?lang=1&level=0&linkid= 45&lid=118&ltypeid=2&domid=6
28. [http://www.sciencedirect.com/science/article/pii/B978012288 1459500565] Women and Health
29. Visakha *v.* State of Rajsthan, (1997) 6 SCC 241.
30. Seema Salgaonkar, 'Violence, Employment and Citizenshiip—A case study of Self employed women in Unorganised Sector in Goa.' *Indian Jounrnal of Gender Studies*, Vol. 14, Jan.-April, 2007. Sage Pub. pp.117-35.
31. 1995 (2) SCC 577. See also T. Damodar Rao and others *v.* Special Officer, Municipal Corporation of Hyderabad, AIR 1987 AP 171.
32. AIR 1991 SC 420, (1991) I SCC 598. See also Shantistar Builders *v.* Narayan Khimalal Totame, (1990) 2 SCJ 10, AIR 1990 SC 630, (1990) 1 SCC, 520 M.C. Mehta *v.* Union of India (1987) 4 SCC 463, AIR 1988 SC 1037; Rural Litigation and Entitlement Kendra *v.* State of U.P., AIR 1987 SC 359.
33. Violence includes exploitation, discrimination, creation of an atmosphere of terror, a situation of threat are parisal and other form of political violence.
34. Indeed, it is difficult to measure the true extent of violence against women as most incidences of domestic violence and sexual assault go unreported.
35. Indian Penal Code deals with the various sexual offences against women in Sections 375 to 376-D and 509. The offence of rape is punishable with seven imprisonment or it may be extended to ten years or even life imprisonment. Bigamy is punishable for a term of ten years- Section 495.
36. Effft Yasmin, 'Enpowring women through eduction: Insights from Jammu and Kashmir', *Journal of Women Studies*, Vol. 111, June 2011, p. 49 at p. 60.

27

Women Health and the Scope for Expansion of Abortion Services

A Medico Legal Analysis

SUNITHA KANIPAKAM, HARIPRIYA SUSMITHA B. AND T. TAGORE DINESH

INTRODUCTION

The fact that the typical female advantage in life expectancy is not seen in India suggests there are systematic problems with women's health. Indian women have high mortality rates, particularly during childhood and in their reproductive years. The health of Indian women is intrinsically linked to their status in society. Research on women's status has found that the contributions Indian women make to families often are overlooked, and instead they are viewed as economic burdens. There is a strong son preference in India, as sons are expected to care for parents as they age. This son preference, along with high dowry costs for daughters, sometimes results in the mistreatment of daughters. Further, Indian women have low levels of both education and formal labor force participation[1]. They typically have little autonomy, living under the control of first their fathers, then their husbands, and finally their sons. Women's health in India can be examined in terms of multiple indicators, which vary by geography, socio-economic standing and culture. Hence, female foeticide at that point of time was, not considered an issue at all which justifies the fact that not a single section in the entire Legislation deals specifically and expressly with the problem.

Abortion data in India is a curious case. Even as the Central Health Management and information System of the National Rural Health Mission (NRHM) recorded 11.06 lakh abortions in India in 2008-09, there is no official data available on unsafe abortions in the country. This, when the Registrar General of India , Sample Registration System (RGI-SRS) estimates that 8 per cent of maternal deaths in India are attributed to abortions, a majority of these to unsafe procedures. Admitting that there was lack of awareness among the people about the legal status of abortion in India. Anuradha Gupta, Mission Director, NRHM, says India has one of the most progressive abortion laws in the world which permit the termination of pregnancy even in the case of a failed contraceptive. But most people believe abortion is illegal and do not approach public health facilities for the procedure.[2]

Health activists and gynaecologists have been demanding more amendments to the MTP Act to permit trained non-MBBS graduates and mid-level healthcare providers like Auxiliary Nurse Midwives (ANMs) and nurses to perform abortions so that these facilities are accessible and confidentiality is maintained. Our estimation based on the sale of drugs suggests over 10 million abortions are performed in India annually. These are reported cases, but the number of procedures performed outside of certified facilities is much more, says Nozier Sheriar, secretary general of the Federation of Obstetric and Gynaecological Societies of India.

There may not be any mala fide intention for non-reporting but the registration system is so complicated and difficult. Even the DLCs which were constituted to simplify the procedure are highly bureaucratic. Appreciating the government for including abortion under the NRHM umbrella, Dr. Sheriar says that unfortunately the States have not followed it up properly during the implementation process. It remains an unfinished business. Claiming that only 15 per cent of women actually misuse the law for sex-selective abortions. Dr. Sheriar says stringent laws to prevent selective abortions were depriving 85 per cent of women, including unmarried women and adolescents, who actually need this facility. "We need to give a woman a choice to plan her family and if she is unable to prevent a pregnancy, she needs to be given a second choice by way of safe abortion," Dr. Sheriar says[3].

CONSTITUTIONAL PROVISIONS AND UDHR

The UDHR[4] guaranteed the right to privacy. No one shall be subject to arbitrary interference with his privacy, family, home or correspondence, nor to attacks upon his honour and reputation. Everyone has the right to the protection of the law against such interference or attacks.

Article 21 of the Indian constitution ensures every person right to personal liberty and dignity and Article 14 gives equality before law and equal protection of the laws irrespective of their race, caste, sex, religion. Article 39(e)[5] of the Constitution provides that the health and strength of women is not to be abused. Part IV-A, Article 51A (e) of the Constitution under the fundamental duties provides that it shall be the duty of every citizen of India to renounce practices derogatory to the dignity of women. Hence, the object of the MTP Act being to save the life of the pregnant woman or relieve her of any injury to her physical and mental health, then the Act is rather in consonance with Article 21 of the Constitution of India than in conflict with it.

SCOPE AND OBJECT OF THE MTP ACT

The objective of the act, as given at the onset of the act itself, is essentially confined to dealing with the termination of certain pregnancies by registered practitioners and matters connected therewith and incidental thereto and does not extend beyond this.

While the District Level Committees (DLCs)[6] to be established for certification of private and NGO sector facilities to provide quality services, have been constituted in many States, they are ineffective. The result is the lack of certified public and private facilities that pushes women into seeking unsafe procedures performed by untrained personnel.

CONDITIONS FOR TERMINATION OF PREGNANCY UNDER MTP ACT

1) Where any pregnancy is alleged by the pregnant woman to have been caused by rape, the anguish caused by such

pregnancy shall be presumed to constitute a grave injury to the mental health of the pregnant woman.

2) Where any pregnancy occurs as a result of failure of any device or method used by any married woman or her husband for the purpose of limiting the number of children, the anguish caused by such unwanted pregnancy may be presumed to constitute a grave injury to the mental health of the woman.[7]

Amendment to the Medical Termination of Pregnancy Act[8], 2002, (No. 64 of 2002) (18th December 2002).

3) For section 4 of the principal Act, no termination of pregnancy shall be made at any place other than—
   (a) a hospital established or maintained by Government, or
   (b) a place for the time being approved for the purpose of this Act by Government or a District Level Committee constituted by that Government with the Chief Medical Officer or District Health Officer as the Chairperson of the said Committee :
   Provided that the District Level Committee shall consist of not less than three and not more than five members including the Chairperson, as the Government may specify from time to time[9].

Art. 14 and comparative provisions under MTP Act and Prenatal Diagnostic Techniques (Prohibition of Sex Selection) Act, 1994.

It is well settled that when a law is challenged as offending against the guarantee enshrined in Article 14, the first duty of the court is to examine the purpose and the policy of the Act and then to discover whether the classification made by the law has a reasonable relation to the object which the legislature seeks to obtain. The object of the MTP Act being to save the life of the pregnant woman or relieve her of any injury to her physical and mental health, and no other thing, it would appear the Act is rather in consonance with Article 21 of the Constitution of India than in conflict with it.

The Objects and Reasons of the Medical Termination of Pregnancy Act, 1997 read with Section 3(2)(i) thereof permit termination of pregnancy of a woman by a registered medical practitioner if the pregnancy would involve risk to the life of the pregnant woman or grave injury to her physical or mental health.

Explanation II to Section 3 states that where any pregnancy occurs as a result of failure of any devise or method used by any married woman or her husband for the purpose of limiting the number of children, anguish caused by such unwanted pregnancy may be presumed to constitute a grave injury to the mental health of the pregnant woman. However, under the Preconception and Prenatal Diagnostic Techniques (Prohibition of Sex Selection) Act, 1994, a woman having children of the same sex is not allowed to use the prenatal diagnostic techniques to have children of the opposite sex. The legislature has not taken into consideration the fact that having a child of the same sex as that of the existing child/children also causes grave mental injury to a woman.

The above discussed provisions inequality in the two legislations has been rightly pointed by the Apex Court in the case of *In Centre for Enquiry In to Health & Allied Themes (Cehat) and Ors.* v. *Union of India and Ors.*[10], a grievance was made by a Non Governmental organization that the provisions of the Preconception and Prenatal Diagnostic Techniques (Prohibition of Sex Selection) Act, 1994 are not properly implemented. After considering this grievance, the Supreme Court has noted that it has already issued directions to secure compliance of the provisions of the said Act. The Supreme Court has issued further directions to the Central Government, State Government and Union Territories to ensure compliance of its earlier directions. If the said action could be done in the above mentioned act, then why can't it be done in MTP Act.

JUDICIAL ACTIVISM

In *Mr. Vijay Sharma and Mrs. Kirti Sharma* v. *Union of India (UOI)*[11], Bombay High Court, through the Ministry of Law and Justice and Ministry of Health and Family Welfare , the court says that foeticide of girl child is a sin; such tendency offends dignity of women. It undermines their importance. It violates woman's right to life. It violates Article 39(e) of the Constitution which states the principle of state policy that the health and strength of women is not to be abused. It ignores Article 51A(e) of the Constitution which states that it shall be the duty of every citizen of India to renounce practices derogatory to the dignity of women. The architects of the MTPA, 1971, have not taken into consideration the fundamental rights of the foetus to be born. The petitioners are a married couple having two female children. It is their case as disclosed in the petition that they are desirous of expanding their family provided they are in a position to select the sex of the child. It is obvious from the petition that the petitioners are desirous of having a male child. According to them, they can then enjoy the love and affection of both, son and daughter simultaneously and their existing children can enjoy the company of their own brother while growing up if they are allowed to select sex of their child and have a son. The petitioners have approached various clinics for treatment for the selection of the sex of the foetus by prenatal diagnostic techniques. However, all clinics have denied treatment to them on the ground that it is prohibited under the said PIT Act.

In *Centre for Enquiry Into Health & Allied Themes (Cehat) and Ors.* v. *Union of India and Ors.*[12], a grievance was made by a Non-Governmental organization that the provisions of the Preconception and Prenatal Diagnostic Techniques (Prohibition of Sex Selection) Act, 1994 are not properly implemented. After considering this grievance, the Supreme Court has noted that it has already issued directions to secure compliance of the provisions of the said Act. The Supreme Court has issued further directions to the Central Government, State Government and Union Territories to ensure compliance of its earlier directions. If the said action could be done in the above mentioned act, then why can't it be done in MTP Act.

CONCLUSION

Though India has one of the most progressive abortion laws in the world which permit the termination of pregnancy even in the case of a failed contraceptive, there was lack of awareness among the people about the legal status of abortion in India. And most people believe abortion is illegal and do not approach public health facilities for the procedure. The reason is that in India the literacy rate is less and people are having less awareness and relatively weak in this sector, hence, the Government has to launch an information, education and communication campaign on abortion. A strategy must be formulated to educate people on the need for approaching a certified health facility for quality services as it involved woman's health women in India face a multitude of health problems, which ultimately affect the aggregate economy's output.

Notes and References

1. Victoria, A. Velkoff and Arjun Adlakha—Women of the World-Women's health in India; International Programs Center, Issued on December 1998.

2. Aarti Dhar, The Hindu, August 29, 2013.
3. *Ibid.*
4. Article 12 of Universal Declaration of Human Rights.
5. Pandey, J.N., The Constitutional Law of India, Central Law Agency, Allahabad, 2012, 416 (Directive Principles of State Policy).
6. Sec. 4(b)of the Medical Termination of Pregnancy (MTP) Amendment Act, 2002.
7. Section 3(2)of the Medical Termination of Pregnancy Act, 1971.
8. the Medical Termination of Pregnancy Amendment Act, 2002 , (No. 64 of 2002) (18th December 2002).
9. In section 5 of the principal Act, for sub-section (2) and the Explanation thereto, the following shall be substituted, namely :
   (1) Notwithstanding anything contained in the Indian Penal Code, the termination of pregnancy by a person who is not a registered medical practitioner shall be an offence punishable with rigorous imprisonment for a term which shall not be less than two years but which may extend to seven years under that Code, and that Code shall, to this extent, stand modified.
   (2) Whoever terminates any pregnancy in a place other than that mentioned in section 4, shall be punishable with rigorous imprisonment for a term which shall not be less than two years but which may extend to seven years.
   (3) Any person being owner/administrative head of a place which is not approved under clause (b) of section 4 shall be punishable with rigorous imprisonment for a term which shall not be less than two years but which may extend to seven years.
10. (2003) 8 SCC 412.
11. AIR 2008 Bom. 29.
12. AIR (2003) 8 SCC 412.

28

Women Rights as Human Rights

Adapa Sarada

The right to live with human dignity and freedom is a God-given gift to every person born in this world. In 1948, United Nations General Assembly formulated a landmark Universal Declaration of Human Rights, which stands till today as an Icon of hope for all people and especially to women. To be specific, it relates to such matters as security of person, slavery, torture, protection of the law, freedom of movement and speech, religion, assembly, rights to social security, work, health, education, culture and citizenship. It clearly stipulates that these human rights apply to all equally "without distinction of any kind such as race, color, sex, language or other status" (Art. 2). Significantly, a substantial section of Universal Declaration seeks to uplift women and bring about equality. However, tradition, prejudice, social, economic and political interests have combined to exclude women from prevailing definitions of general human rights and downgrade women to secondary positions. The great challenge of this paper is to recognize the importance of Women Rights and give voice to women everywhere whose experiences go unnoticed, whose words go unheard so that this effort may strengthen families and societies by empowering women to take greater control over their own destinities.

The growing concern and awareness among people about Civil liberties and Democratic rights, and the demands of human rights Organizations and activists within the country also influenced the decision of the government to enact a law to establish a Human Rights Commission. For this purpose a new law "The protection of Human Rights Acts 1993" was enacted. Though it has its limits, if implemented properly it can be an effective instrument. This is an important subject which goes to the root of human dignity and the right to life and self-respect which the Constitution guarantees to all persons.

"Human Rights" means the rights relating to life, liberty, equality and dignity of the individual guaranteed by the Constitution or embodied in the International Covenants and enforceable by courts in India.

Fundamental Rights are needed to protect the rights and liberties of the people against encroachments by governments and others. They are made to control the powers of the government Legislature as well as the Executive. They are essential for the preservation of public and private rights. The aim of having the declaration of Fundamental rights is that certain elementary rights, such as right to life, liberty, freedom of speech, freedom of faith, etc., should be regarded as inviolable under all conditions and that the shifting majority in the Legislature of the country should not have a free hand in interfering with these fundamental rights.

They represent the Vedic values cherished by the people of India since Vedic times and they are calculated to protect the dignity of the individual and create conditions in which every human being can develop his personality to the fullest extent. They weave a 'pattern of guarantee' on the basic structure of human rights, and impose negative obligations on the state not to encroach an individual's liberty in its various dimensions. (Justice Bhagwati in *Maneka Gandhi* v. *Union of India*, AIR 1978 SC 597, p. 619).

These rights are regarded Fundamental because they are most essential for the attainment of human dignity. The denial of these rights will keep the moral and spiritual life stunted and ones potentialities undeveloped. The inclusion of these rights in the Constitution vests them a sanctity which the legislators dare not violate so easily.

The object behind the inclusion of the Chapter of Fundamental Rights in the Constitution is also to establish a government of law and a governmental system where the majority does not oppress the minority. The object is not merely to provide security and equality of citizenship to the people living in this land, but also to maintain certain standards of conduct, citizenship, justice and fairness.

CLASSIFICATION OF FUNDAMENTAL RIGHTS

Right to equality (Articles 14-18)
Right to freedom (Articles 19-22)
Right against exploitation (Articles 23-24)
Right to freedom of religion (Articles 25-28)
Cultural and educational rights (Articles 29-30)
Right to constitutional remedies. (Articles 32-35)

It is obvious that the Fundamental Rights of the Constitution of India *per se* does not make specific provisions on women's rights. In fact the word 'women' has been scarcely used in the constitution. However, since the constitution is based on the overriding principle of equality (the preamble and the Right to Equality in Part III) women are protected against any kind of discrimination which is based on sex. Therefore, all the rights and freedoms enshrined in the Indian Constitution belong as much to women as they belong to men. Moreover, certain positive disposition in favour of women is permitted in the constitution. Thus, Article 15(3) stipulates: "Nothing in this article shall prevent the State from making any special provision for women and children". It is from this source that various positive developments and women rights have emerged.

What is a right? A right is a justified claim on others. For example, if I have a right to freedom, then I have a justified claim to be left alone by others. Turned around, I can say that others have a duty or responsibility to leave me alone. If I have a right to an education, then I have a justified claim to be provided with an education by society. The "justification" of a claim is dependent on some standard acknowledged and accepted not just by the claimant, but also by society in general.

The universality of human rights means that human rights apply to every single person by virtue of their humanity; this also means that human rights apply to everyone equally, for everyone is equal in simply being human. The idea of human rights as inalienable means that it is impossible for anyone to abdicate her human rights, even if she wanted to, since every person is accorded those rights by virtue of being human. It also means that no person or group of persons can deprive another individual of her or his human rights. In

Indian context when woman is compared or symbolized as Bharatha Matha or goddess of individual families or as a mother with culmination of all love and sacrifice why is that same attitude is not transferred to all women in all the situations of human nature. It is not enough that few elite enjoy this respect and dignity but every woman who cries out for justice and liberation should be heard and bestowed with dignity.

Moral rights are justified by moral standards that most people acknowledge, but which are not necessarily codified in law; these standards have also, however, been interpreted differently by different people. Kant maintained that each of us has a worth or a dignity that must be respected. This dignity makes it wrong for others to abuse us or to use us against our will. Kant expressed this idea in a moral principle: humanity must always be treated as an end, not merely as a means. To treat a person as a mere means is to use a person to advance one's own interest. But to treat a person as an end is to respect that person's dignity by allowing each the freedom to choose for himself or herself.

Whenever we are confronted with a moral dilemma, we need to consider whether the action would respect the basic rights of each of the individuals involved. Rights, then, play a central role in ethics. Attention to rights ensures that the freedom and well-being of each individual will be protected when others threaten that freedom or well-being. If an individual has a moral right, then it is morally wrong to interfere with that right even if large number of people would benefit from such interference. Moreover, an emphasis on rights tends to limit our vision of what the "moral life" entails. Morality, it's often argued, is not just a matter of not interfering with the rights of others. Relying exclusively on a rights approach to ethics tends to emphasize the individual at the expense of the community. And, while morality does call on us to respect the uniqueness, dignity, and autonomy of each individual, it also invites us to recognize our relatedness–that sense of community, shared values, and the common good which lends itself to an ethics of care, compassion, and concern for others.

The term "women's human rights" and the set of practices that accompany its use are the continuously evolving product of an international movement to improve the status of women. In the 1980s and 1990s, women's movements around the world formed networks and coalitions to give greater visibility both to the problems that women face every day and to the centrality of women's experiences in economic, social, political and environmental issues. In the evolution of what is becoming a global women's movement, the term "women's human rights" has served as a locus for praxis, that is, for the development of political strategies shaped by the interaction between analytical insights and concrete political practices. Further, the critical tools, the concerted activism, and the broad-based international networks that have grown up around movements for women's human rights have become a vehicle for women to develop the political skills necessary for the twenty-first century.

The concept of women's human rights owes its success and the proliferation of its use to the fact that it is simultaneously prosaic and revolutionary. On the one hand, the idea of women's human rights makes common sense. It declares, quite simply, that as human beings women have human rights. Anyone would find her or himself hard-pressed to publicly make and defend the contrary argument that women are not human. So in many ways, the claim that women have human rights seems quite ordinary. On the other hand, "women's human rights" is a revolutionary notion.

This radical reclamation of humanity and the corollary insistence that women's rights are human rights have profound transformative potential. The incorporation of women's perspectives and lives into human rights standards and practice forces recognition of the dismal failure of countries worldwide to accord women the human dignity and respect that they deserve-simply as human beings. A woman's human rights framework equips women with a way to define, analyze, and articulate their experiences of violence, degradation, and marginality. Finally, and very importantly, the idea of women's human rights provides a common framework for developing a vast array of visions and concrete strategies for change.

Ehrenreich notes that gender equality often appears to be limited to allowing women to have equality in a male-dominated world, meaning women struggle to have rights to do what men do. But, if what men are doing is generally seen as negative, then gender equality in that context is not enough. As she ends:

To cite an old, and far from naive, feminist saying: "If you think equality is the goal, your standards are too low." It is not enough to be equal to men, when the men are acting like beasts. It is not enough to assimilate. We need to create a world worth assimilating into. (Barbara Ehrenreich, *What Abu Ghraib Taught Me,* Alternet, May 20, 2004)

Gender equality is not only morally right, it is pivotal to human progress and sustainable development. It will not only empower women to overcome poverty and live full and productive lives, but will better the lives of children, families and countries as well. Women's equal rights and influence in the key decisions that shape their lives and those of children must be enhanced in three distinct arenas: the household, the workplace and the political sphere.

Women's rights around the world are an important indicator to understand global well-being. A major global women's rights treaty was ratified by the majority of the world's nations a few decades ago. Yet, despite many successes in empowering women, numerous issues still exist in all areas of life, ranging from the cultural and political to the economic. For example, women often work more than men, yet are paid less; gender discrimination affects girls and women throughout their lifetime; and women and girls are often the ones that suffer the most poverty.

Woman, the very creation of God that makes living beautiful is often at the receiving end of trauma. Not necessarily do criminals live around rural thatched roofs only. They are found in sky rises and posh suites too. In 2009, rape cases have reached 2,497, domestic violence has crossed the 10,000 mark. In short, women are still treated as a lesser person.

Around 2.8 million social workers have been employed by the government to reach into villages and homes across the country, to make women aware of their rights. Article 14 of the Constitution of India says that no person will be denied equality before the law. Article 42 states that women should be provided just and human work atmosphere and maternity relief. Sati laws have been abolished, child marriages are legally punishable. The girl now has to be of 18 years when she is married and her consent has to be taken. Using force is punishable. To her relief eve teasing too is considered a crime. It can be reported and offenders will be put behind bars immediately.

Some of the visible and reported gender bias malpractices prevalent in Indian societies are female fetus termination, killing the girl, child at birth, less nutrition, medical care, education and freedom due to preference for the male child, marriage before puberty, dowry death, legal discrimination, professions exclusively earmarked for men, precarious widow-life, etc. While such practices and activities are prevalent in Indian Society, they are fortunately not the lot of every Indian women and are confined to certain communities and sections of society. Even in such a situation the important role of women in procreation, upkeep, management and development of the family, as well as in performing diverse economic, social, political, religious, national and international roles, cannot be denied. Despite the fact that they deserve equal status, honour, dignity, rights and consideration, certain complex factors have reduced the status of women in human society to a lower level, leading to gender biases generally manifested in a loss of freedom, drudgery, malnutrition, and economic and sex exploitation.

Women have been serving India admirably as doctors and nurses. Lady Doctors have been found to perform efficient surgery by virtue of their soft and accurate fingers. They have monopolized as nurses in the hospitals and nursing homes. Very few men have been able to compete with them in this sphere because women have natural tendency to serve and clean. It is such a natural tendency found in women which motivated Florence Nightingale to make nursing popular among the women of the upper classes in England and in Europe. She showed the way to womankind how nobly they can serve humanity in the hours of sufferings and agonies. There is no denying the fact that women in India have made a considerable progress in the last fifty years but yet they have to struggle against many handicaps and social evils in the male dominated society.

The dowry deaths are really heinous and barbarous crimes committed by the cruel and inhumane persons. The young girls should be bold enough in not marrying the boys who demand dowry through their parents. The boys should also refuse to marry if their parents demand dowry. But unfortunately the number of such bold and conscientious boys is very few. Even the doctors, engineers, teachers and the administrative officers do not hesitate in allowing themselves to be sold to the wealthy fathers of shy and timid girls. Such persons have really brought disgrace to their cadres in particular and society in general.

Medieval India saw many foreign conquests, which resulted in the decline in women's status. When foreign conquerors like Muslim Kings invaded India they brought with them their own culture. As polygamy was a norm for these invaders they picked up any woman they wanted and kept her in their custody. The original Indians wanted to shield their women folk from the barbarous Muslim invaders. In order to protect them, Indian women started using 'Purdah' (a veil), which covers body. Due to this reason their freedom also became affected. They were not allowed to move freely and this led to the further deterioration of their status. These problems related with women resulted in a changed mindset of people. Now they began to consider a girl as misery and a burden, which has to be shielded from the eyes of intruders and needs extra care. Whereas a boy child will not need such extra care and instead will be helpful as an earning hand. Thus, a vicious circle started in which women were at the receiving end. All this gave rise to some new evils such as Child Marriage, Sati, Jauhar and restriction on girl education.

The plight of women in medieval India and at the starting of modern India can be summed up in the words of great poet Rabindranath Tagore: "O Lord Why have you not given woman the right to conquer her destiny? Why does she have to wait head bowed, by the roadside, waiting with tired patience, hoping for a miracle in the morrow?"

The status of women in modern India is a sort of a paradox. On the one hand she is at the peak of the ladder of success; on the other hand, she is mutely suffering the violence afflicted on her by her own family members. In comparison to the past, women in modern times have achieved a lot but in reality they still have to travel a long way. Their path is full of roadblocks and thorns. Today women have left the secured domain of their home and are now in the battlefield of life, fully armored with their talents. They had proven themselves. But in India they are yet to get their dues. The sex ratio of India shows that the Indian society is still prejudiced against female. There are 933 females per thousand males in India according to the census of 2001, which is much below the world average of 990 females. There are many problems which women in India have to go through daily. These problems have become part and parcel of the life of Indian women and some of them have accepted them as their fate.

Women are the primary caretakers for most of the world's children and elderly. Yet much of the work women do is not valued — not by economists, not by historians, not by popular culture, not by government. Women around the world are giving birth, raising children, cooking meals, washing clothes, cleaning houses, planting crops, working on assembly lines, running companies, and running countries. The truth is that most women around the world work both inside and outside the home, usually by necessity. We need to understand that there is no formula for how women should lead their lives. That is why we must respect the choices that each woman makes for herself and her family.

Indian women have not just made their mark on earth but they have engraved their name in the whole universe by flying to space. Kalpana Chawla, who was the member of Colombia Space Shuttle, which exploded on its way back, was the first Indian women astronaut who visited space station. And now following on her footsteps another woman of Indian origin Sunita Williams has become the second one to be the member of International Space Station crew.

- India has world's largest number of professionally qualified women.
- India has largest population of working women in the world.
- India has more number of doctors, surgeons, scientists, professors than the United States.

Today, Indian women excel in each and every field from social work to visiting space station. There is no arena, which remained unconquered by Indian women. Whether it is politics, sports, entertainment, literature, technology everywhere we can hear applauses for her.

These achievements of women and the constant struggle against inequality and discrimination against women call for a celebration—a celebration of the contributions women make in every aspect of life: in the home, on the job, in their communities, as mothers, wives, sisters, daughters, learners, workers, citizens and leaders. What we are learning around the world is that if women are healthy and educated, their families will flourish. If women are free from violence, their families will flourish. If women have a chance to work and earn as full and equal partners in society, their families will flourish. And when families flourish, communities and nations will flourish. Every woman deserves the chance to realize her God-given potential. We also must recognize that women will never gain full dignity until their human rights are respected and protected.

The only one message that echoes forth from my reflection is that, that human rights are women's rights—and women's rights are human rights. Our nation will shine brightly only when men and women join together to combat the forces of tyranny and build a better world. If we take bold steps to better the lives of women, we will be taking bold steps to better the lives of children, families and the whole nation and world at large. As long as discrimination and inequities remain so common around the world — as long as girls and women are valued less, fed less, fed last, overworked, underpaid, not schooled and subjected to violence in and out of their homes — the potential of the human family to create a peaceful, prosperous world will not be realized. Anyone who has patriotism that their nation and community should be a prosperous and peaceful one should work and support causes of women's human rights. And let us heed the call so that we can create a world in which every woman is treated with respect and dignity, every boy and girl is loved and cared for equally, and every family has the hope of a strong and stable future.

Notes and References

Barbara Ehrenreich, What Abu Ghraib Taught Me, Alternet, May 20, 2004.

Charlotte Bunch and Samantha Frost, *Encyclopedia of Women: Global Women's Issues and Knowledge*. Published in Routledge International 2000.

Chatterji, Angana, Women in Search of Human Equality, Social Action, Vol. 40, 46-56, (1990).

Giri V. Mohini, *Kanya: Exploitation of Little Angels*. Gyan Publishing House, New Delhi: 1999.

Kishwar Madhu, Where Daughters are Unwanted, *Manushi*, No. 86, Jan.-Feb., 1995, pp. 15-22

Mathew, P.D., *Do You Know Your Fundamental Rights?* Indian Social Institute, New Delhi, 2004.

——, *The Law to Protect Human Rights in India*. New Delhi, 2004.

——, *Measures for Eradication of Child Labour Fundamental Right to Primary Education*. Legal Education Series No. 45, Indian Social Institution, New Delhi, 2003.

——, *Women and the Constitution*. Legal Education Series No. 17, New Delhi, 2004.

Madhu Kishwar, *Economic and Political Weekly*, Vol. XXXV, No. 47, November 18, 2000, pp. 4151-56.

Meena Dhanda, *Economic and Political Weekly*, Vol. XXV, No. 33, August 12, 2000, pp. 2969-76.

Mita Bhadra, ed. *Girl Child in Indian Society*. Rawat Publications, New Delhi: 1999.

Nivedita Menon, Ed., *Gender and Politics in India*. Oxford University press: Delhi, 1999.

Pal, R.M. (ed.), *Child Labour And Compulsory Basic Education*. Indian Institute, New Delhi, 1999.

Pylee, M.V., Constitutional Government in India. Rev.edition, 6, S. Chand & company Ltd. New Delhi, 2006.

Radha Kumar, *The History of Doing, An illustrated Account of Movements for Women's Rights and Feminism in India*, Delhi, 1990.

Sarkar, Lotika, National Specialised Agencies and women's equality, Law Commission of India (CWDS), 1998.

Venkatesan, Jayshree, Women's Multiple Roles and Coping Strategies; Myths and Realities , *Indian Journal of Gender Studies*, Vols. 3-4, 39-56, (96-97).

www.cwgl.rutgers.edu/globalcenter/whr.html
http://www.youtube.com/watch?v=1hBd1HN7WJM
http://www.globalissues.org/article/166/womens-rights
http://minoroutside.blogspot.com/2006/11/short-note-on-human-rights.html
http://www.alternet.org/story.html?StoryID=18740
http://www.mapsofindia.com/culture/indian-women.html

29

Women Rights as Human Rights

M. DEENADAYAL

"Women Rights are declared as Human Rights".

INTRODUCTION

Human beings should have rights which help them to live a Good, comfortable and meaningful life. These rights should be guaranteed by the Government, by the Society and by the individuals also. In most constitutions of the World, these rights belong to the citizens. There are special institutions which are brought into existence to ensure that these rights are enjoyed by the citizens without hindrance.

The struggle to preserve, protect and promote Human Rights is as old as Human Civilization. A complex International Machinery specifically developed for the promotion and protection of Human Rights and Fundamental Freedoms constitute the cornerstone of all the United Nations. Efforts for the implementation of all such treaties and norms. There have been so many conventions in human rights bodies, besides Commission on human rights forming the operational system. We are entering into a new phase in the field of observing Human Rights after about forty years of the adoption of universal declaration on Human Rights. All out efforts are being made at the united nations to produce the binding Human Rights instrumentsit well as some significant methods for their implementation.

Universal declaration of Human Rights and the conventions on Human Rights define the human rights and provide measures for their protection and preservation at the International level Right to life mean not to be deprived of life by the state without following the due process of life. The stateshould not take the life of a citizen unless it is empowered to do so, for punishing the citizen for a crime committed by him and that too by following the procedure laid down for that purpose. It also means that his life should not be extinguished by other citizens.

Citizens have no right to punish others. They can appeal to the Government to punish any citizen who has committed a crime. The fear in the minds of Human beings is a sort of shield which protects them from the long hand of law for the crimes. They have committedand their nefarious activities like drug trafficking, smuggling, arms trafficking etc. State should enact appropriate laws for the protection of Human Rights of the citizens. At the same time state should also ensure the balance so that laws do not become an instrument of oppression.

The protection of human personality and of its Fundamental rights is the ultimate purpose of alllaw, National and International. Indeed, International Human Rights is one of International relations and represents Revolutionary Development. Human Rights have historically appeared to be morally attractive and practically in practicable.

HUMAN RIGHTS AND ATROCITIES AGAINST WOMEN

Though constituting half the population of the World and often euphemistically referred to the "Better half of Man". Women is fact, had the worst deal at the hands of society, till very recently the reasons for the law not status of worries through out the ages are not for to seek lack of education, deep-rooted false notions, emotional and economic dependence and a tendency to promote male dominance make women submissive and slavish. We should never forget that a country where the prospects are bleak for women can not hope to have a bright future.

WOMEN'S RIGHTS AND INTERNATIONAL ORGANISATIONS

The Fifth International Conference of American States held in

Santiago in 1923 voiced the concern over the "Legal Inequality of Women". The Seventh Conference in Montevideo in 1933 approved the convention on the Nationality of Women Ratified by with establishment of the National Commission for women. Gender issues are receiving proper attention.

RIGHTS OF WOMEN UNDER THE CONSTITUTION OF INDIA

To conclude Articles 14, 15 and 16 of the Indian Constitution as also Article 39(d) guarantee equality of sexes and assure equal pay for equal work to women along with men. This is mainly due to Poverty, Illiteracy, Feudal Outlook, Social mores and lack of public awareness. A disturbing factor of modern era is the increase in crime against women in India.

PROPERTY RIGHTS OF WOMEN

Women are undoubtedly equal to men in all spheres of life. But unfortunately there is discrimination between men and women in all societies through out the world. As men happen to be mostly earning members women have to obey them and lead a slavish or dependable life. They face the discriminatory and secondary status in every society or country women constitute about fifty percent of the total population in all the countries and constitute a considerable labour force in the productivity of the economy both in the traditional status and in the economic status. She extends an invaluable service to the society with her invisible hand shaping and supporting her family members explicit economic activity and therefore the Human Resource Development of country. She accepts the traditional role of house keeping with a pride but her inner mind scores over her to transcend the traditional barriers and she plays an increasing role in the development process of her economy.

According the report of United Nations Organization Women today do two-thirds of the worlds work but receive only five percent of the world's income and own loss than one percent of the worlds assets. By this we understand the fate of the women. We can observe in our society in many families, parents are giving much importance to male child's education. Female children are not encouraged to gofor higher studies even they are interested. Whereas male children even they are not interested in studies. They are encouraged by paying Capitation Fees, Donations.

Legislative recognition of equal property right of female heirs of a Hindu along with their male counterparts under Hindu Succession Act 1956 was an important landmark towards the cause of gender equaly in India. However, section 23 of the Act by putting Bar on the right to claim partition by female heir in respect of a dwelling house until the male heirs choose to divide their respective share is it perpetuation of the male bias under prevailing ancient Hindu Law Section 23 of the Act reads as follows.

Where a Hindu intestate has left surviving male and female heir of class I of the schedule and property included dwelling house. Then the Right of any of such female heir claim partition shall not arise until male heirs choose to divide their respective shares". If not only debars the female heirs to claim partition but also postpone her substantive right till her life time. Her getting property is made dependent upon the sole whims of the male heirs if and when they choose to divide.

In view of the Socio-economic transformation and the changed perception of the Hindu concept of family and the status of women there is a need to reconsider the necessity and relevance of continuing the Archaic view of putting disabilities on female right to property. Supreme Court in *Narasimha Murthy* v. *Susheela Bai* had the ample opportunity to put a Gloss of gender equality upon Sec. 23 of the Act. But it failed to appreciate the statutory provision in its proper perspective. The facts of the case were simple. The disputed property belonged to Narsoju Rao who died intestate leaving behind him and three daughters male heir let out a portion of the house under the circumstances the court had rightly held that sec. 23 is clearly not applicable and the female heirs right to claim partition upheld.

However, Supreme Court has gone into much detail to review the earlier decision on the point and expressed its opinion about Sec. 23 of the Act and its relevance. As a matter of fact, in view of the Supreme Court on Sec. 23 of the Act, AIR 1996 SC 1826 Act was uncalled for and amounts to mere obiter. Still the detailed analysis made by Supreme Court is required to be examined thoroughly.

In a situation where intestate left behind only two heirs one male and another female, the decision clearly stated that female heir of the same class of an intestate Hindu is not entitled to claim partition. Even against a single male heir in respect of a dwelling house. Had there been two male heirs instead of one male and another female heir of the same class the Right to claim. Partition could have been exercised by male heirs. The discrimination on the basis of sex is quite obvious. As the female heir just because of her being female heir is not being allowed to claim partition. There is no rational basis to put the female. Heirs of the same class under a severe disability in respect of a dwelling house. Andhra Pradesh Government made an amendment in 1986 to Hindu Succession Act 1956. By this amendment a new chapter, Chapter II has been inserted and it deemed to have come into force on 5th September 1985.

According to this Amendment any joint family governed by Mithakshara daughter is made a coparcener equating her status to a son subjected to exception that marriage of daughter should not have taken place. The parliament obviously after taking cognizance of the amendments made by states of Andhra Pradesh besides Tamilnadu, Karnataka and Maharastra amended section 6 of the Hindu Succession Act in tune with section 29-A barring some exceptions by way of Amendments Act 39 of 2005 to the Hindu Succession Act 1956 which came into Force with effect from 9th September, 2005.

Central Act 39 of 2005 was introduced in order to bring out uniformity throughout the country. The stipulation that the marriage of the daughter should not have been performed before 5th September, 1985 was removed. Therefore irrespective of the dates of marriage all the daughters would be deemed to be coparceners with one exception that portion should not have taken place before 20th December, 2004. The expression partition means that partition under a duly registered partition deed or partition affected by a decree of court.

In introducing Act 39 of 2005 parliament intends to set right the law. It further bestowed some more rights. In the statement of the objects and reasons it was mentioned the Hindu Succession Act, 1956 has amended and codified the law relating to intestate succession among Hindus and gave rights which were till then known in relating to women's property.

Section 6 of the Act deals with devolution of interest of a male Hindu in coparcenery property and recognizes the rule of devolution by survivorship among the members of the coparcenery. The retention of the Mithakshara Coparcenary property without including the female in its means that females can not inherit in ancestral property to their male counterparts do. The law by excluding the daughter from participating in the coparcenery ownership not only contributes to her discrimination on the ground of Gender, but also has led to oppression and negation of her fundamental rights of equality guaranteed by the constitution having regard to the need to render social justice the women the states of Andhra Pradesh, Tamil Nadu, Karnataka and Maharashtra have made necessarychanges in the law giving equal rights to daughters in Hindu Mitakshara Coparcenary property.

It is proposed to remove thediscrimination as and contained in Sec. 6 of Hindu Succession Act 1956 by giving equal Rights to daughters in the Hindu "Mitakshara Coparcenery" property as sons have Sec. 23 of the Act disentitles a female heir to ask for partition in respect of dwelling house wholly occupied by a joint family until the male heirs choose to divide their respective shares therein. It is also proposed to omit the said section so as to remove the disability on female heirs contained in that section.

The above proposals are based on the recommendations of the Law Commission of India which is contained in its 174th Report on property Rights of Women proposed to reform under the Hindu Law.

To conclude obviously the central Act, 390 of 2005 was introduced in order to bring out uniformity throughout the country. By introducing Act 39 Parliament intends to correct the anomaly created between male and female children. Now the daughter is declared as a Coparcener she will naturally takes a share in the family along with the other male Coparceners.

Thus latest amendments to Hindu Succession Act facilitated women to get coparcenery property Rights absolutely.

RIGHT TO MAINTENANCE OF MUSLIM WOMEN ON DIVORCE

The contract of marriage under the Mohammedam law may be dissolved in any one as the following was:

1. By the Husband at his will, without the interventions of a court.
2. By mutual consent of the husband and wife.
3. By a judicial decree at the suit of the husband or wife, without the intervention of a court.

The wife can not divorce herself from her husband without his consent except under a contract whether made before or after marriage. But she may, in some cases obtain a divorce by judicial decree.

CONCLUSION

1. The merit of a rights approach is that it identifies the different protagonists who are involved in the violation of the right.
2. Many women's efforts to escape domestic violence are hampered by a lack of information on available services.
3. By a great deal of struggle and hard work, women's organisations have won a measure of social legitimacy in pursuing the society, especially law-makers, to recognize the serious threat Women's lives due to domestic violence.
4. Preventive services have enormous potential for becoming more prevalent and effective, for example in the area of legal literacy.
5. The Legal Aid system in India is entirely in adequate to deal with the number of people who require legal aid.
6. Communities in society also can prevent domestic violence by the following ways. Expand education and awareness efforts to increase positive attitudes toward non-violence, and encourage individuals to report family violence. Forum or task forces to asses the problem develop action, monitor progress, mandate training in domestic violence for all social services and criminal justice professionals, advocate laws and judicial procedures at the state and local levels that support and protect battered women.
7. Strengthen the National Commission for Women and ensuring the strengthening of the state Women's Commissions will go a long way in this regard.
8. Domestic violence against women is a violation of Human Rights that can not be justified by any political, religious of cultural claim. A Global culture of discrimination against allows domestic violence to occur daily and with impunity to eradicate violence against women and help women to achieve lives of equality and human dignity.

REFERENCES

Dr. A.M. Abdul Rub, Dr. Abdul Rayees Khan, *Orient Journal of Law and Social Sciences,* Volume I, Issue 10, September 2007.

B.P. Singh Sehgal, Professor of Law & Head, Department of Law, University of Jammu, Jammu, Human Rights in India.

Women & Law by: National Commission for Women, Pub., 2005 Constitutional Amendment Act, 2000.
Human Rights International Challenges, 1997 Ed., Madras Publication, p. 172. Women and Law, Dr. P.D. Upasani, SNDT University Publications, p. 6, 1989.
The Endangered Sex, Miller Barbara, Corneil University Press, Ithaca, 1981.
Women and Law, Nagia, B.K., Rawat Publication, Jaipur, 1991.
Women in a Changing Society, Anjana Maitran, Ashish Publications, Delhi, 1993.
Women and development—the Indian Experience Micra Seth, Sage Publications, New Delhi.
Violence against women, Ram Ahuja, Rawat Publications, Jaipur, 1998.
Girl child in India ed. Mita Bhadra, Ravat Publications, Jaipur, 1999.
Basu, D.D., Human Rights and Constitutional Law, 1995.
Bhatt, J.N., Gender Equality Turmoil or Triumph, AIR, 1998.
Certification of criminal laws relating to women, National Commission for Women.
Dowry Prohibition Act, 1961.
Equal Remuneration Act, 1976
Gupta, V.K., Perspectives on Human Rights, 1996.
Indian Bar Review, 1998.
Indian Constitution.
International Women's Rights Action Watch, CEDAW, 1992.
Kurukshethra, Sept. 1990.
Maternity Benefit Act, 1981.
Medical Termination of Pregnancy Act, 1971.
Shyamal Kumar Mukerjee, 'Protection of Women's Rights under Constitution of India', AIR, Journal, 1988, *The Hindu.*
The Protection of Human Rights Act, 1993.
Women's Link, 1996.
Human Rights International Challenges, 1997 ed., Madras Publication, p. 172.
Women and Law—Dr. P.D. Upasani, SNDT University Publication, p. 6, 1989.
Art. 16(3/4) constitution of India.
Art. 17 constitution of India.
AIR 1954 Sc. 179, p. 12.

30

Impact of Globalisation on Empowerment of Women in India

N.B. Chandrakala and G. Indira Priyadarsini

INTRODUCTION

We are living in the era of globalization. Though the concept of globalization hailed as a weapon to bring all the countries in the world closure to each other as a family and thereby making world as **"Vasudika kutumbam"**, it has its own merits and demerits. In our present discussion leaving the merits and we are concerned with the demerits that will affect the status of different sections of the society including women and their empowerment. Globalization brings with it many changes in India both economically and politically. In the changed scenario women have become pawns in the process of transformation of Indian society from welfare society to capitalistic society. It is the women who are more affected, socially, politically and economically during the process of transformation. The struggle for empowerment of women found place long back, it gains more importance now due to globalization. Hence, an attempt is made in this paper to discuss how globalization effects empowerment of women in India.

GLOBALIZATION

Globalization is a process of interaction and integration among the people, companies, and governments of different nations. It is a process driven by international trade and investment and aided by information technology. This process has effects on the environment, on culture, on political systems, on economic development and prosperity, and on human physical well-being in societies around the world.

This current wave of globalization has been driven by policies that have opened economies domestically and internationally. In the years since the Second World War, and especially during the past two decades, many governments have adopted free-market economic systems, vastly increasing their own productive potential and creating myriad new opportunities for international trade and investment. Governments also have negotiated dramatic reductions in barriers to commerce and have established international agreements to promote trade in goods, services, and investment. Taking advantage of new opportunities in foreign markets, corporations have built foreign factories and established production and marketing arrangements with foreign partners. A defining feature of globalization, therefore, is an international industrial and financial business structure.

There are different types of Technologies. Technology has been the other principal driver of globalization. Advances in information technology, in particular, have dramatically transformed economic life of the people in the world. Information technologies involve all sorts of individual economic actors—consumers, investors, businesses—valuable new tools for identifying and pursuing economic opportunities, including faster and more informed analyses of economic trends around the world, easy transfers of assets, and collaboration with far-flung partners.

Thus, Globalization is deeply controversial. However, Proponents of globalization argue that it allows poor countries and their citizens to develop economically and raise their standards of living, while opponents of globalization claim that the creation of an unfettered international free market has benefited multinational corporations in the western world at the expense of local enterprises, local cultures, and common people. Resistance to globalization has therefore taken shape both at a popular and at a governmental level as people and governments try to manage the flow of capital, labour, goods, and ideas that constitute the current wave of globalization.[1]

IMPACTS OF GLOBALIZATION

The impact of globalization as it becomes evident in economic sphere has not left social and political sphere untouched. In the economic sphere, there is greater emphasis on privatization and opening of economy for foreign capital. Individualism is re-emphasized in recognition of not only a form of individual's freedom of creating wealth and property but also as living a life of dignity that entails availability of basic necessities of life like food, water and shelter.

The rising poverty and unemployment, the mal-treatment of dalits and women in society, rampant child labour, illiteracy, high dropout of children from school, burgeoning corruption, non-transparent bureaucracy and unaccountable police force all have come to stand out in light of fruits of globalization in form of acquired and manifested riches of a section of society that has benefited from the opening of economy and privatization.

The bells heralding death of socialism, injected capitalism with a new vigour which assisted in assuming a new form that is globally pervasive in the form of Globalization. Even the Indian experience with mixed economy, with state having a significant part in the economic affairs and failing miserably, testifies to this contention. But to the credit of socialism, it presents with a mechanism of distribution of whatever little it produces. Even if one accepts the argument that the Globalization would usher an era of prosperity, an even distribution of wealth among the nations, regions and people of the world would be a real challenge before it.

Indian constitution sets out goal for the nation to strive forward to a democratic and socialist republic securing social, economic and political justice for its citizens. A welfare society involves the concept of social justice wherein the marginalized sections of society and the working class get protection from the state. For this it is pertinent that welfare measures of the state as a matter of policy and strong labor laws for the protection of the working class are in place. Any deviation from such a policy would place these sections in a state of vulnerability of exploitation at the hands of big business. State must meet the challenge of striking the fine balance between the economic interests of its people and forces of globalization.[2]

GLOBALIZATION AND ITS IMPACT ON EMPOWERMENT OF WOMEN

Empowerment is analyzed in terms of increasing women's access to services and participation in community affairs, and their number in political and administrative decision-making positions.[3] It is a multi-dimensional process, encompassing all spheres of life, including the social context and is an ongoing dynamic process which enhances women's and any marginalized and alienated group's abilities to change the structures and ideologies that keep them subordinated. It is a process of making present power structure more inclusive to all women and men of various creed, caste, class, ethnicity and race.[4]

The final goal of empowerment is to transform the ideology and practice of domination and subordination, challenge and transfer existing power structures, systems and institutions which have upheld and reinforced this discrimination and gain access to and control over material and knowledge resources. In summary, the process may be viewed in the following three dimensions:

- Increasing women's relative access to economic opportunities and resources—such as, employment, credit and wealth including land and technology and apparently non-economic resources such as education, knowledge, and health which are primary to human development.
- Raising social consciousness of women and men about the symptoms and causes of the oppressive religious, economic, cultural, familial, and legal practices, changing the perceived social images of women as individuals, strengthening their capacity to take action for changing the gender roles.
- Finally, increasing women's political power—through women's organisations, solidarity, and collective action and effective voice and presence at decision making positions.

While economic and social empowerment is a necessary condition for attaining the position of political power, political power enhances the opportunities for economic and social empowerment. Political ability to bring about changes in women's legal status, to direct resources to women, and to get access to positions of power is of crucial importance.[5]

There are four main processes that could lead to women's empowerment, as defined by the IFAD evaluation, were:

- changes in women's mobility and social interaction;
- changes in women's labour patterns;
- changes in women's access to and control over resources; and
- changes in women's control over decision-making.[6]

To bring out the comprehensive empowerment of women, the economic empowerment is a fundamental precondition. But despite the initiation First Five Year Plan in 1951 and many subsequent plans, a considerable part of the people of our country are living below poverty line. Majority of them are women. The effects of poverty and its burden are heavier on the women. In our country, the women depend principally on agriculture for their earning through toil. In the agrarian sector, land relations play the key role. As the implementation of land reforms is nominal, even today the land is concentrated in the hands of few people. Even from 1947 our economic policies have been formulated so as to serve indirectly the interest of imperialists. These policies have been instrumental in increasing the wealth of landlords, compradors and imperialists and making the poor further poor.

In the industrial sector majority of women are employed as casual workers, contract workers and unskilled workers. Out of total workers employed in our country, 41 percent are women, while those of regular employment are only 2%. Even in this sector, lakhs of industries have downed their shutters due to the implementation of policies of globalization. Due to opening up the economy to the competition from the multinational companies, lakhs of small and medium industries have been closed down and the women employers were thrown on to the roads as the first choice of removal. Due to automation, computerization and closure of factories and implementation of various schemes of retrenchments, the worst and first hits are women. In the case of livelihood, the women are in a perpetual state of uncertainty and indignity. The growth of employment opportunities for the women in basic sectors like mines, quarrying and electricity is negative. Down-sizing the work-force, disinvestments and closure of public sector units and such other policies are nothing but driving the people forcefully to the private sector. Uncontrolled and unregulated private sector is expanding without giving any job security, rights and amenities to the women workers.

As a consequence of implementation of globalization, the Indian government is withdrawing from the social welfare sectors like education, health and medical services and civil supply. To women, who utilize everything sparingly except her labour and plays key role in the life of the family and society, the nominal services provided by the government in education and medical facilities were useful to some extent. With the entry of corporate interests in education and health sectors, as a way of their emancipation, without any radical change in the existing social system, their burden is being increased manifold turning their situation akin to falling from frying pan into fire itself. The nature of patriarchal power and harassment has percolated into social sectors and the number of individuals, institutions and percolated into social structures that control the women are also increasing. Under these circumstances, the women are forced to exist and work in social sectors with all their energy, and thus falling victims to physical and mental illness. This gain has become a pretext to restrict their entry and active part in social sectors and to strengthen the prevailing view of weaker sex (ABALA). This is the dangerous consequence of joint attack by the imperialist and feudal cultures.[7]

In social matters both self-reliance of women economically and empowerment are inter-related. If the women have to achieve the social empowerment:

- they have to fight against the patriarchal ideology existing in the society. and
- they have to fight against the economic policies that make their lives miserable.

The globalization is promoting the culture of market that is centered around the individual not the community. This culture of globalization, on the one hand prepares the ground for exploitation of labour of women widely at cheaper rates and on the other hand, restricts the women and subdue them to the confines of patriarchy making them incapable of enjoying their rights and questioning any injustice meted out to them. As a result, dowry harassments have been on the rise. While the unemployment is growing, dowry has become an easy way to earn property. While it is considered that the participation of women, who are being looked down as second rate citizens and are being subjected to exploitation and patriarchal oppression, in social, economic and production sectors attain the empowerment of women.

CONCLUSION

Unless we consolidate, fight unitedly and make the attempts of the imperialists and exploiting landlords to drag and sacrifice us at the altar of the blind world that can not visualize anything other than profits, women can not attain free, independent dignified lives with respect and livelihood. Let us not wait till the "worst" comes to us, and till we learn from our own experience. Let us free from fetters of individualism. It is the immediate task before women to understand the conditions, situation and root causes that impede the real empowerment of women and to unite, to oppose and to fight against such hindering real causes. Thus women should dismantle the iron curtain of tradition and also impacts of globalization:

- to transform the ideology and practice of domination and subordination.
- challenge and transfer existing power structures.
- challenge the discrimination and get access to and control over material and knowledge resources. and
- get access to positions of power.

NOTES AND REFERENCES

1. Globalization101.org.
2. Pushkar Raj, "Globalization and Human Rights", *PUCL Bulletin*, July 2002.
3. "Nepal Human Development Report, 2004: Empowerment and Poverty Reduction", United Nations Development Programme, Kathmandu.
4. Basin, K. and Dhar, S., 1998, "Joining hands to Develop Women Power, A Report of a South Asian Workshop on Gender and Sustainable Development, Koitta, Bangladesh. NPC/UNDP, 2004.
5. Acharya, M., "Empowerment under Globalization—Making Markets Work for Women", Tanka Prasad Acharya Memorial Foundation, Kathmandu, New Banewswore, Nepal, 2005.
6. IFAD/OE, 2000, The Republic of India: Tamil Nadu Women's Development Project: Completion Evaluation, Report 340IN, Rome, April 2000.
7. Regi P. George, "Empowerment of Women—Globalization", India Thinkers Net. Nov., 14, 2005.

31

Sexual Harassment of Women at Work Places

SRIDHAR GANJI

Now-a-day, Sexual harassment of women at work places is a common phenomena right from rural to urban areas. In India, women have come a long way from sages, scholars in the Rig Vedic period to modern in the armed forces, IT sector, politics, industry and other significant areas. This journey towards modernization has not been easy. Therefore, women have to fight the traditional male dominated society to emerge as stronger and independent entities. However, some cases of rape, sexual harassment, etc., are still uncontrolled the reason is illiteracy and ignorance about their rights in most cases. That is why in sexual harassment cases, women feel raped psychologically. Fearing from such an outcome, women offer getting embarrassed from speaking out against their tormentors. To help these women's problem, groups of organizations have released a manual relating to sexual harassment at work place[1].

Meaning: The expression like 'sexual harassment' has been defined in different manner viz., obscene acts or songs[2], assault of criminal force intent to outrage her modesty[3], word, gesture or act intended to insult the modesty of women[4], any man who in order to satisfy his lust in an improper manner[5], any unwelcome sexually determined behavior[6], the repeated making of an unwanted sexual advances or obscene remarks to a person[7]. Sexually intended terrorism against a person, which includes a male and a female[8].

Hence, we can say in a simple manner, "it is an unwanted conduct of a sexual nature based on sex affecting the dignity of women at work place".

Therefore, an act that is a sexual harassment must satisfy the following conditions: The conduct must be unwanted, improper or offensive, refusal or acceptance of influence decisions concerning a job. It creates a working climate that is intimidating hostiles or humiliating the woman[9]. When these conditions be satisfied then, that there is a sexual harassment. Hence, a person may be liable for the same and the law will take its own course against the violators.

CLASSIFICATION OF SEXUAL HARASSMENT

It has different nomenclature in nature and classify into a sexual intended molestation, use of foul language, outrage the modesty, obscene gesture[10] eve teasing, leering, dirty jokes, physical conduct and advances, demand or request for sexual favours sexually colored remarks about a person's body, showing pornography, any other unwelcome physical verbal and non-verbal conduct of sexual nature, etc.[11]

POSITION OF SEXUAL HARASSMENT IN INDIA

As far as sexual harassment is concerned, it is a sensitive and pathetic one and year by year increasing against women. The number of sexual harassment cases includes eve teasing in India in 2009 was 17,155. It increases of 5.2 percent over the previous year (9946). But Andhra Pradesh reported the highest number of cases 2024 (19.9%) followed by U.P. 1,1887 (18.6) and Tamilnadu 1,718 (16.9%) Haryana had the highest rate of 6.6 per 1,00,000 population, compared to national level rate of 1.0%[12]. Therefore, from the above said statistical, report, every day more or less 47 Sexual Harassment cases are happening in all over India in general, six cases in Andhra Pradesh alone in particular. In order to restrict the same Supreme Court of India has given widest guidelines to the states and centre to follow their direction in a strict manner until a new law comes into force i.e., a law under Article 141 of the constitution[13]. Inspire of that guidelines day-by-day, the sexual harassment is increasing and the law enforcement machinery did not effectively follows.[14] Therefore, very frequently, sexual harassment cases are occurring and the same reported by several newspapers, magazines, etc., In 1997, the Supreme Court (SC) in its famous judgment laid down what is known as the Vishakha guidelines to prevent sexual harassment at workplace. The SC clearly stated that these guidelines would have the force of law until a separate law on sexual harassment is passed by the Parliament. Almost ten years since the judgment, the draft bill on sexual harassment is still pending in the Parliament. Supreme Court results in violating of the fundamental rights of gender equality and the right to life and liberty under Articles 14, 15 and 21 of the constitution.

One of the logical consequences of such an incident is also the violating of the victims' rights to practice any profession or to carry on any occupation, trade or business[15]. Hence, these attract the remedy under Article 32 for the enforcement of the rights of women even, in the absence of domestic law occupying the field to formulate an effective measure to check this evil practice, the contents of international conventions[16] and norms are significant for the purpose of interpretation of the guarantee of gender equality right to work with human dignity and the safeguards against. Sexual harassment, therefore, these rights are enforceable under Article 32 read with the provisions of international conventions[17]. The same once again confirmed by the Supreme Court Rupan Deo Bajaj against the former D.G.P. of Punjab Mr. K.P.S. Gill[18] and former D.G.P. of Haryana SPS Rathod convicted for 6 months imprisonment with fine of Rs. 1000 by the Haryana Court[19]. That is why Supreme Court and UNO directing all state parties to make appropriate legislation on the basis of the UN conventions for preventing all forms of discrimination against women.

Those who are meeting out the sexual harassment either from employer or from employee or any other person they can have two remedies: 1. Self-help, and 2. To invoke relevant provisions of the law. Under self-help, women may tackle this evil practice in their own manner like through karate, Khunfu, yoga, meditation etc.,[20] then they can able to face any adverse situation with boldness and confidence. Therefore, women become stronger not only physically but also psychologically, under the second category, she can able to set in motion the various law enforcement agencies through the law like IPC, CrPC, the women and children Act, 2000, the protection of Human Rights Act, 1993, state and central commissions for women self-help groups, NGOs, courts and other law enforcement agencies. However, these legislations are not exhaustive one; hence, we need a separate and comprehensive for the sexual harassment.

DO WE NEED AN EXHAUSTIVE LEGISLATION ON SEXUAL HARASSMENT?

As far as Sexual Harassment is concerned, we need an exhaustive legislation on rather than an exhausted one. Whereas the proposed bill as is pending before the parliament, which has deliberately avoided to consider certain important aspects like, sexual harassment in police station, armed forces in addition, prison, men's complaint, common definition for sexual harassment, common complaint committee and appointing authority, from rural to state level, supervising cell within a department, special courts with more powers. Hierarchy of punishment like from warning to dismissal, common law for all the sexual harassment victims[21] therefore, we have certain questions for the welfare of the victims. Because, this is essential for equitable justice and free from discrimination. Those questions are as follows:

1. Does the Sexual harassment constitute an act of unlearning of good conduct?
2. Is there any distinction between liability of a male and a female supervisor officer against his or her subordinate employee?
3. Is the punishment of removal from job common surety with the gravity of the offence? If so,
4. Is not a too harsh in the present day of economic hardship?
5. Shall we apply the same yardstick to both a male and female employee?
6. Therefore, do we need a comprehensive legislation on sexual harassment for both men and women alike?

For these questions, the answer is 'yes'. Hence, the above said laws from the Bill must be rectified and provide a comprehensive legislation rather than a complimentary legislation to check that evil practice while in service. Therefore, I have no other option except to give some suggestions to prevent the sexual harassment at work place and the same to be taken into consideration either personally or legally.

SUGGESTIONS FOR PREVENTING THE SEXUAL HARASSMENT

There are some suggestions to prevent the sexual harassment at work places to be taken into consideration either personally or legally, therefore, personally some behaviours that must be avoided, because it could be misinterpreted and perceived as unwelcome. Those behaviors are:

- When meeting a person for the first time, holding the hand shake longer than normal.
- Standing behind a co-worker and putting your hand on his/her shoulder.
- Staring at some one's body.
- Looking someone up and down at close proximity.
- Making remarks about some one's body during conversation.
- Frequent compliments on the person and seldom on the performance.
- Risqué human in mixed company.
- Offensive language, picture, calendars, etc. in the office.

There is the most obvious behavior to exclude it. Legally also we have to take some action i.e.,

- Common comprehensive law for the entire abusing person.
- Establish special courts[22].
- Hierarchy of Punishment[23].
- Appoint women Judges for hearing cases of crimes against women.
- Recording of statement of the victims at her home with due protection.
- In-camera proceeding, in case of any urgency.
- Set-up a committee of women advocates examining the sequence of events in the case if there is any attempts to scuttle or impede the probe[24].
- Strict and exemplary action against any state and non-state functionaries who conspire to deny justice to the victims.[25]
- Jail for longer period of time.
- Trial must be a fast track rather than fast track.
- To suspend and withdraw the benefits, if he continues the sexual.harassment[26].

- All complaints are to be handled in a confidential manner.
- Common complaint committee and appointing authority.
- Dismissal only on rare and rarest occasion.
- To create special women police cell.
- Amend the relevant legislation including conduct and service rules.
- Annual report must be prepared and submits to the departments concerned.
- Appoint equal number of women to the state and NHRC and national commission for women and minorities with more powers, right to sue and have compensation and sexual harassment fund.
- Then to ensure the early enactment of pending legislation.

Therefore, we need a comprehensive law for strict and exemplary action against any state and non-state functionaries who conspire to deny justice to victims of sexual violence. "Merely bringing in a law to fast tract cases through the proposed "sexual offence (special courts) Bill" making character evidence illegal or sexual offences cognizable would not solve the difficulties beyond the immediate context going by the endless histories of those victims' sexual violence unless the definitional and substantive aspect of the rape law and those dealing with Sexual harassment, molestation, unnatural offences and abduction of girls and women in every day context where amended, the proposed law would remind a hollow gesture[27].

Therefore, the said suggestions that must be incorporated in a separate legislation and widened the scope of sexual harassment as a comprehensive one for protecting women from sexual harassment. Then only they feel like a safe and healthy atmosphere at the work place.

Notes and References

1. www.nationalcommission for women.com.
2. Sec. 294 of IPC.
3. Sec. 354 of IPC.
4. Sec. 509 of IPC.
5. The Suppression of Violence against Women and Children Act of 31 January 2000, Sec: 10(2) of the Woman and Children Act, 2000.
6. Vishakha *v.* State of Rajasthan, AIR 1997 SC.
7. The concise Oxford Dictionary, 10th edn., 1999.
8. The writer's own opinion.
9. European Commission, 1991 cited in Timmerman and Bajema: 423. Emphasis added.

10. Refer to IPC.
11. Refer to Vishaka case.
12. www.mational commission for women.org
13. Supreme Court guidelines in Vishaka case: preventive steps, criminal proceedings, disciplinary action, complaint mechanism, complaint committee, workers' initiative, awareness, third party harassment.
14. Guidelines given by the centre-ignored in some criminal cases against Women Union Home Minister Mr. P. Chidambaram replied to a questions in parliament, *The Hindu*, dated 16th Dec. 2009, p. 11.
15. (a) The suicide of High Court Advocate Sangeeta Sharma in A.P., the new *Indian Express*, July 3, 2000 online edn.
    (b) In A.P. TDP MLA Kovvur constituency Mr. T.V. Rama Rao, guilty of outraging the modesty of girl students from Kerala at the Nursing College run by him at Nidadavole, says west Godavari of S.P's report, *The Hindu*, dated on July 11, 2009 A.P. edition.
    (c) Tribal women raped by the DIG of Rajesthan Mr. Madhukar Tandon, *The Hindu*, Dec. 31, 2009.
    (d) 14 years old tennis girl was driven to commit suicide by the former DGP of Haryana Mr. SPS Rathode, *The Hindu*, dated Dec. 2009.
    (e) A molestation charge against three players of the Chenchil Brothers foot ball club i.e., outranging the airhostess against her colleague Mahesh Kumar Lala in Mumbai modesty of a spice jet hostess on a flight form Goa to Kolkata, *The Hindu*, Jan. 7, 2010, p. 20.
    (f) Karnataka Govt. ordered an enquiry against P.K. Ramaswamy, Director, mass education, for alleged Sexual Harasssment of a widow in Bangalore. The senior IAS officer who sought sexual favours from the woman, *The Hindu*, dated Jan. 07, 2010, A.P. edition.
16. Art. 19(1)(g) of the constitution of India.
17. Vishaka case AIR 1997 SC.
18. Rupan Deol Bajaj *vs.* Kanwar Pal Singh Gil, 1996 (1) All PLR 49 (SC); AIR 1996 SC (1) 309.
19. Ruchika Gil Malhotra, 14 years old tennis player's molestation case reported by *The Hindu*, 22 Dec. 2009.
20. BBCNews, Friday, 14 January 2000, 14:37 GMT Karate for women conductors, Lawyers, Collective Law for the People, December 2000
21. In USA, the Civil Rights Act, 1964 under sec. 703 which is common for all the victims cited by K.D. Gaur's criminal law—cases and material, 4th edition, 2005.
22. Separate sexual offence [special courts] Bill is pending in the parliament *The Hindu*, 06.01.2010, A.P. edition, p. 11.
23. Warning like transfer, closer of supervision, suspension and dismissal including suspend the benefits.
24. The suggestion given by NCW, *The Hindu*, Dec. 24, 2009 A.P. edi. p. 20.
25. The Former DGP of Haryana Mr. S.P.S. Rathore, who conspired to deny justice to the family of Ruchika for 19 years.
26. The Union Home Ministry issued show cause notice to the former D.G.P. Haryana, S.P.S. Rathore to take away the police medals and reduce pension, *The Hindu*, Dec. 27, 2009 A.P. [edn.].
27. Several women's groups complaint to law minister to amend the laws on sexual violence report by *The Hindu* on 06.01.2010, p. 11, A.P. edn.

Index